God's Mission *in* Asia

American Society of Missiology Monograph Series

THE ASM MONOGRAPH SERIES provides a forum for publishing quality dissertations and studies in the field of missiology. Collaborating with Pickwick Publications—a division of Wipf and Stock Publishers of Eugene, Oregon—the American Society of Missiology selects high quality dissertations and other monographic studies that offer research materials in mission studies for scholars, mission and church leaders, and the academic community at large. The ASM seeks scholarly work for publication in the Series that throws light on issues confronting Christian world mission in its cultural, social, historical, biblical, and theological dimensions.

Missiology is an academic field that brings together scholars whose professional training ranges from doctoral-level preparation in areas such as scripture, history and sociology of religions, anthropology, theology, international relations, interreligious interchange, mission history, inculturation, and church law. The American Society of Missiology, which sponsors this series, is an ecumenical body drawing members from Independent and Ecumenical Protestant, Catholic, Orthodox, and other traditions. Members of the ASM are united by their commitment to reflect on and do scholarly work relating to both mission history and the present-day mission of the church. The ASM Monograph Series aims to publish works of exceptional merit on specialized topics, with particular attention given to work by younger scholars, the dissemination and publication of which is difficult under the economic pressures of standard publishing models.

Persons seeking information about the ASM or the guidelines for having their dissertations considered for publication in the ASM Monograph Series should consult the Society's website—www.asmweb.org.

Members of the ASM Monograph Committee who approved this book are:

Gary B. McGee
Assemblies of God Theological Seminary, Springfield, Missouri

Anthony Gittins
Catholic Theological Union, Chicago

Dana Lee Robert
Boston University School of Theology

God's Mission *in* Asia

*A Comparative and Contextual Study
of This-Worldly Holiness
and the
Theology of* Missio Dei
in M. M. Thomas and C. S. Song

KEN CHRISTOPH MIYAMOTO

American Society of Missiology
Monograph Series

1

Pickwick *Publications*
An imprint of *Wipf and Stock Publishers*
199 West 8th Avenue • Eugene OR 97401

GOD'S MISSION IN ASIA
American Society of Missiology Monograph Series 1

Copyright © 2007 by Ken Christoph Miyamoto. All rights reserved. No part of this publication may be reproduced or transmitted in any form, electronic or mechanical, or stored on any information storage and retrieval system without prior permission in writing from the publishers. For permissions write to Wipf & Stock Publishers, 199 W. 8th Avenue, Suite 3, Eugene OR 97401.

Pickwick Publications
A Division of Wipf and Stock Publishers
199 W. 8th Ave., Suite 3
Eugene, OR 97401

ISBN 13: 978-1-59752-713-2

Cataloguing-in-Publication data:

Miyamoto, Ken Christoph

God's mission in Asia : a comparative and contextual study of this-worldly holiness and the theology of *missio dei* in M. M. Thomas and C. S. Song / Ken Christoph Miyamoto.

American Society of Missiology Monograph Series 1

x + 234 p.; 23 cm.

ISBN 13: 978-1-59752-713-2

1. Missions—Asia. 2. Missions—theory—Comparative studies. 3. Thomas, M. M. (Madathilparampil M.), 1916–. 4. Song, Choan-Seng, 1929–. I. Title. II. Series.

BV3151 .M58 2007

Manufactured in the U.S.A.

Books published in the American Society of Missiology Scholarly monograph series are chosen on the basis of their academic quality as responsible contributions to debate and dialogue about issues in mission studies. The opinions expressed in the book are those of the authors and are not represented to be those of the American Society of Missiology or its members.

Contents

Acknowledgments vii
List of Abbreviations ix

1. Modernization and Christianity in Asia:
   Some Theoretical Issues Related to Today's Contextual Theology 1

   Modernization, Religion, and the Problem of Meaning 2
   Christian Theology in Modernizing Asia 12
   The Subject of This Study 23

2. This-Worldly Holiness and the *Missio Dei* Concept
   in Ecumenical Mission Thinking 31

   Ecumenism as the Search for Wholeness 32
   *The Search for the Theological Foundation of Christian
   Mission and the Emergence of the* Missio Dei *Concept* 34
   The Rise of the World-Centric Approach to the Missio Dei 42
   *The Continuing Tension between the Church-Centric
   and the World-Centric Views of the* Missio Dei 51
   Conclusion 61

3. This-Worldly Holiness and the *Missio Dei* Concept
   in Asian Ecumenical Thinking 63

   Christian Witness in the Midst of Rapid Social Changes 64
   Christian Presence in the Process of Modernization 70
   "Peoples of Asia, People of God" 74
   Conclusion 83

4 The Theology of God's This-Worldly
   Presence in M. M. Thomas   89

   The Context and Early Life of M. M. Thomas   89

   *An Emergence of the Motif of God's This-Worldly
      Presence in Thomas's Thinking*   104

   Discerning the Signs of God in Christ at Work in History   112

   Conclusion   132

5 The Theology of God's Mission
   of Incarnation in C. S. Song   137

   Taiwan and C. S. Song's Earlier Life   137

   Primary Questions: The Churches in Asia and the West   146

   *A Search for a Missiological Alternative
      from an Asian Perspective*   155

   A Search for a New Framework of Theology in Asia   167

   The People-Centered Approach towards Christology   177

   Conclusion   188

6 Conclusion   193

Bibliography   203
Index   221

Acknowledgments

MANY PEOPLE CONTRIBUTED TO the completion of this research project in a variety of ways. Although I would like to acknowledge all their contributions, I can only mention here those few who most closely helped me to accomplish this work. First, I would like to express my deep gratitude to Dr. Charles A. Ryerson III, the late Dr. Alan Preston Neely, and Dr. Kathleen E. McVey of Princeton Theological Seminary for their guidance and support. In particular, Dr. Ryerson, my supervisor, and Dr. Neely graciously devoted their time and scholarship to my work from the day I arrived at Princeton as a new doctoral student, and continued to assist me with their inspiration, encouragement, and patience on numerous occasions. I am also grateful to Dr. Charles C. West and Dr. Mark Lewis Taylor for their guidance in the early stage of this project.

I also want to acknowledge the encouragement of Dr. Gonzalo Castillo-Cardenas. While I was doing my M.Div. program at Pittsburgh Theological Seminary, he opened my eyes toward contemporary Third World theologies with his commitment to liberation theology in Latin America. My interest in M. M. Thomas and C. S. Song goes back to the research papers I wrote in some of his courses.

I would like to mention two of my good friends and colleagues at Princeton, Dr. Lalsangkima Pachuau and Dr. Chandra Shekar Soans. I was inspired by Kima on various occasions through our lively academic discussions, and Chandra gave me precious assistance in obtaining Thomas's manuscript writings held at the United Theological College in Bangalore, India. Special thanks are due to another good friend, Deborah M. Cordonnier, for her generous offer to proofread the entire work in manuscript. Of course, I am responsible for all errors and mistakes that may still be found in it, whether typographical or not.

During the last stage of my research, I suffered a serious retinal detachment and went through several eye operations over ten months. This unexpected illness, and the consequent recuperation period, halted the progress of the project for almost a year. I was, however, tremendously encouraged by the professors and colleagues at Princeton Seminary who warmly surrounded me with sincere concern and constant prayers. I am also grateful to my friends at All Saints' Episcopal Church in Princeton who were always willing to provide my family and me with assistance, both spiritual and material, thereby showing us the riches of Christian fellowship.

I am most grateful to the ASM Dissertation Series Committee for approving the inclusion of this work in the ASM Scholarly Monograph Series and especially to Dr. William R. Burrows, ASM Publisher, for his patient and continual assistance through e-mail correspondence during its preparation for publication.

Finally, I must express my thankfulness to my parents in Yokohama, Japan, as well as to my wife Maylene for their support. In particular, Maylene accompanied me throughout the years at Princeton and constantly encouraged me with her love, understanding, patience, and prayer. Without her cooperation, this work would never have been finished. In July 1998, we were blessed by the birth of our daughter Migiwa Immanuelle, who brought an abundance of joy and hope to our life. With my deepest love and gratitude, I would like to dedicate this work to both Maylene and Migiwa.

Abbreviations

CCA	Christian Conference of Asia
EACC	East Asian Christian Conference
IMC	International Missionary Council
PCT	Presbyterian Church in Taiwan
SCM	Student Christian Movement
TEF	Theological Education Fund
TTC	Tainan Theological College
WCC	World Council of Churches
WSCF	World Student Christian Federation
WUFI	World United Formosans for Independence
YCCA	Youth Christian Council of Action

CHAPTER I

Modernization and Christianity in Asia

*Some Theoretical Issues Related to
Today's Contextual Theology*

IN THE LAST SEVERAL centuries, most peoples in Asia were constantly exposed to the expansion of the Western powers. The Second World War brought the colonial rule of the West to an end, and the postwar period was marked by the emergence of many new independent nations in Asia. Yet the process of globalization has become predominant in the past several decades, and Western values and worldview have become deeply intertwined with the indigenous ones. Thus, the influence of the West has transformed Asian societies profoundly. Modern science and technology have thoroughly reorganized their political and economic systems and brought about urbanization and industrialization. Modern education has created the new type of intellectuals and national leaders which was unknown in pre-modern Asia. Still modernization has not always resulted in the improvement of the material conditions of human life. In many nations, modern capitalism has radically accelerated the maldistribution of wealth and widened the gap between the rich and the poor. Indeed, the "underdevelopment" of many countries in Asia, Africa, and Latin America is merely the other side of the prosperity of modern capitalism in the North.[1]

---

1. Peter Worsley, *The Three Worlds: Culture and World Development* (Chicago: University of Chicago Press, 1984), 3; Eric R. Wolf, *Europe and the People without History* (Berkeley and Los Angeles: University of California Press, 1982), 22–23. This view of underdevelopment was presented by an economic theory usually referred to as "dependency theory." This theory was developed as the critique of Western "modernization theory" that argued the lack of development in the Third World was chiefly caused by internal factors inherent in a traditional society. According to Kofi Buenor Hadjor, "dependency theory played a pioneering role in exposing the ethnocentric assumptions of modernization theory" (Kofi Buenor Hadjor, *Dictionary of Third World Terms* [London: Penguin Books, 1993], s.v. "Dependency Theory"; Richard D. N. Dickinson, *Poor, Yet Making Many Rich: The Poor as Agents of Creative Justice* [Geneva: WCC, Commission on the Churches' Participation in Development, 1983], 27–28).

The impact of the West is also evident in the religious and cultural aspects of social life in Asia. Both reform movements within traditional religions and religious fundamentalism have emerged as responses to, or reactions against, the Western values and worldview transplanted by colonialism, Christian missions, and secular ideologies. Nationalism, enlivened by Western secular ideologies, often inspired the struggle of Asian nations for independence and nation-building. Since the end of the Cold War, another type of nationalism—"religious nationalism" inspired by traditional religious sentiments transformed by Western influences—has emerged as a major cause both for international and domestic conflicts in various parts of the world.

Still another important development was the emergence of the Christian communities in Asia as a result of the Western missionary movement. These communities are mostly small. Yet they have frequently exercised a significant influence on the transformation of their societies. In what way then have Christians in Asia responded to the historical reality of their societies rapidly changing under the dynamic impact of the West? This is the question I want to deal with in this study. To address this question, the study will focus on two leading Christian intellectuals from Asia, namely, M. M. Thomas of India and C. S. Song from Taiwan, and look into the ways in which they tried to bridge and reconcile the discrepancy between the historical reality of Asia and their religious faith rooted in the West. In this introductory chapter, however, I will first discuss some theoretical issues underlying the study and define several important concepts. Then, a conceptual framework will be provided for understanding contemporary Christian theology in Asia. In the last section, I will briefly discuss the subject and outline of this study.

Modernization, Religion, and the Problem of Meaning

The essence of the Western influence on world history is the impact of modernity. The significance of modernity is well summarized by the sociologist Anthony Giddens:

> The modes of life brought into being by modernity have swept us away from *all* traditional types of social order, in quite unprecedented fashion. In both their extensionality and their intensionality the transformations involved in modernity are more profound than most sorts of change characteristic of prior periods.[2]

2. Anthony Giddens, *The Consequences of Modernity* (Stanford, Calif.: Stanford University Press, 1990), 4.

In recent years, the confidence in modernity, particularly in the ideas of rationalism and progress conceptualized in the framework of the Enlightenment, has increasingly weakened. The impact of modernity is, nonetheless, deeply felt everywhere on earth, and much of its effect is most likely irreversible. An example for this situation is a growing number of ethno-religious conflicts in today's world. Most of them arise from traditional ethno-religious sentiments awakened and intensified by modernization. Thus, the complex and multifaceted effect of modernization on traditional religions and cultures is drawing more and more attention.

The question of traditional and modern societies has always attracted the interest of Western social scientists.[3] Two founders of social science, Max Weber and Emile Durkheim, dealt with the question extensively. Weber, who considered history as the process of rationalization, contrasted a "magical" traditional society with a "rationalized" or "disenchanted" modern society.[4] Durkheim similarly distinguished between two types of society: a society where homogeneity and resemblance are predominant, and a society dominated by a high degree of differentiation and interdependence. He thought that it was a "historical law" that the society of the first type (primitive and traditional societies) would gradually be replaced by that of the second type (modern society).[5] History was thus conceived by him as a process toward a greater differentiation.

Generally speaking, it is not easy to define the notions of modernity and modernization with precision. As Charles Ryerson writes,

> Structurally, modernisation has often been described as increasing complexity, differentiation, and adaptability of organizational units. Recruitment to occupations on the basis of achievement

---

3. According to the sociologist S. N. Eisenstadt, the sociological conception of tradition has its "strong roots . . . in the central concern of modern sociology about the distinctiveness of modern social order." It is "especially prevalent in the work of many of the founding fathers of sociology—de Toqueville, Marx, Durkheim, Weber, and others" (S. N. Eisenstadt, "Intellectuals and Tradition," *Daedalus* 101 [Spring 1992]: 2). This fact implies that the distinction between tradition and modernity is a product of the intellectual effort of the modern West to understand itself in terms of its relationship with the rest of the world, and that it is as such a Eurocentric distinction. If so, then one must re-examine the universal validity of these two conceptions critically, taking into account non-Western perspectives. Such a re-examination is, however, not within the scope of this study.

4. Charles Ryerson, *Regionalism and Religion: The Tamil Renaissance and Popular Hinduism* (Madras: Christian Literature Society for the Christian Institute for the Study of Religion and Society, Bangalore, 1988), 4.

5. Emile Durkheim, *On Morality and Society*, ed. Robert N. Bellah (Chicago: University of Chicago Press, 1973), 63.

rather than by ascriptive criteria and the spread of potential power to wider groups in the society have also often been stressed as the indices of modernisation.⁶

Modernization has been explained also in terms of the attainment of higher efficiency in the political and economic life of society. The Philippine scholar Josefa M. Saniel thus defined the notion as "the process of transforming a society's traditional political, economic, and social systems into modern systems ideally characterized by the highest possible degree of efficiency with the least expenditure of energy."⁷ In this type of definition, technical efficiency is considered as the key feature of modernity.

After the Second World War, especially in the 1960s, the modernization process of newly independent nations in Asia confronted scholars as well as politicians with a new question: this question was about the relationship between traditional values and modernization in the midst of social change.⁸ Among the scholars who devoted themselves to this question, the American sociologist Robert N. Bellah contributed greatly to the discussion of modernization by pointing out the significance of the cultural dimension of the modernization process. Distinguishing the "rationalization of means" from the "rationalization of ends," Bellah wrote:

> The modernization of societies and personalities is not concerned solely . . . with maximization of technical efficiency. Such modernization has increased the possibility of rational conscious choice of ends. It is this point, indeed, that our definition of "progress" . . . as an increase in learning capacity primarily implies. Modernization involves the increased capacity for rational goal-setting because it gives the system—society, organization, personality—a more comprehensive communications network through which it is possible to access the needs and potentialities of all parts of the system.⁹

Bellah thus considered modernization not only as the "maximization of technical efficiency" but also as "the increased capacity for rational goal-

---

6. Ryerson, *Regionalism and Religion*, 5.

7. Josefa M. Saniel, "The Mobilization of Traditional Values in the Modernization of Japan," in *Religion and Progress in Modern Asia*, ed. Robert N. Bellah (New York: Free Press, 1965; London: Collier-Macmillan, 1965), 124.

8. See Soedjatmoko, "Memorandum on Scope and Purpose of Seminar," quoted in Robert N. Bellah, "Introduction," in *Religion and Progress in Modern Asia*, ed. Robert N. Bellah (New York: Free Press, 1965; London: Collier-Macmillan, 1965), x–xiv.

9. Robert N. Bellah, "Epilogue: Religion and Progress in Modern Asia," in *Religion and Progress in Modern Asia*, ed. Robert N. Bellah (New York: Free Press, 1965; London: Collier-Macmillan, 1965), 195.

setting," and he argued that such a new capacity must entail "the changed sense of identity and a new way of posing limit images." Defined in this way, modernization was now seen as the "internal problem for religion" as well as culture for "it involves the heart of religious concerns."[10]

Such an approach of Bellah's to modernization was based on his understanding of modernity, which even today remains helpful. Emphasizing its cultural dimension, he primarily viewed modernity "as a spiritual phenomenon or a kind of mentality" rather than "as a form of political or economic system." He thus defined it "as a new attitude toward the phenomenon of change."[11] Following Weber's Protestant ethic thesis, Bellah considered that such an attitude originated in Protestantism, in particular in Puritanism. According to him,

> This new mentality, which was found among small groups of enlightened spirits all over Europe in the sixteenth and seventeenth centuries and was to some extent socially institutionalized in Holland and England by the end of the seventeenth century, can best be characterized as a new attitude toward the phenomenon of change. Change was seen as something not to be feared but to be welcomed, to be responsibly and intelligently guided.[12]

This new openness toward change was accompanied by "a new attitude toward authority." Change was now not to be directed "by reference to any fixed or given authority in the past, but only through reason and discussion, through intelligent inquiry and tentative consensus." In other words, change was to be guided by rational conscious choice rather than by reference to traditional authority. Thus, change came to be seen as "a primary human responsibility."[13] This new spiritual orientation of modernity radically revolutionized the Western world. Its impact on the political, economic, and technological spheres was tremendous and far-reaching. The new attitude no less profoundly affected the cultural and religious life of the West. Its new ethos deeply challenged the worldview of traditional Christianity and triggered the secularization of the Western culture.

A similar confrontation between traditional societies and modernity took place outside the West. Concerning the encounter between tradi-

---

10. Ibid., 196.

11. Robert N. Bellah, *Beyond Belief: Essays on Religion in a Post-Traditionalist World* (New York: Harper & Row, 1970; reprint, Berkeley and Los Angeles: University of California Press, 1991), 66.

12. Ibid.

13. Ibid., 66–67.

tional religions and modern "secular nationalism," Mark Juergensmeyer observed:

> In the West this encounter, and the ideological, economic, and political transitions that accompanied it, took place over many years. Though fundamental, these changes were not complicated by the intrusion of foreign control of a colonial or neocolonial sort. The new nations of this century have had to confront the same challenges in a short period of time and simultaneously contend with new forms of politics forced on them as by-products of colonial rule. As in the West, however, the challenge they have faced is fundamental: it involves a religious worldview and one shaped by secular nationalism.[14]

This conflict has been far more tense among the new nations than in the West due to the reasons Juergensmeyer pointed out here: that modernization has been a relatively recent phenomenon among them, and that the Western colonial rule has left in its wake political complications even after national independence. Furthermore, as the product of the historical development inside the Western world, modernity confronted the rest of the world from outside as something alien. The effect of this confrontation has been to break up the stability, continuity, and solidarity of traditional societies maintained by what Clifford Geertz called "primordial attachments" or "primordial sentiments."

The concept of "primordial attachments" helps to clarify the problems caused by the impact of modernity upon traditional societies. According to Geertz, a primordial attachment is an attachment

> that stems from the "givens"—or, more precisely, as culture is inevitably involved in such matters, the assumed "givens"—of social existence: immediate contiguity and kin connection mainly, but beyond them the givenness that stems from being born into a particular religious community, speaking a particular language, or even a dialect of a language, and following particular social practices. These congruities of blood, speech, custom, and so on, are

---

14. Mark Juergensmeyer, *The New Cold War?: Religious Nationalism Confronts the Secular State* (Berkeley and Los Angeles: University of California Press, 1993), 28–29. In this work, Juergensmeyer uses the term "nationalism" in a broad sense, defining it as follows: "The modern nation-state is morally and politically justified by a concept of *nationalism*, by which I mean not only the xenophobic extremes of patriotism but also the more subdued expression of identity based on shared assumptions regarding why a community constitutes a nation and why the state that rules it is legitimate" (ibid., 6).

seen to have an ineffable, and at times overpowering, coerciveness in and of themselves.[15]

With such coerciveness, these primordial attachments—blood ties, races, languages, religions, and customs[16]—can produce a sense of being naturally connected. They, therefore, provide a society and person with a sense of identity, that is, the sense of who you really are, and of where you came and where you are going.

Among the primordial attachments, religion is particularly important as a mechanism for the production of identity. Religion is the dimension of culture that relates life to ultimate meaning. It is a system of symbols that establishes the general orientation in human life by manifesting an ultimate dimension of reality that transcends the realm of everyday experience.[17] In Eliade's language, religion makes the world "apprehensible as world, as cosmos," by symbolically creating the opposition between the "sacred" and the "profane," and thus ordering the world around the sacred as the "Center of the World."[18] According to Bellah, the fundamental function of religion is to provide a society and its members with "a stable set of definitions of the world and . . . the self," that is, a set of values and ideas with which the society and its members maintain their integrity, coherence, and solidarity. Such values and ideas define their identity that gives a sense of stability and continuity to the society as well as its members.[19]

In his work written with Thomas Luckmann, the sociologist Peter Berger called these values and ideas "legitimations." According to them, legitimations are "ways by which it [i.e., the social order] can be 'explained' and justified."[20] In other words, they are "answers to any questions about

15. Clifford Geertz, *The Interpretation of Cultures: Selected Essays* (New York: Basic Books, 1973), 259.

16. Ibid., 261–63.

17. See Bellah, "Epilogue," 172; idem, *Beyond Belief*, 21; Peter L. Berger, *The Sacred Canopy: Elements of a Sociological Theory of Religion* (Garden City, N.Y.: Doubleday, 1967; reprint, New York: Anchor Books, Doubleday, 1990), 25, 51; Geertz, *Interpretation*, 90. As for the definition of culture, I will follow the one given by Geertz, that is, "an historically transmitted pattern of meanings embodied in symbols, a system of inherited conceptions expressed in symbolic forms by means of which men communicate, perpetuate, and develop their knowledge about and attitudes toward life" (*Interpretation*, 89).

18. Mircea Eliade, *The Sacred and the Profane: The Nature of Religion*, trans. Williard R. Trask (San Diego: A Harvest/HBJ Book, Harcourt Brace Jovanovich, 1987), chap. 1 passim.

19. Bellah, "Epilogue," 173.

20. Peter L Berger and Thomas Luckmann, *The Social Construction of Reality: A Treatise*

the 'why' of institutional arrangements."[21] Elements of the reality we daily experience are ostensibly fragmented and have no mutual relationship. Legitimations relate these elements to each other on various levels, and make them intelligible within certain areas of everyday reality. The entirety of reality is eventually made comprehensible on the highest level of legitimations that Berger called "symbolic universes."[22] Legitimations thus arrange seemingly fragmented empirical realities into a meaningful whole, transforming the chaotic world into a web of meanings. This is why legitimations are capable of producing a sense of coherence and integrity and of defining the identity of a society or person.

Derived from the sociology of knowledge developed by Berger and Luckmann,[23] the notion of legitimation is not confined to religion alone. The notion is used with a much broader sense than religion, and religion is in fact merely "a type of symbolic universe."[24] Nevertheless, according to Berger, religion is particularly important among legitimations because

> religion has been the historically most widespread and effective instrumentality of legitimation. All legitimation maintains socially defined reality. Religion legitimates so effectively because it relates the precarious reality constructions of empirical societies with ultimate reality. The tenuous realities of the social world are grounded in the sacred *realissimum*, which by definition is beyond the contingencies of human meanings and human activity.[25]

In other words, the capability of religion to produce a particularly strong identity and to maintain integrity, coherence, and solidarity comes from the transcendental nature of religious legitimation. Berger thus continues:

---

in the Sociology of Knowledge (Garden City, N.Y.: Doubleday, 1966; reprint, New York: Anchor Books, Doubleday, 1989), 61.

21. Berger, *Sacred Canopy*, 29.

22. Berger and Luckmann, *Social Construction*, 95–97; Robert Wuthnow, *Rediscovering the Sacred: Perspectives on Religion in Contemporary Society* (Grand Rapids, Mich.: Eerdmans, 1992), 16–18. Berger and Luckmann define "symbolic universes" as "bodies of theoretical tradition that integrate different provinces of meaning and encompass the institutional order in a symbolic totality" (*Social Construction*, 95).

23. According to Berger and Luckmann, the term "legitimation" was originally taken from Max Weber (Berger and Luckmann, *Social Construction*, 201; Berger, *Sacred Canopy*, 191).

24. Wuthnow, *Rediscovering*, 18. To Berger, religion is the legitimation particularly related to a sacred order as he defines it "the establishment, through human activity, of an all-embracing sacred order, that is, of a sacred cosmos that will be capable of maintaining itself in the ever-present face of chaos" (*Sacred Canopy*, 51).

25. Berger, *Sacred Canopy*, 32.

"Religion legitimates social institutions by bestowing upon them an ultimately valid ontological status, that is, by *locating* them within a sacred and cosmic frame of reference."[26] Such is the function of religion or "sacred canopy." He calls this function "world-maintenance." Thus, religion may be understood as "a symbolic system that imposes order ('cosmos') on the entire universe, on life itself, and thereby holds chaos (disorder) at bay."[27]

The impact of modernity on the traditional society has seriously undermined precisely this function of religion. In the society that maintained its order with the traditional "sacred canopy," a phenomenon of change was viewed as something negative as Bellah pointed out: "In all the great traditional civilizations the notion of change was charged with horror and fear and was contrasted with that which is eternal, which does not change, and which alone is of value, as in the Christian idea of God."[28] The West has profoundly challenged this negative attitude by its belief in change and has radically destabilized the traditional order; the new openness toward change has loosened up the cohesion of society based on the primordial attachments and broken up the coherence of traditional religious symbolism and the values and worldview expressed and organized by it. This development has inevitably weakened the hold of traditional authority over society as well. Consequently,

> All previous forms of military, political, economic, and ideological organization were called into question. In some cases, premodern forms were quickly destroyed by occupying Western powers. In other cases, they survived in battered form in some kind of uneasy symbiosis with impinging structures. And in some cases, traditional forms were able to adapt modern organization to their own ends or to new syncretic ends. But whatever the particular outcome, traditional assumptions and traditional values could no longer be taken for granted. Each society, as the relentless pressure mounted, found its own identity becoming problematic.[29]

The Western impact has, thus, resulted in the crisis of traditional legitimations. Inevitably, religion as a symbolic universe has also become problematic.

---

26. Ibid., 33.
27. Wuthnow, *Rediscovering*, 18.
28. Bellah, *Beyond Belief*, 67.
29. Bellah, "Epilogue," 200.

This crisis has posed for traditional societies a dual question of how to cope with change and how to reaffirm the sense of identity. As Bellah wrote, the modern conception of change must be integrated with a conception of identity traditionally provided by religion.[30] Similarly, Geertz pointed out "the two powerful, thoroughly interdependent, yet distinct and often actually opposed motives" operative among the peoples of the Third World nations.[31] He called these two motives "a search for an identity" and "a demand for progress,"[32] or "essentialism" and "epochalism."[33] Reform movements within traditional religions, religious fundamentalism, and secular and religious nationalism in Asia, Africa, and Latin America—all these phenomena are manifestations of conscious or unconscious attempts to tackle this tremendous dilemma between identity and change.

In many cases, such a dilemma has particularly been felt by the group of people called "intellectuals." Since Asia encountered the West, the intellectuals in Asian societies have often played the leading role in the attempt of society to respond to the questions raised by the dilemma. Bellah wrote:

> It was, of course, the intellectuals who felt earliest and most severely the cultural trauma of the modern pressure. They were forced into a re-examination of their own cultural identity symbols, which meant, in most traditional societies, . . . religious symbols.[34]

They have also tried hard to interpret Western symbols, including religious ones, to their own people amid the rapidly changing social reality. As a result, cultural responses to the Western influence and modernization have often been initiated and carried out by the intellectuals.

This fact derives from the peculiar relationship of the intellectuals with culture. Weber defined the intellectuals as "a group of men who by virtue of their peculiarity have special access to certain achievements considered to be 'culture values,' and who therefore usurp the leadership of a 'culture community.'"[35] According to the British sociologist Tom Bottomore, the intellectuals in a modern society comprise a smaller group within the population called the "intelligentsia"—those who have received higher educa-

---

30. Bellah, *Beyond Belief*, 67.
31. Geertz, *Interpretation*, 258.
32. Ibid.
33. Ibid., 240–41, 243–44.
34. Bellah, "Epilogue," 200–201.
35. H. H. Gerth and C. Wright Mills, eds. and trans., *From Max Weber: Essays in Sociology* (New York: Oxford University Press, 1946), 176.

tion and are engaged in "non-manual occupations." The intellectuals are usually "writers, artists, scientists and technologists, philosophers, religious thinkers, social theorists, political commentators." School teachers, journalists, and so forth, could also be counted among the intellectuals as the precise boundaries of the group are ambiguous. Wherever its boundaries may be drawn, according to Bottomore, "its characteristic feature—direct concern with the culture of a society—is sufficiently clear."[36]

This relationship between the intellectuals and culture assigns them a special role in society. In his discussion of the rationalization of religion and the intellectuals' role in it, Weber wrote:

> Behind them [i.e., various beliefs] always lies a stand towards something in the actual world which is experienced as specifically 'senseless.' Thus, the demand has been implied: that the world order in its totality is, could, and should somehow be a meaningful 'cosmos.' This quest, the core of genuine religious rationalism, has been borne precisely by strata of intellectuals.[37]

In other words, the primary questions that the intellectuals ask in their engagement with culture are the questions about the meaning of the world. Following Weber, Bellah called the intellectuals "those especially responsible for interpreting the meaning of the world."[38] Because of this social function, they are characterized also as "those who contribute directly to the creation, transmission and criticism of cultural products and ideas."[39]

Thus, what is at stake in the attempt of the intellectuals to confront the modern dilemma between identity and change is the so-called "problems of meaning." Bellah observed this point as follows:

> But behind the popular ideologies, implicit or in some cases explicit in them, lie deeper problems of meaning, problems of a historical, philosophical, and even religious nature. The traditional culture had its own view of the world and of man; the modern West has quite a different view. Can the two be reconciled? If so how? What must be given up, what changed? The problem of how

---

36. Tom Bottomore, *Élites and Society*, 2d ed. (London: Routledge, 1993), 53.

37. Gerth and Mills, *From Max Weber*, 281.

38. Robert N. Bellah, "Ienaga Saburo and the Search for Meaning in Modern Japan," in *Changing Japanese Attitudes Toward Modernization*, ed. Marius B. Jansen (Princeton, N.J.: Princeton University Press, 1965), 369.

39. Bottomore, *Élites*, 53.

to act in a given historical situation leads to the deeper problems of what is true, what is good.[40]

These problems are manifestations of a new search for "holistic meaning."[41] Confronted by the modern West with its belief in change, the traditional values and worldviews in Asia were deeply shaken and fragmented. The old world appears to have lost its meaning since, its elements being fragmented, it does not make sense by itself any longer. The world, therefore, neither has worth nor relates "to the subject's feelings of integrity, wholeness, and self-mastery."[42] This apparent loss of meaning drives the intellectuals to a reinterpretation of the traditional symbolic universe as well as the worldview and values of the West. In this way, they try to overcome the fragmentation of the old world and to move toward a larger and more comprehensive whole of meaning.

As Bellah suggests in the above-quoted passage, such an attempt often remains implicit. The bearers of modern ideologies and movements, represented by the intellectuals, are often unaware of them. Only some individuals realize the significance of the problems of meaning and strive to answer them explicitly as in the case of the Japanese historian Saburo Ienaga, whose thought was studied by Bellah himself.[43] Nonetheless, these problems, frequently raised in the past, are still being raised today by those who live in the non-Western world.

Christian Theology in Modernizing Asia

Seen from a sociological point of view, conversion to Christianity in traditional societies is one of the major responses of intellectuals to the pressure of modernity in the process of modernization. According to Bellah, Christian converts were usually those who rejected "more or less vigorously their cultural past under the impact of the missionary critique." In this sense, their response to modernity was unlike that of those who totally rejected the West, insisting on the superiority of their traditional cultures, and of those who tried to come to terms both with tradition and modernity.[44]

40. Bellah, "Ienaga Saburo," 369–70.
41. Robert Wuthnow, *Meaning and Moral Order: Explorations in Cultural Analysis* (Berkeley and Los Angeles: University of California Press, 1987), 40.
42. Ibid., 35.
43. Bellah, "Ienaga Saburo," 370.
44. Bellah, "Epilogue," 201.

In many Asian countries, the acceptance of newly imported Western ideas as well as the missionary critique of traditional society made converts—particularly early converts—"ardent advocates of social and political reform." The rise of nationalism in the twentieth century, however, resulted in the alienation of Christian converts in society due to the intimate association of Christianity with the colonialist and imperialist powers of the West. As a result, Christians in Asia increasingly found themselves "isolated and irrelevant."[45]

In the second half of the twentieth century, some Christian leaders initiated a serious effort to overcome this isolation. The effort was accompanied by the emergence of a new type of Christian thinking that attempted to cope with the particularities of Asian societies and cultures. This intellectual development was a phenomenon parallel to similar developments observed among Christians in the rest of the world, both Western and non-Western.

This new type of Christian thinking is commonly known as "contextual theology." Its major concern has been the "contextualization" of the Christian gospel in the societies in which Christian theology does not traditionally have its roots. The term "contextualization" appeared for the first time in 1972 in the report of the Theological Education Fund (TEF) of the World Council of Churches (WCC).[46] In this report entitled *Ministry in Context*, the TEF defined contextualization as follows:

> It [i.e., contextualization] means all that is implied in the familiar term "indigenization" and yet seeks to press beyond. Contextualization has to do with how we assess the peculiarity of third world [sic] contexts. Indigenization tends to be used in the sense of responding to the Gospel in terms of a traditional culture. Contextualization, while not ignoring this, takes into account the process of secularity, technology, and the struggle for human justice, which characterize the historical moment of nations in the Third World.[47]

---

45. Ibid., 202–4.

46. Krikor Haleblian, "The Problem of Contextualization," *Missiology* 11 (January 1983): 95; David J. Hesselgrave and Edward Rommen, *Contextualization: Meanings, Methods, and Models* (Grand Rapids, Mich.: Baker Book House, 1989), 28; Ruy O. Costa, "Introduction: Inculturation, Indigenization, and Contextualization," in *One Faith, Many Cultures: Inculturation, Indigenization, and Contextualization*, ed. Ruy O. Costa (Maryknoll, N.Y.: Orbis, 1988; Cambridge, Mass.: Boston Theological Institute, 1988), xii.

47. Theological Education Fund, *Ministry in Context: The Third Mandate Programme of the Theological Education Fund (1970–77)* (Bromley, England: Theological Education Fund, 1972), 20.

Thus, the term "contextualization" was initially introduced with an intention to overcome the limitation of "indigenization."

The older concept of "indigenization" goes back to the "concern for indigeneity" in the famous three-self movement formulated by the Protestant missionary leaders Henry Venn and Rufus Anderson in the nineteenth century.[48] In the first half of the twentieth century, Roland Allen advocated evangelization by the "spontaneous expansion" of the indigenous churches free from the control of Western missionaries.[49] This period also witnessed the growing influence of the "younger churches" in Asia and Africa with their increasing representation to the meetings of the International Missionary Council (IMC) held during this period.[50] This development further stimulated the discussion of indigenization among missionary circles as well as the younger churches.

The Tambaram meeting of the IMC held in 1938, for instance, expressly acknowledged the need to take indigenous cultures seriously to communicate the Gospel. Its report stated:

> We strongly affirm that the Gospel should be expressed and interpreted in indigenous forms, and that in methods of worship, institutions, literature, architecture, etc., the spiritual heritage of the nation and country should be taken into use. The Gospel is not necessarily bound up with forms and methods brought in from the older churches.[51]

Tambaram 1938 called this approach "adaptation" and recognized it as "a natural and essential method of approach to the mind and heart of the non-Christian."[52] Much later, in 1960, Eugene A. Nida defined the term

---

48. Haleblian, "Problem of Contextualization," 97; Hesselgrave and Rommen, *Contextualization*, 32. R. Pierce Beaver calls Rufus Anderson a "pioneer advocate of the indigenous church." He, however, observes that "Anderson evidently did not regard cultural adaptation as a necessity to indigenization" (R. Pierce Beaver, "Rufus Anderson's Missionary Principles," in *Christusprediking: studiën op het terrein van de zendingswetenschap gewijd aan de nagedachtenis van Professor Dr. Johan Herman Bavinck* [Kampen: J. H. Kok, 1965], 60).

49. Roland Allen, *The Spontaneous Expansion of the Church and the Causes Which Hinder It* (London: World Dominion Press, 1927).

50. Ruth Rouse and Stephen Charles Neill, eds., *A History of the Ecumenical Movement: 1517–1948*, 4th ed. (Geneva: WCC, 1993), 369.

51. International Missionary Council, *"Madras Series": Presenting Papers Based upon the Meeting of the International Missionary Council, at Tambaram, Madras, India, December 12th to 29th, 1938*, vol. 1, *The Authority of the Faith* (New York: International Missionary Council, 1939), 186.

52. Ibid., 195.

"indigenization" in his *Message and Mission* as follows: "Indigenization consists essentially in the full employment of local indigenous forms of communication, methods of transmission, and communicators, as these means can be prepared and trained."[53] Defined in these ways, however, indigenization was the concept that connoted an orientation toward the past, presupposing indigenous culture in its traditional form. Consequently, indigenous culture was seen as something static and changeless. As the TEF report criticized in the above-quoted passage, the term "indigenization" thus tended "to be used in the sense of responding to the Gospel in terms of a traditional culture." In other words, this approach tended to focus on "the purely cultural dimension of human experience," and to define culture in traditional terms.[54]

The concept of contextualization was introduced to go beyond such a limited approach of indigenization by broadening "the understanding of culture to include social, political, and economic questions," and thereby emphasizing "the process of change and transformation in culture." Contextualization, furthermore, approached human culture more critically than indigenization that inclined to regard it as something good, whether Western or non-Western.[55] Such a difference between indigenization and contextualization is important in terms of the problems of meaning discussed earlier in this chapter. I will come back to this point later.

According to Steven G. Mackie, contextual theologies in Asia emerged in a close connection with the development of transnational organizations, such as the Christian Conference of Asia (CCA).[56] This regional ecumenical body was formally constituted at the Kuala Lumpur Assembly in 1959 as the East Asian Christian Conference (EACC). When it underwent a structural reform in 1973 and received a more centralized administrative system, the EACC also obtained its current name, that is, CCA.[57]

---

53. Eugene A. Nida, *Message and Mission: The Communication of the Christian Faith* (New York: Harper & Bros., 1960), 185.

54. Stephen B. Bevans, *Models of Contextual Theology* (Maryknoll, N.Y.: Orbis, 1992), 22.

55. Bevans, *Models*, 22; Haleblian, "Problem of Contextualization," 98. For the other terms related to contextualization, see Alan Neely, *Christian Mission: A Case Study Approach*, American Society of Missiology Series, No. 21 (Maryknoll, N.Y.: Orbis, 1995), 3–10.

56. Steven G. Mackie, "God's People in Asia: A Key Concept in Asian Theology," *Scottish Journal of Theology* 42 (1989): 216.

57. Nicholas Lossky et al., eds., *Dictionary of the Ecumenical Movement* (Geneva: WCC, 1991; Grand Rapids, Mich.: Eerdmans, 1991), s.v. "Christian Conference of Asia," by Tosh Arai and T. K. Thomas.

Mackie observed that Asian theologians' concern with culture started earlier than their socio-political concern. He summarized the theological development of the EACC/CCA in the 1960s and 1970s as follows:

> The Christian Conference of Asia (CCA) . . . already in the 1960s was concerned with the question of 'Confessing the Faith in Asia Today', and with the relation between 'text' and 'context' in Asian theology and theological education. During this first period, its primary concern was to take seriously the *cultural* context, in order to communicate the Christian message more effectively to Asian people, who tended to see Christianity as a foreign importation. But a worsening in the political climate of many Asian countries during the 1970s brought a new emphasis on the *socio-political* context, which was pioneered by the EACC/CCA teams involved in Urban Industrial Mission in Asian cities.[58]

As we shall see in the third chapter, however, this observation is not correct. From the very beginning of its formation, the EACC did have a strong concern for the socio-political situations in Asia. The shift that Mackie referred to was actually the one that occurred in the approach to the socio-political questions, namely, the shift from the modernization project with the emphasis on nation-building and economic development towards the liberation project with the emphasis on social justice and the people's struggle against poverty and oppression. It is obviously no coincidence that this shift occurred almost simultaneously with the introduction of the term "contextualization."

A strong concern with culture and religion has, nonetheless, remained one of the major features that make Asian theologies distinct among contemporary Third World theologies. To quote Mackie once more,

> Asian Christian theology is not new, but in recent years a new kind of *contextual* theology has begun to emerge in Asia, with obvious similarities to other Third World theologians, especially as regards methodology, and yet with certain notable differences. The familiar Third World emphasis on liberation is indeed often present, but there is also a widespread concern with culture; and even more important is the concern, which prevails everywhere apart from the Philippines, to relate theologically to other Asian religions.[59]

---

58. Mackie, "God's People," 216. Emphasis mine.

59. Ibid., 215. As for similar observations, see also Theo Witvliet, *A Place in the Sun: An Introduction to Liberation Theology in the Third World* (Maryknoll, N.Y.: Orbis, 1985), 154; Charles C. West, "Culture, Power and Ideology in Third World Theologies," *Missiology* 12 (October 1984): 412.

Some Asian theologians are quite aware of the significance of such a double emphasis on the religio-cultural as well as the socio-political dimensions. This awareness was well expressed by Aloysius Pieris, a Sri Lankan Jesuit and one of the leading theologians in Asia, when he argued:

> Any discussion about Asian theology has to move between two poles: the *Third Worldness* of our continent and its peculiar *Asian* character. More realistically and precisely, the common denominator linking Asia with the rest of the Third World is its overwhelming poverty. The specific character defining Asia within the other poor countries is its multifaceted religiousness. These two inseparable realities constitute in their interpenetration what might be designated as *Asian context*, the matrix of any theology truly Asian.... In fact, history attests... that the *theological* attempts to encounter Asian religions with no radical concern for Asia's poor and the *ideological* programs that presume to eradicate Asia's poverty with naive disregard for its religiousness, have both proved to be misdirected zeal.[60]

Based on this observation, Pieris criticized the "antithetical attitudes" toward religions held by some Asian Christians who had uncritically accepted the Latin American model of liberation theology that he called the "Christ-against-religions" theology.[61]

The concern with culture and religion so evident among Christians in Asia is not a new phenomenon. It is well known that two early Jesuit missionaries to Asia, Matteo Ricci to China and Roberto de Nobili to India, displayed a remarkable sensitivity to Asian cultures. They developed a missionary method that aimed at cultural adaptation to communicate the Gospel to indigenous people.[62]

60. Aloysius Pieris, *An Asian Theology of Liberation* (Maryknoll, N.Y.: Orbis, 1988), 69.

61. Ibid., 88, 90. Regarding the emphasis both on the religio-cultural and socio-political dimensions among Asian Christians, see also Gaudencio B. Rosales and C. G. Arévalo, eds., *For All the Peoples of Asia: Federation of Asian Bishops' Conferences, Documents from 1970 to 1991* (Maryknoll, N.Y.: Orbis, 1992; Quezon City, Philippines: Claretian Publications, 1992), xxv–xxvi, 14–16, 135–48; Samuel Rayan, "Reconceiving Theology in the Asian Context," in *Doing Theology in a Divided World: Papers from the Sixth International Conference of the Ecumenical Association of Third World Theologians, January 5–13, 1983, Geneva, Switzerland*, ed. Virginia Fabella and Sergio Torres (Maryknoll, N.Y.: Orbis, 1985), 125–28; R. S. Sugirtharajah, "Introduction," in *Frontiers in Asian Christian Theology: Emerging Trends*, ed. R. S. Sugirtharajah (Maryknoll, N.Y.: Orbis, 1994), 3.

62. See Stephen Neill, *A History of Christian Missions*, 2d ed., revised by Owen Chadwick (London: Penguin Books, 1986), 139–41, 156–59; Kenneth Scott Latourette, *A History of the Expansion of Christianity*, vol. 3, *Three Centuries of Advance: A.D. 1500–A.D. 1800* (Grand Rapids, Mich.: Zondervan, 1970), 259–62, 339–42.

Asian Christians today live in the context totally different from the one that confronted Ricci and de Nobili. Today's context is the modern Asian world with many nation-states: these nation-states, which came into being after the collapse of the Western colonial powers, have experienced the process of rapid modernization and yet are still in search for a more democratic and stable polity. As we have already discussed, Western influence forever shattered the coherence of traditional orders and legitimations. Yet neither truly stable social orders nor legitimations have fully emerged in most Asian societies. Thus, the impact of modernity remains vital to Asia in spite of the widespread talk of post-modernity.

Such a historical context has confronted both Christians and non-Christians commonly in postwar Asia. Christians' social status has, however, been particular because in Asian countries, except for the Philippines, they comprise a tiny group of those who rejected their traditional culture in favor of the religion alien to their societies. This situation has given Asian Christians a sense of double belonging. They were born and raised in societies whose cultures were shaped by the ethos and worldviews of traditional religions of Asia. Even though they have rejected traditional cultures, they are still bound to their societies by primordial attachments. As members of their own societies, they still share corporate historic memories with their non-Christian compatriots. Nevertheless, as Christians, they are committed to the values and worldview of the community built by Christian missionaries from Europe and North America. Due to this double belonging, Asian Christians are very susceptible to the problem of identity.

The sense of such double belonging was typically articulated by Kosuke Koyama, a Japanese Christian theologian and retired professor of Union Theological Seminary in New York. Being a Japanese, Koyama was aware that he was deeply rooted in the tradition of Japan in spite of his commitment to the Christian faith. In his *Mount Fuji and Mount Sinai*, he wrote: "When I came to Mount Calvary I brought my Japanese language, culture and psychology to Jesus Christ. No matter what I do, 'Prince Shotoku' is within me, just as Moses is found in every Jew."[63] This awareness led him to identify himself with this Japanese tradition. Contrasting himself with Martin Buber, who experienced "his identity in terms of the sacred tradition of Mount Sinai with the memory of all that happened there,"[64] Koyama explicitly confessed his identity as a Japanese as follows:

---

63. Kosuke Koyama, *Mount Fuji and Mount Sinai: A Critique of Idols* (Maryknoll, N.Y.: Orbis, 1985), 6–7.

64. Ibid., 8.

> A gentile and Japanese, I stand outside of that corporeality of sacred memory [of Israel]. But I do not find my spiritual home base in the tradition of the Christian cathedral either. The graveyard . . . in which I find my *identity* would be that of Mahayana Buddhism. I am proud of this great tradition. Its memory reaches back to the Enlightenment of Gotama Buddha. Born in a land which has embraced Mahayana Buddhism for thirteen centuries, I am invited to achieve Enlightenment in emulation of this great son of Asia. This profound memory is not to be scorned.[65]

Koyama is, however, a Christian. He converted to the Christian faith in his early teens. This experience gave him a new identity in addition to his primordial identity as a Japanese. Thus, he wrote:

> When I was baptized I sensed that I was moving from the cultural world of Mount Fuji to that of Mount Sinai. . . . [However,] Mount Calvary is more central than Mount Sinai for me as a Christian. It is in the name of Jesus Christ that I received a new *self-identity* both spiritual and cultural. With this new *identity* I began to appreciate the tradition presented by the name of Moses.[66]

Here again, Koyama explicitly spoke of his identity. His personal conversion and commitment to "Mount Calvary"—Jesus Christ—led him to the identification with the entire tradition that flows from "Mount Sinai," namely, the Judaeo-Christian tradition.

These passages reveal Koyama's awareness of the presence of two identities within himself. One is the national or ethnic identity based on the primordial sentiments. This identity stems from the "givens" of social existence; it both expresses and sustains itself in the symbolic systems peculiar to the indigenous tradition. The other is the Christian identity. This second identity could also be considered as primordial. In Asia, however, it often arises, as in Koyama's case, from a personal commitment to Christ that is not the given of society but the result of conscious conversion.[67]

---

65. Ibid. Emphasis mine.

66. Ibid., 6. Emphasis mine.

67. The awareness of double identity is also expressed in the following two passages: the first from the Japanese-American theologian Roy Sano, and the second from the Korean feminist Chung Hyun Kyung: "Because of warnings against syncretism, I once asked myself: 'How can I be Christian and yet Buddhist?' Through time, however, as I became aware of the extent to which Buddhism permeated my Japanese cultural heritage and I recognized how impossible it was to eliminate everything from that heritage, my question changed. I now asked: 'How can I be Christian without being Buddhist?'" (Roy Sano, "'Holy Moments' at Canberra," *Christianity and Crisis* 51 [15 July 1991]: 228); "I discovered my bowel is shamanist bowel, my heart is Buddhist heart and my head is

Such dual identification implies that two conflicting symbolic systems coexist within the world of an individual believer, as well as the Christian community, as distinct frames of reference, yet without being integrated. The consequence of this conflict is a fragmentation of the symbolic universe in which a believer and community live. Such a fragmentation drove Koyama to a conscious search for the integration of the two identities—the theological effort that he called a "creative two-way traffic" between "Mount Fuji" and "Mount Sinai."[68]

Many Christians in Asia, particularly Christian intellectuals and leaders, are likewise trying to reconcile and integrate these two conflicting systems of symbols.[69] In their attempts, they often "appropriate the religious symbols of their social and cultural environment in dealing with their own religious problems."[70] Simultaneously, they often break the established link between a Christian symbol and its classical meaning and give it a new interpretation.

Such a search of Asian Christians for holistic meaning can be either conscious or unconscious. In either case, it is complicated by the modern dilemma between identity and change, as discussed earlier, posed by the modernization process. That is to say, the Christian search for identity is intersected by the tension that exists in modernizing societies at large between their own search for identity and a demand for change. Christians' primordial identification, consequently, takes place between these two conflicting motives and locates itself somewhere within the wider spectrum of the attempt of modernizing nations to integrate the traditional identity based on primordial sentiments with the modern quest for change. This fact implies that the Christian search for identity entails the tension between two distinct orientations: one toward the past or the traditional, and the other toward the future or the modern.

A passage from Shoki Coe (C. H. Hwang), a Taiwanese Presbyterian theologian, serves as a telling example that reveals the presence of the different orientations within the Christian search for identity. As the direc-

---

Christian head" (Events and People, *Christian Century* 109 [11 March 1992]: 272).

68. Koyama, *Mount Fuji and Mount Sinai*, 7.

69. The Chinese theologian Archie Lee Chi Chung's "cross-textual" approach is another example for this attempt. He wrote: "A cross-textual approach aims at going beyond comparative studies and interfaith dialogue. It is a way to do theology which is meaningful to Asian Christians and theologians who have *both the identity of being Asian as well as being Christian* and who value both their cultural-religious text and the biblical text" (Archie Lee Chi Chung, "Cross-Textual Hermeneutics in Asian Context," *PTCA Bulletin* 5, no. 1 [1992]: 5, quoted in Sugirtharajah, "Introduction," 4. Emphasis mine.).

70. Bellah, *Beyond Belief*, 12.

tor of the TEF, Coe contributed greatly to the formulation of the idea of contextualization in the 1970s. In his 1973 article entitled "In Search of Renewal in Theological Education," he discussed why the idea of "indigenization" had become inadequate, and why the TEF report of 1972 had instead proposed the introduction of the idea of "contextualization."[71] According to him,

> Indigenous, indigeneity, and indigenization all derive from a nature metaphor, that is, of the soil, or taking root in the soil. It is only right that the younger churches, in search of their own identity, should take seriously their own cultural milieu. However, because of the static nature of the metaphor, indigenization tends to be used in the sense of responding to the Gospel in terms of traditional culture. Therefore, it is in danger of being past-oriented. Furthermore, the impression has been given that it is only applicable to Asia and Africa, for elsewhere it was felt that the danger lay in over-indigenization, an uncritical accommodation such as expressed by the culture faiths, the American Way of Life, etc. But the most important factor, especially since the last war, has been the new phenomenon of radical change. The new context is not that of static culture, but the search for the new, which at the same time has involved the culture itself.[72]

In this passage, Coe admitted that Christians' search for identity would demand their primordial identification, that is, "taking seriously their own cultural milieu." In the case of indigenization, this primordial identification was done in relation to the past, that is, a statically conceived "traditional culture." To Coe, however, such identification was insufficient since it resulted in ignoring a more important factor at work in a modernizing society, that is, the "phenomenon of radical change." He thus argued: "The new context is not that of static culture, but the search for the new, which at the same has involved the culture itself."

In other words, Coe held that Christians ought to identify themselves not only with the legitimations that traditionally gave identity and solidarity to their society, but with the demand of their society for social, political, and cultural change. Thus, he wrote: "So in using the word *contextualization*, we try to convey all that is implied in the familiar term *indigenization*, yet seek to press beyond for a more dynamic concept

---

71. Shoki Coe, "In Search of Renewal in Theological Education," *Theological Education* 9 (Summer 1973): 233–43. See p. 13 above.

72. Ibid., 240.

which is open to change and which is also future-oriented."[73] To Coe, Christians in modernizing societies were supposed to identify themselves with the dynamics of the modern operative in the midst of the traditional. Traditional culture and religion were also to be seen from this perspective. Such was the point that he tried to make by the term "contextualization." Contextualization was thus the idea which was primarily meant to be oriented toward modernity rather than tradition.[74]

Thus, Asian Christians' search for identity and holistic meaning is confronted by a question of how they should relate to the problems of meaning in their society at large. Should Christians relate to the search of their society for its own primordial identity? In this case, their quest would take a "romantic" tone[75] and emphasize the relationship between the Christian faith and traditional legitimations in Asia. Should they instead identify themselves with the demand for change, for modernization and progress? In this case, they would embark on the attempt to make sense of their religious commitment in terms of the process of socio-political transformation, modern secular ideologies, and the reform movement of traditional religion. There could also be an option that is a counterpart of what Bellah called the "radical socialist ideology," one of the "secondary ideologies of modernization." In this case, Christians would relate to the "disfavored strata and groups" in modernizing societies who have traditionally been oppressed by and, therefore, hostile toward "the established authorities and their charisma."[76] In recent years, some Christian intellectuals who themselves came from these strata are taking the initiative in a theological development in this direction.[77]

73. Ibid., 241.

74. To illustrate the difference between the context for indigenization and the one for contextualization, Coe uses Koyama's imagery of two contemporary Thailands. The first is "Thailand One, saturated by its nature, the seasons with which the rural community is tied up, symbolized by the leisurely pace of the water buffaloes, and impregnated religiously and culturally by Hinayana Buddhism." The second is "Thailand Two, undergoing rapid social change, urbanization, industrialization, modernization, symbolized by the cars crowding the cities and the jet planes coming in from all over the world." In addition to this, "the Lord of the Hosts is conducting the controversy with Thailand One (the unchanging one) through Thailand Two, which is crying out for change" ("In Search for Renewal," 240–41). This imagery graphically displays that the central issue at stake here is the relation between the modern and the traditional.

75. Bellah, *Beyond Belief,* 71.

76. Ibid.

77. See, for instance, Kuribayashi Teruo, "Recovering Jesus for Outcasts in Japan: From a Theology of the Crown of Thorns," *The Japanese Christian Review* 58 (1992): 19–32; John Parratt, "Recent Writing on Dalit Theology: A Bibliographical Essay," *International*

To sum it up, Asian Christians live at the intersection between two distinct problems of identity. One problem is the relationship between primordial and Christian identities. This problem is peculiar to the Christian community. The other is the problem of how to integrate the traditional with the modern, or the search for identity with the demand for change. Unlike the first one, this problem is shared commonly by both Christians and non-Christians. The primordial identity in the first problem and the search for identity in the second problem are both rooted in primordial attachments. To avoid confusion, therefore, the term "primordial identity" or "primordial identification" will be used in the rest of the study only when we refer to Christians' national or ethnic identity based on the primordial sentiments; otherwise, the identity that arises from these sentiments will generally be referred to as the "traditional identity."

Christian theology is a rational, systematic discourse that arises out of the religious experience of the Christian community mainly by the small group of intellectuals who belong to it. Whether context-sensitive or not, Christian theology in Asia takes its shape at the point where the two problems of identity intersect. This fact becomes especially evident when theologians attempt to take the socio-cultural milieu of Asia seriously, no matter whether this attempt is called indigenization, contextualization, or something else.

Geertz gave the term "integrative revolution" to the process in which a modernizing state tries to reconcile primordial attachments with the "unfolding civil order," and to contain "diverse primordial communities under a single sovereignty."[78] Likewise, the discourse through which a thinker tries to reconcile and integrate the conflicting symbolic systems in the process of modernization may be called "integrative" discourse. Developing Christian theologies in Asia as well as the rest of the Third World are thus considered as examples for such integrative discourse.

The Subject of This Study

In this study, I will argue that the idea that God is redemptively at work in world history has helped Christian intellectuals in postwar Asia to integrate two distinct symbolic systems, Christian and Asian, and make sense of their religious commitments in the cultural and social milieu of modernizing Asia. In other words, the thesis of the study is that the symbolism of "this-worldly presence of God" has played a central role in the search

---

Review of Mission 83 (April 1994): 329–37.

78. Geertz, *Interpretation*, 277.

of Asian Christians for identity and holistic meaning in the second half of the twentieth century.

To examine this thesis, I will concentrate on and compare the thought of two leading Christian intellectuals in contemporary Asia, namely, the Indian lay theologian M. M. Thomas (1916–96) and the overseas Taiwanese theologian C. S. Song (1929–). Because I am neither Indologist nor Sinologist, I will devote my attention to the formation of their theologies in response to the reality of their societies rather than extensively analyzing the cultural and social environments in which they operated. Thus, the study will mainly be concerned with questions, such as: How did these two thinkers perceive the reality or problems of their societies confronting them as Christians and attempt to overcome these problems intellectually?; how did the idea of God's this-worldly presence arise in this process?; and, what were the theological devices they developed for the discernment of God's presence in Asia?

Thomas and Song were chosen because they are leading Christian intellectuals who vigorously advocated the idea of God's this-worldly presence and thereby typically represented the world-centric orientation in the churches in postwar Asia.[79] As prolific writers and original thinkers, both of them significantly contributed to the Christian interpretation of Asian culture and society as well as the rise and development of ecumenical Christian theology from the Asian perspective. Their backgrounds were different; they were associated with different civilizations of Asia; their major concerns and approaches to theology and mission were also quite different. Nonetheless, the idea of God's this-worldly presence played a central role in their thinking.

Thomas belongs to the generation of Christians who developed the world-centric orientation in the Asian churches. From the late 1940s on, he made a tireless effort to formulate a theological and ideological basis for the Christian participation in the ongoing Asian revolution. This effort brought him to affirm: "God in Christ is present in the Asian revolution and his creative, judging and redemptive will is its essential dynamic."[80] In the 1960s, he pressed the WCC together with some Western Christian leaders to adopt the world-centric approach to mission.

---

79. Thomas and Song were chosen partly because of my personal favor. I regard their ways of thinking as personally inspiring and have had a desire to do an in-depth research into their theological thought.

80. M. M. Thomas, *The Christian Response to the Asian Revolution* (London: SCM, 1966), 27.

Song belongs to the generation of Asian theologians who began formulating their theology in the early 1970s with the help of this world-centric approach to mission. He rejected the classical view of salvation history and affirmed a "direct relationship" between God and the whole world. Using the *missio Dei* concept, he wrote: "The world has been God's mission field before the church was enlisted to serve the mission. And the world has not ceased to be God's mission field after the church has come to share that mission."[81] The affirmation of God's direct involvement in human history became fundamental to Song's construction of people-oriented theology.

Although the idea that the world is the arena of God's activity is certainly not extrinsic to Christianity,[82] it gained special momentum in ecumenical mission thinking in the 1960s. The idea of God's this-worldly presence was, subsequently, expressed on various occasions by many conciliar mission thinkers. This development was closely related to the debate over the world-centric view of *missio Dei* in the conciliar circle in the decade. As David J. Bosch observed, Christian mission thinking during the second half of the twentieth century experienced "a subtle but nevertheless decisive shift toward understanding mission as *God's* mission," or *missio Dei*.[83] The term *missio Dei* emerged in the 1950s in the West. The concept was initially intended to emphasize the Trinitarian origin of the mission of the Church; it was, therefore, theocentric as well as Church-centric. The emphasis, however, shifted in the 1960s from the Triune God as the source of mission towards the world as the locus of God's mission. The WCC study project entitled "The Missionary Structure of the Congregation" played an important role in this shift toward the world-centric *missio Dei*. Two study groups in North America and Europe attempted to reformulate Christian mission, affirming that God was at work in world history even outside the Church. They also affirmed that in God's saving act "God's primary relationship is to the world," and that "it is the world and not the Church that is the focus of God's plan." The groups thus declared that Christians had to allow "actual life situations" of modern society "to provide the agenda for the churches" and direct the renewal and mission of congregations.[84]

81. C. S. Song, *Tell Us Our Name: Story Theology from an Asian Perspective* (Maryknoll, N.Y.: Orbis, 1984), 13.

82. David J. Bosch, *Transforming Mission: Paradigm Shifts in Theology of Mission* (Maryknoll, N.Y.: Orbis, 1991), 426.

83. Ibid., 389.

84. *The Church for Others and the Church for the World: A Quest for Structures for*

Because the 1960s were the decade when the Third World theologies began to emerge in many parts of the world, it was not strange that the *missio Dei* concept gained wide current among Third World theologians.[85] Unlike Western traditional theology that never took into account their culture and society, the world-centric *missio Dei* concept helped them to see their own world in relation to God's redemption.

The wide circulation of the concept among Third World theologians resulted in a belief among some Western missiologists that the *missio Dei* concept was first formed in the West and then spread into the rest of the world, giving a rise to various types of contextual theology. Dietrich Werner of Germany, for instance, wrote: "Through the medium of Uppsala the idea of the *missio Dei* and historical theology continued to have an effect in the contextual theologies of Asia and Latin America."[86] The Lutheran missiologist James A. Scherer also shares a similar view. He condemned the world-centric view of *missio Dei* as "the wrong interpretations [*sic*] of *Missio Dei*"[87] and wrote:

> In the decade of the 1960s, *Missio Dei* was to become the play-thing of armchair theologians with little more than an academic

---

Missionary Congregations, Final Report of the Western European Working Group and North American Working Group of the Department on Studies in Evangelism (Geneva: WCC, 1968), 16–17, 20–23.

85. See, for instance, Coe, "In Search of Renewal," 241–43; D. T. Niles, *Upon the Earth: The Mission of God and the Missionary Enterprise of the Churches* (New York: McGraw-Hill, 1962); Shoki Coe, "Across the Frontiers: Text and Context of Mission," in *Christian Action in the Asian Struggle*, by Christian Conference of Asia (Singapore: CCA, [1973?]), 70–80; Emerito Nacpil, "Mission and Modernization," in *What Asian Christians Are Thinking: A Theological Source Book*, ed. Douglas J. Elwood (Quezon City: New Day Publishers, 1976), 277–88; Orlando E. Costas, *Christ Outside the Gate: Mission Beyond Christendom* (Maryknoll, N.Y.: Orbis, 1982), 43–44, 52–53, 88–91; Emilio Castro, *Sent Free: Mission and Unity in the Perspective of the Kingdom* (Grand Rapids, Mich.: Eerdmans, 1985); M. Azariah, *Mission in Christ's Way in India* (Madras: Christian Literature Society for the Church of South India, 1989), 9; Kim Yong-Bock, "Keynote Address: The Mission of God in the Context of the Suffering and Struggling Peoples of Asia," in *Peoples of Asia, People of God: A Report of the Asia Mission Conference 1989* (Osaka: CCA, 1989), 5–32.

86. Dietrich Werner, "Missionary Structure of the Congregation," in *Dictionary of the Ecumenical Movement*, ed. Nicholas Lossky et al. (Geneva: WCC, 1991; Grand Rapids, Mich.: Eerdmans, 1991).

87. James A. Scherer, "Church, Kingdom, and *Missio Dei*: Lutheran and Orthodox Correctives to Recent Ecumenical Mission Theology," in *The Good News of the Kingdom: Mission Theology for the Third Millennium*, ed. Charles Van Engen, Dean S. Gilliland, and Paul Pierson (Maryknoll, N.Y.: Orbis, 1993), 85.

interest in the practical mission of the church but with a considerable penchant for theological speculation and mischief making.[88]

The meaning of "armchair theologians" is clear, for Scherer also calls them "armchair mission strategists from Western Europe and the United States, operating under a mandate to examine the 'missionary structure of the local congregation' in the period before Uppsala."[89] Obviously, he referred to those who worked for the above-mentioned WCC project and published the reports *The Church for Others and the Church for the World* in 1967. Whether or not it is fair to label them "armchair theologians," his presupposition was obviously that the world-centric *missio Dei* was a product of Western theological thinking.

In Asia, however, the idea expressed by the world-centric *missio Dei* concept already existed before this Latin term and its English equivalent "God's mission" emerged in the West and gained wide currency among Asian Christians. In his study of the ecumenical movement in Asia, Hans-Ruedi Weber distinguished two types of spirituality observable among Asian Christians: "other-worldly holiness" and "this-worldly holiness."[90] The first was the attitude that "seeks union with God by mediation, Christian *yoga*, often expressing itself in an other-worldly attitude." To Weber, this trend, sometimes referred to as "the mystic way of life," was particularly strong in India before the Second World War.[91] This-worldly holiness was, in contrast, the spirituality that emphasized "the presence of God in *this* world."[92] Weber described this spirituality as follows:

> It calls thus for a 'secular holiness,' the participation in God's life and mission by living in and for this world. The spokesmen for this trend fight the other-worldly tendency in Asian church life and oppose what they call pietism. A life submitted to the living Lord means for them active participation in the struggles of this time in costly obedience to God's will and in discerning co-operation with

---

88. Ibid.

89. Ibid.

90. The terms "other-worldly" and "this-worldly" are here used merely descriptively. They should not be understood to imply any value judgment on these spiritualities. This terminology also applies to the rest of this study.

91. Hans-Ruedi Weber, *Asia and the Ecumenical Movement 1895–1961* (London: SCM Press, 1966), 294. Weber refers to Sadhu Sundar Singh and A. J. Appasamy, both from India, as examples for this trend. See also Robin Boyd, *An Introduction to Indian Christian Theology*, rev. ed. (Delhi: ISPCK, 1989), 19–185.

92. Weber, *Asia and the Ecumenical Movement*, 295.

his judging and redeeming work in the religions, cultures, nations and revolutions of men.[93]

Weber noted that this type of spirituality had already been "present among the early *samurai* converts of Japan" and in the life of people like Chengting Wang of China and K. T. Paul of India before the war.[94]

Weber noted further that this-worldly holiness had "gained force especially since the war" in Asian churches, though he left the reader with no detailed account of this development.[95] As we shall see in the third chapter, the ecumenical movement in Asia has indeed been characterized by a steady emphasis on the world since the first ecumenical meeting in Asia held in Bangkok in 1949. In this aspect, ecumenism in Asia has been in a remarkable contrast with the ecumenical movement in general centered on the West, for the latter has, as we shall see in the second chapter, displayed a constant oscillation and tension between the Church-centric and the world-centric approaches to mission. In fact, this-worldly holiness in Asian churches did significantly contribute to the formulation of the world-centric *missio Dei* through their increasing influence on the ecumenical movement in general. Therefore, it would be too simplistic to presuppose, as Werner and Scherer did, that the idea expressed by the *missio Dei* in the 1960s originated in the West alone. Rather, the concept developed over years through dialogical interactions between Asian Christians, such as Thomas,[96] and Western Christians. For a better understanding of the development of ecumenical thinking, it is essential to look into the interactions that occurred among regional variations of Christian thinking at different localities of the world long before the emergence of the Third World theologies.

To understand and compare Thomas and Song adequately, we have to situate them in the above-discussed context of the ecumenical movement. First, therefore, we will survey the development of this-worldly holiness in ecumenical mission thinking centered on the West, more specifically in the IMC and the WCC. Then, we will look into the development of this-worldly holiness in ecumenical thinking in Asia, particularly in the CCA, to which both Thomas and Song greatly contributed. Thus, the global—in

---

93. Ibid.

94. Ibid.

95. Ibid., 295–98.

96. Weber mentioned Thomas, as well as Masao Takenaka of Japan, as representing the this-worldly holiness after the Second World War (*Asia and the Ecumenical Movement*, 295).

fact mostly Western—ecumenical movement and the regional ecumenism in Asia will be the subjects of the second and third chapters of this study.

After the surveys of ecumenical mission thinking, I will analyze Thomas in the fourth chapter and Song in the fifth chapter. In both cases, the chapters will begin with a brief sketch of the theologian's background, including society, church, and early life. I will then discuss his primary concerns and motives for the intellectual search and examine his attempt to respond to the questions arising from them. Because our theme in this study is this-worldly holiness, these chapters will basically focus on the question of the kinds of theological understandings that these two theologians developed regarding the relationship between God and the world.

Finally, Thomas's and Song's this-worldly holiness will be compared briefly in the conclusion of the study. This comparison will be made in the light of my view that Christian theologies in Asia may be viewed as integrative discourse for the sake of the intellectual search of Asian Christians for identity and holistic meaning.

CHAPTER 2

This-Worldly Holiness and the *Missio Dei* Concept in Ecumenical Mission Thinking

THE GOAL OF THIS and the following chapters is to trace the development of this-worldly holiness in ecumenical mission thinking in the West as well as Asia after the Second World War. This-worldly holiness is a type of spirituality that takes the world seriously. It does not confine the divine or ultimate reality to certain spheres of human life, such as the sphere outside of human history, in the interior of a person, or inside of the church or any other religious group. Instead, it considers the divine reality to be related to the entire world, including its ordinary, secular sphere, and seeks and experiences the reality in the midst of secular life. This-worldly holiness, thus, assumes a positive attitude toward worldly affairs.

In the history of Christianity, such a spirituality was by no means peculiar to the period after the Second World War. As Max Weber's famous study of the rise of modern capitalism shows, for instance, Protestantism in the sixteenth and seventeenth centuries, particularly Puritanism, displayed a remarkable world-affirming ethos.[1] A this-worldly spirituality is, nonetheless, one of the outstanding features of the postwar Christian thinking in the ecumenical movement that was marked by a growing concern for world history and creation. The theological renewal of Asian churches led by the Christian leaders, including M. M. Thomas and C. S. Song, who gathered in the EACC/CCA was also a manifestation of such a trend. The ecumenical organizations, both worldwide and regional, played a crucial role in the development of a this-worldly spirituality.

In this chapter, I will concentrate my effort on the questions of how this-worldly holiness developed in the IMC and the WCC, and what role the *missio Dei* concept played in this development. These international organizations originated in the West. While the WCC membership and

---

1. Max Weber, *The Protestant Ethic and the Spirit of Capitalism*, trans. Talcott Parsons, with an introduction by Anthony Giddens (New York: Scribner, 1976), 79–81, 95–154.

staff have grown to become global, the WCC is geographically and linguistically still centered in the West.[2] The survey will, therefore, trace the unfolding of this-worldly holiness in ecumenical mission thinking not on the global level, but mainly in the West. As ecumenism in Asia has constantly been interacting with the development in the West, this survey will provide the background for the understanding of this-worldly spirituality in the EACC/CCA that will be dealt with in the next chapter.

Ecumenism as the Search for Wholeness

At the Nairobi Assembly of the WCC in 1975, the then moderator of the Central Committee, M. M. Thomas, referred to the "emphasis on the whole gospel for the whole man in the whole world" as one aspect of the theological convergence taking place in the early 1970s among conciliar-ecumenical, evangelical, Roman Catholic, and Eastern Orthodox circles.[3]

---

2. The fact that the ecumenical movement is still dominated by some major Western languages has a significant cultural and ideological implication. Following the linguist Benjamin L. Whorf's tradition, Robert Hodge and Gunther Kress write: "Whatever has a name can become familiar, and is easier to classify and remember. Only what has a name can be shared. Communicable perception has to be coded in language. So language, which is given by society, determines which perceptions are potentially social ones. These perceptions, fixed in language, become a kind of second nature. We inevitably impose our classifications on others, and on ourselves. Language plays a vital role in what has been called the 'social construction of reality.' . . . But language, typically, is immersed in the ongoing life of a society, as a practical consciousness of that society. This consciousness is inevitably a partial and false consciousness. We can call it ideology, defining 'ideology' as a systematic body of ideas, organized from a particular point of view. . . . Language is an instrument of control as well as communication. Linguistic forms allow significance to be conveyed and to be distorted. In this way hearers can be both manipulated and informed, preferably manipulated while they suppose they are being informed. Language is ideological in another, more political, sense of that word: it involves systematic distortion in the service of class interests" (*Language as Ideology*, 2d ed. [London: Routledge, 1993], 5–6). This observation regarding the intrinsic relationship between language, thought, and ideology sheds light on a serious problem of the ecumenical movement: that is, the continuing use of the Western languages as the common languages in the WCC inevitably implies the continuing Western dominance over ecumenism on the cultural and ideological level, even though the WCC has become increasingly non-Western on the organizational level. The observation also reveals the inherent problem of using English as the common language in the ecumenical movement in Asia. Although this issue is important, its impact on ecumenical mission thinking is beyond the scope of the current study.

3. David M. Paton, ed., *Breaking Barriers, Nairobi 1975: The Official Report of the Fifth Assembly of the World Council of Churches, Nairobi, 23 November–10 December, 1975* (London: SPCK, 1976; Grand Rapids, Mich.: Eerdmans, 1976), 231–32; James A. Scherer, *Gospel, Church, and Kingdom: Comparative Studies in World Mission Theology* (Minneapolis: Augsburg, 1987), 127.

This phrase "the whole gospel for the whole man in the whole world" goes back to a meeting of the Central Committee of the WCC held in Rolle, Switzerland, in 1951. There, a proposal was made that the term "ecumenical" should be used "to describe everything that relates to the whole task of the whole Church to bring the Gospel to the whole world."[4] Since then, this phrase and its variations were constantly repeated by the leaders of the ecumenical movement on various occasions as the reminder for the indissoluble connection between mission and unity within the movement.

The phrase thus served as a symbolic expression for the holistic vision that the movement attempted to materialize through its endeavors. It implies that the movement may be understood as a search for the authentic Christian identity. In other words, ecumenism was a movement that tried to answer the question of what it meant to be Christian in the broadest perspective imaginable and overcome the historical fragmentation of Christianity on the intellectual, cultic, and organizational levels.[5]

This-worldly holiness in mission thinking in the West was an outcome of such a search for wholeness and totality. The modern Protestant missionary movement originated in German Pietism in the early eighteenth century and reached its climax in the late nineteenth-century in the wake of the Second Great Awakening in the Anglo-Saxon world. A result was the pietistic emphasis on the personal salvation of the individual envisioned as a separation from the world. This "other-worldly" view of salvation was typically expressed by Dwight L. Moody in his statement, "I look upon this world as a wrecked vessel. God has given me a lifeboat and said to me, 'Moody, save all you can.'"[6] The concern for wholeness in ecumenical mission thinking increasingly manifested itself as the emphasis on this-worldliness in its continuous attempt to counterbalance such a one-sided tendency.

Another outcome of the search for wholeness and totality in ecumenism was the encounter and integration of mission thinking with both Christian theology and social thinking. In the nineteenth century, Christian social action, or the *Innere Mission*, and foreign missions devel-

---

4. "The Calling of the Church to Mission and to Unity," *Ecumenical Review* 4 (October 1951): 68; Rodger C. Bassham, *Mission Theology: 1948–1975 Years of Worldwide Creative Tension Ecumenical, Evangelical, and Roman Catholic* (Pasadena, Calif.: William Carey Library, 1979), 31–32.

5. As for this three distinct levels of religion, see Thomas F. O'Dea and Janet O'Dea Aviad, *The Sociology of Religion*, 2d ed. (Englewood Cliffs, N.J.: Prentice-Hall, 1983), 40–41.

6. Bosch, *Transforming Mission*, 318.

oped separately. After the World Missionary Conference at Edinburgh in 1910, this development resulted in the formation of two distinct branches of the ecumenical movement, namely, the IMC and the Life and Work movement.[7] A traditional rift also existed between Christian theology and the missionary enterprise. Christian theology, on one hand, rarely paid attention to missions. As the church historian Wilhelm Pauck commented,

> with the possible exception of the early Church, whose theology was decisively shaped by the missionary spirit, no part of Christendom has produced major theological responsibility and creativeness in connection with evangelistic endeavors.[8]

The missionary movement, on the other hand, did not take much interest in theology since it did not arise from the conscious theological reflection of the Church.[9] As a result, missiology also came into being as a discipline independent of theology. The ecumenical movement initiated in Edinburgh in 1910 gradually brought together these differentiated spheres of Christian life. This development was a process of the mutual rediscovery of social action, foreign missions, and theology in Christianity.

The Search for the Theological Foundation of Christian Mission and the Emergence of the *Missio Dei* Concept

The process for integration of the different spheres of Christian life was made possible by a more fundamental discovery, that is, the mutual discovery between the Church and mission.[10] In the nineteenth century, Protestant foreign missions were chiefly carried out by missionary societies. In the middle of the century, however, the Church began to play a crucial role in the missionary practice. Mission was then defined in terms

---

7. M. M. Thomas, *Recalling Ecumenical Beginnings* (Delhi: I.S.P.C.K., 1987), 10–11, 15.

8. Wilhelm Pauck, "Theology in the Life of Contemporary American Protestantism," in *Religion and Culture: Essays in Honor of Paul Tillich*, ed. Walter Leibrecht (New York: Harper and Bros., 1959), 278, quoted in Gerald H. Anderson, ed., *The Theology of the Christian Mission* (New York: McGraw-Hill, 1961), 3–4.

9. Wilhelm Andersen, *Towards a Theology of Mission: A Study of the Encounter between the Missionary Enterprise and the Church and its Theology*, I.M.C. Research Pamphlet No. 2 (London: SCM Press, 1955), 13.

10. Ibid., 12, 15; Gerald A. Anderson, "Introduction: The Theology of Mission among Protestants in the Twentieth Century," in *The Theology of the Christian Mission*, ed. Gerald A. Anderson (New York: McGraw-Hill, 1961), 4.

of *plantatio ecclesiae* (church planting). The planting of "self-governing," "self-supporting," and "self-propagating" indigenous churches came to be considered as the main missionary goal under the leadership of Henry Venn and Rufus Anderson.[11]

After Edinburgh 1910, the role of the Church increasingly became central also to missionary thinking.[12] The IMC conference at Tambaram in 1938 was especially significant in this development. There it was affirmed that "the Church . . . is ultimately the bearer of the Christian mission and of the evangelistic task."[13] Various historical factors, such as the growth of the "younger" churches, the resurgent paganism in Europe, the political crises in the world, and the influence of Karl Barth, contributed to the Tambaram emphasis on the Church.[14] This emphasis was the recognition—theological as well as practical—that "mission and Church are indissolubly related to one another."[15] After the Second World War, the conviction that the Church and mission belonged together was strengthened by the recognition of the partnership between the "younger" and the "older" churches at the IMC conference at Whitby in 1947 and the formation of the WCC in 1948.

The move towards the discovery of the inseparable relationship between the Church and mission, quite naturally, impelled mission thinkers to seek the theological foundation common to both of them. An urge for such a search was well articulated by Wilhelm Andersen:

> If we wish to discover anew the theological basis of the missionary enterprise, if it is our purpose to formulate a theology of missions, it is not the Church which should be the starting-point of our investigation, and our thought must not remain confined within the boundaries and limits of the Church. Theologically, we must dig deeper; we must trace out the originating impulse in faith in the triune God; from that standpoint alone can we see the missionary

---

11. Bosch, *Transforming Mission*, 331–32; Scherer, "Church, Kingdom, and *Missio Dei*," 82–83.

12. Andersen, *Theology of Mission*, 15–22.

13. Feliciano V. Carino, "Partnership in Obedience," *International Review of Mission* 67 (July 1978): 318.

14. Rouse and Neill, *History of the Ecumenical Movement*, 369–70; Lesslie Newbigin, "The Call to Mission—A Call to Unity?" in *The Church Crossing Frontiers: Essays on the Nature of Mission in Honour of Bengt Sundkler*, ed. Peter Beyerhaus and Carl F. Hallencreutz, Studia Missionalia Upsaliensia ([Lund]: Gleerup, 1969), 255; Andersen, *Theology of Mission*, 21; Evert Jansen Schoonhoven, "Tambaram 1938," *International Review of Mission* 67 (July 1978): 303–4.

15. Andersen, *Theology of Mission*, 20, 29.

enterprise synoptically in its relationship to the Kingdom of God and in its relationship to the world.[16]

The urgent necessity for the reorientation of Christian mission was intensified by other historical factors that radically shook the traditional missionary approach: the collapse of Western colonialism and the decline of "Christendom," the rise of nationalism among Third World nations and the resurgence of traditional local religions, the victory of the militant Marxism in many parts of the world, particularly in China and Eastern Europe, and the change of the relationship between the "sending" and "receiving" churches as the result of the growth of the latter.[17] Thus, the serious question about the missionary task emerged as to "whether our present patterns of carrying out that task and the conceptions behind such patterns are the right expression of the obedience God wants from us today."[18]

It is in this junction that the concept of *missio Dei* came into being as a clue to the new understanding of mission. According to L. A. Hoedemaker, the term *missio Dei* had already been used in 1934 by the German missiologist Karl Hartenstein.[19] Under Barth's influence, Hartenstein grounded missionary sending in the Word of God and argued that mission takes place when and where Christ gathers his Church through the Word of God.[20] It was, however, in the 1950s that the *missio*

16. Ibid., 10.

17. Ibid., 12–13; Anderson, "Introduction," 3; Arthur F. Glasser and Donald A. McGavran, *Contemporary Theologies of Mission* (Grand Rapids, Mich.: Baker Book House, 1983), 85–90; Scherer, *Gospel, Church, and Kingdom*, 19–34.

18. W[alter] Freytag, "Changes in the Patterns of Western Missions," in *The Ghana Assembly of the International Missionary Council, 28th December, 1957 to 8th January, 1958: Selected Papers, with an Essay on the Rôle of the I.M.C.*, ed. Ronald K. Orchard (London: Edinburgh House Press for the International Missionary Council, 1958), 139.

19. L[ibertus] A. Hoedemaker, "The People of God and the Ends of the Earth," in *Missiology: An Ecumenical Introduction: Texts and Contexts of Global Christianity*, ed. F. J. Verstraelen, A. Camps, L. A. Hoedemaker, and M. R. Spindler (Grand Rapids, Mich.: Eerdmans, 1995), 163.

20. Karl Hartenstein, *Die Mission als theologisches Problem: Beiträge zum grundsätzlichen Verständnis der Mission* (Berlin: Furche-Verlag, 1933), 13–14. As to Barth's influence on Hartenstein, see Michael W. Stroope, "Eschatological Mission: Its Reality and Possibility in the Theology of Karl Barth and Its Influence on Modern Mission Theology" (Ph.D. diss., Southwestern Baptist Theological Seminary, 1985), 172–79. The significance of Barth was also discussed by Johannes Aagaard. In his excellent analysis of modern Protestant missiology, Aagaard referred to the Trinitarian definition of mission presented by Barth in his lecture in 1932 as the *missio Dei* and argued that the subsequent development of the *missio Dei* concept was the result of Barth's "decisive" influence on the twentieth-century

Dei concept as well as the Latin term became widely used. The IMC conference held at Willingen, Germany, in 1952 played an important role in this development. It was a catalyst to the emergence of the concept.[21] Held under the theme "The Missionary Obligation of the Church," the conference examined afresh "the Biblical and theological basis of the Church's missionary obligation" and "the role of the missionary movement at this particular moment in history."[22]

Willingen 1952 was, however, not necessarily successful. Its participants failed to reach an agreement regarding the theological basis for Christian mission. The failure was due to the heated debate that the preparatory documents incited, which had been composed by a number of individuals, and the differences the study groups generated with their contrasting approaches.[23] The Dutch missiologist J. C. Hoekendijk's critical thinking also contributed to this debate. He criticized the dominant Church-centric approach as nothing but an attempt to restore the *Corpus Christianum*.[24] He then proposed to take the relationship between God and the world as the primary determinant for Christian mission.[25] The Church was to be seen as "a function of the Apostolate, that is, an instrument of God's redemptive action in this world."[26] In other words, "the

---

Protestant missiology (Johannes Aagaard, "Some Main Trends in Modern Protestant Missiology," *Studia Theologica* 19 [1965]: 238–39, 244–46). See also Bosch, *Transforming Mission*, 390; Karsten Nissen, Review of *Missio Dei*, by H. H. Rosin, in *International Review of Mission* 62 (1973): 496.

21. Bassham, *Mission Theology*, 167; Bosch, *Transforming Mission*, 390; Glasser and McGavran, *Theologies of Mission*, 91; Scherer, *Gospel, Church, and Kingdom*, 96; Eric J. Sharpe, "New Directions in the Theology of Mission," *Evangelical Quarterly* 46 (January–March 1974): 11; Johannes Verkuyl, *Contemporary Missiology: An Introduction*, tr. and ed. Dale Cooper (Grand Rapids, Mich.: Eerdmans, 1978), 3. According to Bosch (*Transforming Mission*, 390), Aagaard ("Some Main Trends," 251–52), and Stroope ("Eschatological Mission," 197, 200–207), the Barthian influence was crucial at this conference. Stroope writes that "Willingen represents the general acknowledgment and the summary statement of Barth's thought in modern mission thought" (ibid., 197).

22. International Missionary Council, "A New Study of the Missionary Obligation of the Church," TD [mimeographed], The Missionary Obligation of the Church: (Papers and Reports), Speer Library, Princeton Theological Seminary, Princeton, N.J., 1.

23. Bassham, *Mission Theology*, 33–34; idem, "Seeking a Deeper Theological Basis for Mission," *The International Review of Mission* 67 (1978): 329–30.

24. J. C. Hoekendijk, "The Call to Evangelism," *International Review of Missions* 39 (1950): 163.

25. J. C. Hoekendijk, "The Church in Missionary Thinking," *International Review of Missions* 41 (1952): 333–34.

26. Hoekendijk, "Call to Evangelism," 170.

nature of the Church can be sufficiently defined by its *function*, i.e. its participation in Christ's apostolic ministry. . . . it lives only in so far as it partakes actively in the 'economy of witness.'"[27] This radical view of Hoekendijk's was resisted by other participants. The conference was still unable to adopt the report produced by the group that worked on the theological basis of the missionary obligation. It only received the report and instead adopted a document entitled "A Statement on the Missionary Calling of the Church"[28] prepared by Lesslie Newbigin, Paul Lehmann, Russell Chandran, and Karl Hartenstein.[29]

This "failure," however, did not mean that Willingen 1952 really failed. Rather, it marked an important step forward towards the emerging theology of mission. Willingen was particularly successful in giving the solid Trinitarian foundation to Christian mission. It gained this insight from the North American preparatory study document entitled "Why Missions?" The study suggested that Christian mission was shifting "from vigorous Christo-centricity to thoroughgoing trinitarianism,"[30] and stated:

> Missionary theology, centered upon the reconciling action of the triune God, is . . . a living way of thinking about and of understanding life in the Church and in the world. . . . Missionary obligation, grounded in the reconciling action of the triune God, is . . . the sensitive and total response of the Church to what the triune God has done and is doing in the world.[31]

Following this way of thinking, Willingen affirmed: "The missionary movement of which we are a part has its sources in the Triune God Himself."[32] The statement continued:

> Out of the depths of His love for us, the Father has sent forth His own beloved Son to reconcile all things to Himself, that we and

27. Hoekendijk, "Church in Missionary Thinking," 334–35.

28. Norman Goodall, ed., *Missions under the Cross: Addresses Delivered at the Enlarged Meeting of the Committee of the International Missionary Council at Willingen, in Germany, 1952; with Statements Issued by the Meeting* (London: Edinburgh House Press for the International Missionary Council, 1953), 188–92.

29. Bassham, *Mission Theology*, 34.

30. Committee on Research in Foreign Missions, Division of Foreign Missions and the Central Department of Research and Survey, National Council of the Churches of Christ in the U.S.A., "The Missionary Obligation of the Church: Why Missions?" Report of Commission I on the Biblical and Theological Basis of Missions, 26 February 1952, mimeographed, 6; Bassham, "Seeking a Deeper Basis," 330.

31. Committee on Research in Foreign Missions, "Why Missions?" 6.

32. Goodall, *Missions under the Cross*, 189.

all men might, through the Spirit, be made one in Him with the Father in that perfect love which is the very nature of God.... On the foundation of this accomplished work [of atonement in Jesus Christ] God has sent forth His Spirit, the Spirit of Jesus, to gather us together in one Body in Him, to guide us into all truth, to enable us to worship the Father in spirit and in truth, to empower us for the continuance of His mission as His witnesses and ambassadors, the first fruits and earnest of its completion.[33]

Thus, it was maintained that the missionary obligation of the Church came from the very nature of the Church as the community of those who are chosen in Christ and reconciled to God. The mission of the Church was essentially a commitment "to full participation in His redeeming mission to the world," that is, "there is no participation in Christ without participation in His mission to the world."[34] Here, one can see Hoekendijk's influence clearly.

This was the *missio Dei* as Willingen formulated it.[35] It shows a clear shift from Church-centrism to theocentrism. Christian mission now ceased to be seen as *our* work or the Church's work. It was instead understood as the reconciling action of the Triune God who, in Christ, sends forth the Church to the world through the Holy Spirit. Five years later, the Ghana Assembly of the IMC confirmed this understanding of mission, declaring: "The Christian world mission is Christ's, not ours."[36]

33. Ibid.

34. Ibid., 190.

35. According to H. H. Rosin, the documents produced by the conference never used the Latin term *missio Dei*. The term was revived by Hartenstein immediately after Willingen 1952 in his conference report entitled "Theologische Besinnung." The English phrases "God's mission" and "his mission" were, however, used in some Willingen documents. According to Rosin's study, these phrases were given a greater emphasis in the unpublished draft documents produced at Willingen by the group working on the theological basis of mission (H. H. Rosin, *'Missio Dei': An Examination of Origin, Contents and Function of the Term in Protestant Missiological Discussion* [Leiden: Interuniversity Institute for Missiological and Ecumenical Research, Department of Missiology, [Foreword 1972]], 6–7, 17; Karl Hartenstein, "Theologische Besinnung," in *Mission zwischen Gestern und Morgen: Vom Gestaltwandel der Weltmission der Christenheit im Licht der Konferenz des Internationalen Missionsrats in Willingen*, ed. Walter Freytag, G. Brennecke, K. Hartenstein, C. Ihmels, A. Lehmann, and E. Verwiebe [Stuttgart: Evang. Missionsverlag, 1952], 54, 62; Johannes Aagaard, "Trends in Missiological Thinking during the Sixties," *International Review of Mission* 62 [1973]: 12; Goodall, *Missions under the Cross*, 189; Committee on Research in Foreign Missions, "Why Missions?" 11, 13).

36. Ronald K. Orchard, ed., *The Ghana Assembly of the International Missionary Council, 28th December, 1957 to 8th January, 1958: Selected Papers, with an Essay on the Role of the I.M.C.* (London: Edinburgh House Press for the International Missionary Council, 1958), 180.

Despite such a shift at Willingen, the Church-centric approach to mission remained dominant, and the *missio Dei* was thought to be mediated by the Church as its bearer. One of the proponents of this position was the German missiologist Georg F. Vicedom who popularized the term *missio Dei* among the ecumenical missionary circles with the publication of his book entitled *Missio Dei*.[37] He held that the *missio Dei* was God's redemptive activity to incorporate humankind into the Kingdom of God of which he conceived as utterly transcending all the human spheres where satanic powers were at work.[38] Rejecting Hoekendijk's view of the Church as a function of the apostolate, Vicedom argued that the Church was "the bearer of the apostolate."[39] According to him, the apostolate was the office that belonged to the discipleship of the people of God, that is, to the Church.[40] It was a basic function of the Church. The Church as its bearer was "privileged to act in God's stead" by proclaiming the Word of God to the world and thus performing the *missio Dei*.[41] His Church-centric position was made plain in his statement: "The church's mission is at the same time the *missio Dei* at the present time, included and formed by the *missio Dei*."[42]

Lesslie Newbigin was another proponent of the Church-centric notion of *missio Dei*. In 1958, he published a booklet entitled *One Body, One Gospel, One World* and tried to prepare the ecumenical missionary circles for the imminent integration of the IMC and the WCC with a new missionary vision centered on the idea of unity.[43] In this work, Newbigin stated: "The Church's mission is none other than the carrying on of the mission of Christ Himself." In other words, Christian mission is "the continuing work of Christ Himself through Holy Spirit," and "the Church participates in the mission only by virtue of its participation in the Holy Spirit."[44]

---

37. Georg F. Vicedom, *Missio Dei: Einführung in eine Theologie der Mission* (Munich: Chr. Kaiser Verlag, 1958); Aagaard, "Trends during the Sixties," 12. The English version of Vicedom's work is *The Mission of God: An Introduction to a Theology of Mission*, tr. Gilbert A. Thiele and Dennis Hilgendorf (St. Louis: Concordia Publishing House, 1965).

38. Vicedom, *Mission of God*, 14, 17–26.

39. Ibid., 81.

40. Ibid., 77–80.

41. Ibid., 83.

42. Ibid.

43. Lesslie Newbigin, *One Body, One Gospel, One World: The Christian Mission Today* (London: International Missionary Council, 1958).

44. Ibid., 17–19.

Newbigin thus strongly emphasized the relation between the Church and the Holy Spirit and called the former "the community of the Holy Spirit."[45] Such a pneumatological approach made it possible for him to give the Church a prominent role in the *missio Dei*. To Newbigin, the significance of the Church was threefold. The Church was first "the place where the fruit of Christ's mission is already present in foretaste." Secondly, it was "the place where the powers of the Holy Spirit are available to serve men in all their needs." Finally, it was the community that bore witness to that which transcended it, that is, to God's mercy and judgment in Jesus Christ.[46] Newbigin, however, held that the witness to God's reconciling mission became both authentic and effective only when the Church united all Christians. Thus, Newbigin called Christians to unity and urged them to take seriously the idea of "the whole Church with one Gospel for the whole world."[47]

The Church-centric approach to Christian mission reached its culmination with the integration of the WCC and the IMC and the creation of the Commission of World Mission and Evangelism (CWME) at the New Delhi Assembly in 1961. The Assembly reaffirmed the *missio Dei* concept saying: "God is his own witness; that is to say, God has been and is at work authenticating his own message to men."[48] Quite naturally, the emphasis was placed on the Church, for the merger of two bodies, one representing the Church and the other mission, provided the ecumenical movement with an occasion to reassert the inseparable relationship between the Church and mission. The report of the section on witness stated that "in the very existence of the Church, there is a constant witness . . . to the

---

45. Ibid., 19. In the emphasis on the Holy Spirit, Newbigin was clearly influenced by the thought of Roland Allen. He explicitly referred to Allen in this work (45) as well as his John R. Mott Memorial Lecture delivered at Kuala Lumpur in 1959, the lecture that dealt with the work of the Holy Spirit in the mission of the Church. According to his own later account, Newbigin consciously followed Allen's thought in this lecture (J. E. Lesslie Newbigin, "The Work of the Holy Spirit in the Life of the Asian Churches," in *A Decisive Hour for the Christian Mission: The East Asia Christian Conference 1959 and the John R. Mott Memorial Lectures,* by Norman Goodall, J. E. Lesslie Newbigin, W. A. Visser't Hooft, and D. T. Niles [London: SCM Press, 1960], 32; Lesslie Newbigin, *Unfinished Agenda: An Autobiography* [Grand Rapids, Mich.: Eerdmans, 1985], 166).

46. Newbigin, *One Body, One Gospel, One World,* 19–20.

47. Ibid., 15. Newbigin's Trinitarian view of *missio Dei* and its relation both to the Church's mission and the world were presented in further detail in his *The Relevance of Trinitarian Doctrine for Today's Mission* (London: Edinburgh House Press for the World Council of Churches, Commission on World Mission and Evangelism, 1963), 31–51.

48. *The New Delhi Report: The Third Assembly of the World Council of Churches, 1961* (New York: Association Press, 1962), 79.

reality of God's dealing with men in Jesus Christ,"[49] and that "through his Church God witnesses to his purpose to gather all nations, peoples and tongues, all sorts and conditions of men into his city."[50] Commenting on the significance of the Church-centric approach to this historical event, Newbigin, the last general secretary of the IMC and the first director of the CWME, wrote:

> The Tambaram meeting marked the beginning of an exceedingly necessary and fruitful period during which missionary thinking was, to use the oft repeated phrase, church-centric. . . . We must grant that the period of missionary history dominated by the 'church-centric' understanding of missions has been fruitful. It has brought us to our present consensus regarding the unity and mission of the Church and it has been the presupposition of the events that have led to the integration of the World Council of Churches and the International Missionary Council.[51]

The Rise of the World-Centric Approach to the *Missio Dei*

Despite its emphasis on the Church, New Delhi 1961 was the beginning of a new climate in ecumenical mission thinking. This new period was marked by a highly this-worldly orientation and the interpretation of the *missio Dei* with the primary focus on the world rather than the Church. The shift had already surfaced in 1960 in the conference of the World Student Christian Federation (WSCF) at Strasbourg. At this meeting, Hoekendijk's call for "full identification with man in the modern world" was enthusiastically received by the students, whereas other speakers, such as D. T. Niles, Newbigin, Barth, and Visser't Hooft, failed to speak to and for them.[52] Throughout the 1960s, Hoekendijk increasingly became influential with his criticism of Church-centrism and insistence on the need to take an "ex-centric" approach with the world as its starting point.[53]

The integration of the two ecumenical bodies also had a significant impact on the shift since ecumenical social thinking thus far represented by

---

49. Ibid.

50. Ibid., 81.

51. Newbigin, *Relevance of Trinitarian Doctrine*, 23–24. See also Newbigin, "Word of the Holy Spirit," 19–20.

52. Bassham, *Mission Theology*, 47; Bosch, *Transforming Mission*, 382.

53. J. C. Hoekendijk,, "Notes on the Meaning of Mission (-ary)," in *Planning for Mission: Working Papers on the New Quest for Missionary Communities*, ed. Thomas Wieser (New York: U.S. Conference for the World Council of Churches, 1966), 44–45.

the Life and Work movement began to influence mission thinking directly. The influence was already visible at New Delhi. Basing Christian service on God's love, the New Delhi report of the section on service strongly advocated the secular engagement of the Church for social justice in several areas, such as technological and social changes, racial and ethnic tensions, international relations, and nuclear armaments and world peace.[54]

The contribution of Asian mission thinking was particularly important in this regard. In Asia, social concerns had been integral to mission thinking since the Eastern Asian Christian Conference held at Bangkok in 1949. This tendency was strongly present at the EACC Assembly at Kuala Lumpur in 1959. It was also manifested at New Delhi 1961 by certain Asian delegates, such as Paul D. Devanandan of India and Masao Takenaka of Japan. In his address on Christian witness, Devanandan called the churches to the "identification with the present concerns of secular life" and in particular to the dialogical encounter with non-Christian faiths.[55] Takenaka also challenged the delegates with the idea that Christian service to the world must embrace "secular engagement and participation in worldly affairs" since it is related to the totality of human life, including the "conditions of social justice."[56]

In 1963, the first meeting of the CWME was held at Mexico City under the theme "God's Mission and Our Task." This theme indicated that the *missio Dei* concept had become widely accepted among the ecumenical mission circles by that time. It was no coincidence that the concept also appeared for the first time in the documents produced by the EACC on the occasion of its Bangkok Assembly in the following year. The theme also reflected the recognition that "the old 'sending and receiving' model of mission was past," and that the emphasis should instead be placed on "God's mission in every part of the world, 'mission in six continents.'"[57]

Interestingly, the Trinitarian language that had always been associated with the *missio Dei* concept since Willingen 1952 disappeared at the

54. *New Delhi Report*, 94.

55. P. D. Devanandan, "Called to Witness," in *Preparation for Dialogue: A Collection of Essays on Hinduism and Christianity in New India*, ed. Nalini Devanandan and M. M. Thomas, Devanandan Memorial Volume No. 2 (Bangalore, India: Christian Institute for the Study of Religion and Society, 1964), 186–91. The call to interfaith dialogue expressed by Devanandan in this address to New Delhi 1961 was reflected in its report on witness (S. Wesley Ariarajah, *Hindus and Christians: A Century of Protestant Ecumenical Thought* [Amsterdam: Editions Rodopi, 1991; Grand Rapids, Mich.: Eerdmans, 1991], 115–16).

56. *New Delhi Report*, 13.

57. Timothy Yates, *Christian Mission in the Twentieth Century* (Cambridge: Cambridge University Press, 1994), 165.

Mexico City meeting. Christian mission was instead grounded on the doctrine of creation and covenant.[58] This change went together with another significant change, namely, a new tendency to approach the secular, material world positively. The Mexico City report stated:

> The writers who began to express it [i.e. the doctrine of creation] in the Old Testament were men who already knew God in human history. The world is spiritual because God made it. But there is widespread a debased religiosity which divides the sacred and the secular in a way that is opposed to the Christian doctrine of creation. The process of secularization helps us to see that the material world is God's creation, the place where he calls men to play their part in his continuing work.[59]

Such a rejection of the dichotomy between the sacred and the secular implied the refusal of the traditional distinction between the Christian and non-Christian worlds—the refusal on which the idea of "mission in six continents" was based. As this passage indicates, the rejection also meant a positive attitude toward the phenomenon of secularization. Mexico City defined secularization as "the revolutionary attempt of man to become emancipated from all forms of dependency"[60] and spoke of Christian mission as follows:

> Christian witness participates in the common agony and hope which men experience in the process of secularization. It should articulate questions and answers *from within the modern world* and take up the points of decision which God himself has provided through secularization. Thus we can come to deeper understanding of the presence of Jesus Christ in the world and communicate the Gospel.[61]

---

58. Ronald K. Orchard, ed., *Witness in Six Continents: Records of the Meeting of the Commission on World Mission and Evangelism of the World Council of Churches Held in Mexico City, December 8th to 19th, 1963* (London: Edinburgh House Press for Division of World Mission and Evangelism of the World Council of Churches, 1964), 144.

59. Ibid., 152.

60. Orchard, *Witness in Six Continents*, 151. The Christian attempt to give a positive evaluation to the significance of secularization goes back to the Jerusalem meeting of the IMC in 1928. Though no clear consensus was reached there, "Jerusalem tried to understand it, to do justice to its positive aspects and to discern its implications for Christian mission" (David M. Gill, "The Secularization Debate Foreshadowed. Jerusalem 1928." *International Review of Missions* 57 [1968]: 354).

61. Orchard, *Witness in Six Continents*, 153–54. Emphasis mine.

The idea "from within the modern world" well expresses this-worldly holiness evident at Mexico City. This important contribution of the meeting to Christian mission was to have a far-reaching impact on ecumenical mission thinking. The idea also revealed the influence that Hoekendijk's ex-centric approach began to exercise on the ecumenical movement.

The new emphasis on the world, however, provoked resistance and became the occasion for a difficult theological debate on the relationship between God's redemption, the Church, and the world. The Mexico City report referred to this debate stating:

> Debate returned again and again to the relationship between God's action in and through the Church and everything God is doing in the world apparently independently of the Christian community. Can a distinction be drawn between God's providential action and God's redeeming action? If the restoration and reconciliation of human life is being achieved by the action of God through secular agencies, what is the place and significance of faith? If the Church is to be wholly involved in the world and its history, what is the true nature of its separateness? We were able to state thesis and antithesis in this debate, but we could not see our way through to the truth we feel lies beyond this dialectic.[62]

The debate was particularly related to a sentence in the report which read: "The evidence of changed lives is often to be found in other areas than a recognized congregation." Some participants opposed this sentence and proposed a far more explicit expression: "God is at work also in the activities of secular agencies."[63] Despite such a difficulty, the Mexico City report acknowledged that "the concern of the Church is not only for those things which it does as a separate community but also for the whole of God's work in the world," and that Christians are "to watch for the signs of Christ's presence in the communities of the world."[64] Thus, as Bassham

---

62. Ibid., 157.

63. Ibid. The expression "God is at work" was not new. It appeared, for instance, in the report of Amsterdam 1948 as follows: "We acknowledge that He is powerfully at work amongst us to lead us further to goals which we but dimly discern" (*Man's Disorder and God's Design*, vol. 1, *The Universal Church in God's Design: An Ecumenical Study Prepared Under the Auspices of the World Council of Churches* [London: SCM Press, 1948], 216). The difference was, however, that Amsterdam 1948 did not mention world history as the arena for God's work; rather, it implicitly confined God's work to the interior of the Church and, more specifically, to the ecumenical movement.

64. Orchard, *Witness in Six Continents*, 157–58.

pointed out, "the Mexico City CWME gathering took a significant step toward seeing the world as the primary locus for mission."[65]

The ecumenical movement during several years following Mexico City 1963 was marked by the rapid intensification of the approach "from within the modern world." The World Conference on Church and Society held in Geneva in 1966—the third international conference of the Life and Work movement after Stockholm 1925 and Oxford 1937—represented another important step. At Geneva 1966, ecumenical social thinking made a further contribution to the world-centric missionary approach. Chaired by M. M. Thomas, the conference took up the material and social dimension of human life as integral parts of the missionary task of the Church. The concept of revolution formally emerged as part of the language of the ecumenical movement. The participants vigorously discussed the question of Christian witness in a time of revolutionary change. This discussion even included the most sensitive issue of violence.[66] The concept of the "human" also drew attention "as a criterion for judging economic and social change."[67] The final report of the conference called for the responsible participation of Christians in the revolutionary process and the awareness of the ambiguous nature of this process.[68]

The world-centric tendency of ecumenical mission thinking after the New Delhi Assembly was dramatically manifested in the final reports of the study project "The Missionary Structure of the Congregation" pro-

65. Bassham, *Mission Theology*, 67.

66. World Conference on Church and Society, Geneva 1966, *Christians in the Technical and Social Revolutions of Our Time: World Conference on Church and Society, Geneva, July 12–26, 1966: The Official Report*. With a Description of the Conference by M. M. Thomas and Paul Abrecht (Geneva: WCC, 1967), 23–27, 31–33.

67. Ibid., 52–53, 90.

68. As at New Delhi, the Asian factor played an important role at Geneva. Not only was it chaired by Thomas, but its major task was to respond to the challenge that had come from the churches in the new nations since the Ecumenical Study Conference for East Asia held at Lucknow, India, in 1952. It was the challenge that originated in the social revolution taking place among these nations (Paul Abrecht, "The Development of Ecumenical Social Thought and Action," in *The Ecumenical Advance: A History of the Ecumenical Movement, Volume 2, 1948–1968*, ed. Harold E. Fey, 3d. ed. [Geneva: WCC, 1993], 248–50). According to Abrecht, ecumenical social thinking in the West traditionally favored gradual social change, a society influenced by the Christian ethos, and the traditional structures of world economic and political relations. It also maintained a critical attitude toward nationalism. In contrast, Christians from the new nations tended to opt for rapid political and social change, a pluralistic society where Christians could also contribute to the promotion of human values, and a creative role of nationalism and nation-states. They also challenged the Western biases and presuppositions inherent in the traditional structures of international political and economic relations (ibid., 249).

duced by two working groups in Western Europe and North America. These two groups worked in close contact and came to the conclusions that displayed a "remarkable commonality."[69] Published in 1967, the year before the Uppsala Assembly, the reports considered thoroughly the implications of the world-centric approach to Christian mission. Their key concept was "the Church for others"—the idea taken from Dietrich Bonhoeffer who wrote in a Nazi prison: "The church is the church only when it exists for others."[70]

In the reports, the working groups advocated a view that the process of secularization characterized by increasing "differentiation" and "a liberation from the control of metaphysics and theology" was the fundamental, unalterable feature of contemporary world history. Under the influence of Harvey Cox and Arend Th. van Leeuwen, they recognized a theological significance of secularization and argued that it was coherent with the biblical views of Creation and Incarnation.[71] Such thinking made the concept of history far more crucial than ever before. Hoekendijk, who played a major role in the study project, particularly advocated the necessity of taking history seriously.[72] He wrote in his working paper: "It is essential to recognize *history as the decisive context of the* Mission [*sic*]."[73] The idea much debated at Mexico City—the idea that God is at work in world history—played a central role in the thinking of the groups.[74] The world, thus, came to be seen as the locus for God's redeeming act. The groups also affirmed the idea of *Christus extra muros ecclesiae,* or Christ outside the walls of the Church.[75]

---

69. *Church for Others,* 58.

70. Dietrich Bonhoeffer, *Letters and Papers from Prison,* ed. Eberhard Bethge, enlarged ed. (New York: Collier Books, Macmillan, 1972), 382; Bosch, *Transforming Mission,* 375.

71. *Church for Others,* 9–13; Harvey Cox, *The Secular City: Secularization and Urbanization in Theological Perspective* (New York: Macmillan, 1965); Arend Th. van Leeuwen, *Christianity in World History: The Meeting of the Faiths of East and West,* trans. H. H. Hoskins (London: Edinburgh House Press, 1964). Harvey Cox took part in the study project as a member of the North American Working Group.

72. Hoekendijk participated in the project as a consultant of the Western European Working Group and member of the North American Working Group (*Church for Others,* 54, 56).

73. Hoekendijk, "Meaning of Mission," 42.

74. *Church for Others,* 16; Western European Working Group, "Mission in God's Mission," in *Planning for Mission: Working Papers on the New Quest for Missionary Communities,* ed. Thomas Wieser (New York: U.S. Conference for the World Council of Churches, 1966), 52.

75. *Church for Others,* 11; Walter J. Hollenweger, "'Christus extra et intra muros

The novelty of the thinking of the groups was particularly manifest in their proposal to reverse the relationship between God, the Church, and the world. According to them, the relationship was traditionally conceived of in the sequence of "God—Church—world." In this view, God was believed to be "primarily related to the Church and only secondarily to the world by means of the Church." Replacing this view, the groups proposed a reversal of the last two items in the sequence to conceive of the relationship as "God—world—Church." By this new sequence, the groups intended to mean this: "God's primary relationship is to the world, and it is the world and not the Church that is the focus of God's plan."[76]

In their formulation of the *missio Dei,* the groups again placed emphasis on history. The report of the Western European Group stated:

> The God of the bible is a sending God—he sends his prophets; he sends his Son; he sends his Spirit through the Son; he sends the apostles through the Son and by the Spirit. But the context of his sending is always history, since it is his concern to be present in the actual life situation of every man. Participation in God's mission is therefore entering into partnership with God in history, because our knowledge of God in Christ compels us to affirm that God is working out his purpose in the midst of the world and its historical processes.[77]

The Trinitarian view still exists in this formulation. The chief concern was, however, with history as the primary context for God's sending. As for the goal of the *missio Dei,* the North American Group took an anthropological approach and suggested taking the idea of "humanization" seriously. Their report stated:

> We have lifted up humanization as the goal of mission because we believe that more than others it communicates in our period of history the meaning of the messianic goal. In another time the goal of God's redemptive work might best have been described in terms of man turning towards God rather than in terms of God turning towards men.... The fundamental question was that of the true God, and the church responding to that question by pointing to him. It was assuming that the purpose of mission was Christianization, bringing man to God through Christ and

---

ecclesiae,'" in *Planning for Mission: Working Papers on the New Quest for Missionary Communities,* ed. Thomas Wieser (New York: U.S. Conference for the World Council of Churches, 1966), 56–61.

76. *Church for Others,* 16–17, 61, 69–71.

77. Ibid., 13–14.

his church. Today the fundamental question is much more that of true man, and the dominant concern of the missionary congregation must therefore be to point to the humanity in Christ as the goal of mission.[78]

The Western European Group took a theological approach and followed Hoekendijk's thought more closely: they defined the goal of mission as "the establishment of *shalom*," that is, "the realization of the full potentialities of all creation and its ultimate reconciliation and unity in Christ."[79]

In this understanding of the *missio Dei*, the significance of the Church was to be found only in the context of God's direct concern for the world. "In no respect," wrote Hoekendijk, "can the Church regard itself either as the subject of the Mission or as its sole (and exclusive) institutionalized form."[80] The Church was merely "a segment of the world." Therefore, "thinking about the Church should always begin by defining it as part of the world."[81] Using Hoekendijk's concept of "ex-centeredness," the Western European Group declared:

> The Church is only required to be separate in order to be prepared for engagement, that is, the Church exists for the world. It is called to the service of mankind, of the world. . . . The Church lives in order that the world may know its true being. It is *pars pro toto*; it is the first fruits of the new creation. But its centre lies outside itself; it must live "ex-centredly". It has to seek out those situations in the world that calls for loving responsibility and there it must announce and point to *shalom*. This ex-centric position of the Church implies that we must stop thinking from the inside towards the outside.[82]

Such a position instead meant that Christians had to allow "actual life situations" of modern society "to provide the agenda for the churches" and direct the renewal and mission of congregations.[83] Only when the Church began with the world could it participate in the *missio Dei* directly at work in history.

---

78. Ibid., 77–78.

79. Ibid., 14–15; Hoekendijk, "Call to Evangelism," 168, 170–71; idem, "Church in Missionary Thinking," 334; idem, "Meaning of Mission," 43.

80. Hoekendijk, "Meaning of Mission," 44.

81. *Church for Others.*, 17–18.

82. Ibid., 18; Hoekendijk, "Meaning of Mission," 44.

83. *Church for Others*, 20–23.

The affirmation that the mission of the Church is to participate in the mission of God at work in world history inevitably raises the question of discernment. The study itself raised the question asking, "But how do we recognize Christ?" To this question, it responded with an acknowledgment: "the signs of his presence . . . can only be discerned and understood in faith."[84] The study also urged theology to engage in the task of discernment, saying:

> It is the task of theology to learn how to discern what God is doing not only in and through the churches but also in those impulses and forms of God's presence which the "old" church has not yet learned to incorporate—and more, in those places of God's presence which the church is not called to master by drawing them to itself but to serve by giving itself to them.[85]

In the entire study project, Hoekendijk's influence was evident. During the years immediately after Willingen, his critique of Church-centrism as well as his emphasis on God's direct engagement with the world gave in to the more Church-centric understandings of the *missio Dei* advocated by some missiologists, such as Vicedom and Newbigin. At the time, however, his position was accepted by the working groups and played a "determinative" role in their formulation of the new approach to Christian mission.[86]

In 1968, the Uppsala Assembly of the WCC endorsed the secular approach to mission advocated by the study "The Missionary Structure of the Congregation." The Assembly elected M. M. Thomas, a leading non-Western proponent of the Christian participation in the struggle for human society, as moderator of the WCC Central Committee.[87] The Uppsala report entitled "Renewal in Mission" took up humanization as the central concept of its approach to Christian mission.[88] The report began with the anthropological question, "What is man?" rather than the question of God. Emphasizing the wholeness of humanity, Uppsala refused to treat the "concern for physical and social needs as merely secondary to . . .

---

84. Ibid., 11.

85. Ibid., 67.

86. Bassham, 68; Bert [Libertus A.] Hoedemaker, "The Legacy of J. C. Hoekendijk," *International Bulletin of Missionary Research* 19 (October 1995): 168.

87. For the significance of M. M. Thomas for Uppsala 1968, see p. 127 below.

88. Norman Goodall, ed., *The Uppsala Report 1968: Official Report of the Fourth Assembly of the World Council of Churches, Uppsala July 4–20, 1968* (Geneva: WCC, 1968), 21–38.

[the] responsibility for needs of the spirit." Its major concern was on the cries for "a fully human life" that were being expressed in "the worldwide struggle for meaning, dignity, freedom and love."[89] Similarly, the *missio Dei* was described as "the gift of a new creation which is a radical renewal of the old and the invitation to men to grow up into their full humanity in the new man, Jesus Christ."[90] The participation in the mission of God meant the following:

> Our part in evangelism might be described as bringing about the occasions for men's response to Jesus Christ. Often the turning point does not appear as a religious choice at all. Yet it is a new birth. It sets a pattern of dying and rising which will continually be repeated.... We have to «put on the new man» and this change is always embodied in some actual change of attitude and relationship. For there is no turning to God which does not at the same time bring a man face to face with his fellow men in a new way. The new life frees men for community unabling [*sic*] them to break through racial, national, religious and other barriers that divide the unity of mankind.[91]

In other words, the Christian task was to work for "achievements of greater justice, freedom and dignity as a part of the restoration of true manhood in Christ." This work had to be done with a more open and more humble partnership with all people, including those of other faiths or of no faith, who worked for these goals.[92] Thus, Uppsala displayed the degree of mutual integration between ecumenical social thinking and ecumenical mission thinking that had been achieved under the world-centric theology of *missio Dei* after New Delhi 1961.

The Continuing Tension between the Church-Centric and the World-Centric Views of the *Missio Dei*

The focus on secularization and humanization at Uppsala 1968 obviously only reflected concerns of one part of the actual world, namely, the secularized societies of the contemporary West and the secularized sectors of the Third World nations. The reaction in some quarters was immediate and intense. The study on humanity authorized by Uppsala—"the Humanum study"—led to the realization that, to answer the question

89. Ibid., 27–28.
90. Ibid., 28.
91. Ibid.
92. Ibid., 29.

of what the human is, one must take extremely seriously the anguish of men and women in particular cultural and socio-political settings as well as their struggles to fulfill human and cultural identity.[93] As the publications of James H. Cone's *A Black Theology of Liberation* in 1970 and of Gustavo Gutiérrez's *A Theology of Liberation* in 1973 demonstrated,[94] new theological movements generally known as liberation theology became increasingly influential after Uppsala with their common emphasis on the socio-political particularities of the theologians' contexts. The impact of feminist theology in North America also started to be felt during this period with the publication of several works that marked its emergence.[95] Furthermore, the interest in dialogue, which was affirmed "as the most appropriate approach in interfaith relations" at a conference in Kandy, Sri Lanka, in 1967, grew rapidly under the leadership of the Indian theologian Stanley J. Samartha.[96]

These new trends were clearly visible at the Bangkok Assembly of the CWME in 1973 held under the theme "Salvation Today." In his address, Philip Potter, Director of the CWME from 1967 till 1972, criticized the Uppsala emphasis on secularization, saying: "The real error was to assume that the process of secularization would lead to the withering away of religious consciousness, or of the concern for the transcendent."[97] A significant development at Bangkok was that voices from the Third World were clearly heard for the first time. As Scherer wrote, "whereas Uppsala had been marked by a climate of 'old world' unrest, Bangkok was a two-thirds world meeting at which church leaders from Asia and Africa freely spoke

---

93. *The Humanum Studies 1969–1975: A Collection of Documents* (Geneva: WCC, 1975), 26–33, 38–39, 45–46, 75–76, 81–84.

94. James H. Cone, *A Black Theology of Liberation*, C. Eric Lincoln Series in Black Religion (Philadelphia: Lippincott, [1970]); Gustavo Gutiérrez, *A Theology of Liberation: History, Politics, and Salvation* (Maryknoll, N.Y.: Orbis, 1973). Gutiérrez's book was originally published in Spanish in Lima, Peru, in 1971.

95. Mary Daly, *Beyond God the Father: Toward a Philosophy of Women's Liberation* (Boston: Beacon Press, 1973); Letty M. Russell, *Human Liberation in a Feminist Perspective—A Theology* (Philadelphia: Westminster, 1974); Rosemary Radford Ruether, ed., *Religion and Sexism: Images of Women in Jewish and Christian Tradition* (New York: Simon and Schuster, 1974).

96. Lossky et al., *Ecumenical Movement*, s.v. "Dialogue, Interfaith," by S. Wesley Ariarajah; Ariarajah, *Hindus and Christians*, 132–41.

97. Philip Potter, "Christ's Mission and Ours in Today's World: Director's Report," *International Review of Mission* 62 (April 1973): 149.

their minds."⁹⁸ The report of Section I, "Culture and Identity," expressed the painful voice of Third World Christians as follows:

> The problem of personal identity is closely related to the problem of cultural identity. 'Culture shapes the human voice that answers the voice of Christ.' Many Christians who have received the Gospel through Western agents ask the question: 'Is it really I who answer Christ? Is it not another person instead of me:?' Too often, in the history of Western missions, the culture of those who received the Gospel was either ignored or condemned. At best, it was studied as a subject of missiology.⁹⁹

Thus, the significance of culture that Uppsala 1968 had set aside was recognized at Bangkok as an essential factor for Christian mission.

By the same token, the finding of the Humanum studies regarding the importance of contextual particularities also drew attention at Bangkok. Thus, the Bangkok report declared:

> Proper theology is reflection on the experience of the Christian community in a particular place, at a particular time. Thus, it will necessarily be a contextual theology; it will be a relevant and living theology which refuses to be easily universalized because it speaks to and out of a particular situation.¹⁰⁰

The report particularly referred to the emerging Black theology as an example for such a contextual theology and appraised its significance by stating: "It affirms the personhood of the oppressed and asserts that God offers them Salvation in Jesus Christ as the persons for whom Christ died."¹⁰¹

Related to this development was the surfacing of the concept of liberation. In his report on the Salvation study, Thomas Wieser pointed out "the increasing use of the word 'liberation' in interpreting the meaning of salvation for today."¹⁰² Indeed, the Assembly emphasized the holistic nature of salvation. This emphasis was, however, accompanied with an even stronger emphasis on socio-political engagement. In accordance with

---

98. Scherer, *Gospel, Church, and Kingdom*, 121.

99. "Culture and Identity: Report of Section I of the Bangkok Conference," *International Review of Mission* 62 (April 1973): 188.

100. Ibid., 190.

101. Ibid.

102. Thomas Wieser, "Report on the Salvation Study," *International Review of Mission* 62 (April 1973): 172.

M. M. Thomas's opening address,[103] the report of Section II, "Salvation and Social Justice," stated:

> The salvation which Christ brought, and in which we participate, offers a comprehensive wholeness in this divided world. . . . It is salvation of the soul and the body, of the individual and society, mankind and 'the groaning creation' (Rom. 8:19). . . . We have to overcome the dichotomies in our thinking between soul and body, person and society, human kind and creation. Therefore, we see the struggles for economic justice, political freedom and cultural renewal as elements in the total liberation of the world through the mission of God.[104]

As the last sentence shows, this "comprehensive notion of salvation" emphasized by Bangkok simultaneously had a highly this-worldly orientation.[105] Challenging the "pietistic and individualistic" bias of the conventional understanding,[106] the report described salvation in four distinct socio-political dimensions: they were the struggles for economic justice against exploitation; for human dignity against political oppression; for solidarity against alienation; and for hope against despair in personal life. God's mission was defined with the reference to liberation theologians' favorite text, namely, Luke 4:18. Instances of salvation referred to in the report were "the peace of the people in Vietnam, independence in Angola, justice and reconciliation in Northern Ireland and release from the captivity of power in the North Atlantic community."[107] The notion of salvation advocated by Bangkok was, indeed, not other-worldly. It was salvation *today*—here and now.[108]

---

103. M. M. Thomas, "The Meaning of Salvation Today—A Personal Statement," *International Review of Mission* 62 (April 1973): 162, 165–66.

104. "Salvation and Social Justice: Report of Section II of the Bangkok Conference," *International Review of Mission* 62 (April 1973): 199.

105. Ibid., 200; Bosch, *Transforming Mission*, 396–97.

106. Thomas, "Meaning of Salvation Today," 162.

107. "Salvation and Social Justice," 199–201.

108. The world-centric understanding of salvation at Bangkok was strongly challenged by evangelicals. Donald A. McGavran, for instance, criticized Bangkok saying: "The issue at Bangkok is clear: does the word salvation, according to the Bible, mean eternal salvation or does it mean this-worldly improvements? Which is the basic meaning? It appears as if the conciliar forces are set to maintain, on the basis of the Old Testament, that salvation means primarily if not exclusively this-worldly improvements. Evangelicals will maintain, on the basis of the total biblical record (the New Testament as well as the Old) that 'salvation' means a change in status of the soul, the essential person, is achieved through faith in Jesus Christ alone, and results in abundant life in this world" (Donald A. McGavran, "Salvation

These new tendencies at Bangkok—the shift of the CWME leadership away from the West, concern for cultural identity and contextual particularity, and concern for socio-political liberation—indicated a clear departure from the mission thinking in the 1960s. They pointed to the fact that the time of the Western dominance in the ecumenical movement had come to an end. Emilio Castro thus commented:

> *We have seen the end of one missionary era; we are beginning a new one in which the idea of world mission will be fundamental. . . . We are at the end of westernization of the Church and are going through a process in which in a multiplicity of different identities the Church universal will appear.*[109]

However, another development also made Bangkok 1973 significant. Since Uppsala 1968, the tension between the conciliar emphasis on the world and the conservative opposition against it had created a polarization between the conciliar-ecumenical and the evangelical circles. The Uppsala report on mission was sharply criticized by evangelical leaders, such as John R. W. Stott and Donald A. McGavran. In 1970, a group of German missiologists, including Peter Byerhaus and Vicedom, issued a statement called "The Frankfurt Declaration" and rejected the use of socio-political analysis in the task of mission, the idea of humanization as the primary goal of mission, and the view that Christ is at work in world history.[110] After Bangkok 1973, the evangelicals met at Lausanne in 1974 under the leadership of the evangelist Billy Graham to have their own International Congress on World Evangelization. There, they signed the document called "The Lausanne Covenant"[111] and launched the movement known as the "Lausanne Movement."

The development of the polarization had a clear repercussion at Bangkok 1973. The influence of the conservative and traditional groups began to be felt at this Assembly. Its reports contained paragraphs on conversion and church growth.[112] The issue of conversion was discussed in the

---

Today," in *The Evangelical Response to Bangkok*, ed. Ralph Winter [South Pasadena, Calif.: William Carey Library, 1973], 29.)

109. Emilio Castro, "Bangkok, the New Opportunity," *International Review of Mission* 62 (April 1973): 140–42.

110. "The Frankfurt Declaration," *Christianity Today*, 19 June 1970, 3–6.

111. J. D. Douglas, ed., *Proclaim Christ Until He Comes: Calling the Whole Church to Take the Whole Gospel to the Whole World, Lausanne II in Manila, International Congress on World Evangelization, 1989* (Minneapolis: World Wide Publication, 1990), 19–24.

112. "Culture and Identity," 191–94; "Church Renewed in Mission: Report of Section III of the Bangkok Conference," *International Review of Mission* 62 (April 1973): 219–20.

report of Section I, which, interestingly, expressed a hesitation to take up the question of discernment: "We believe that he [i.e., God] is present in his whole creation. But we do not want to make this belief an operative principle for pointing out exactly where he is at work, lest we say: here is the Messiah, or there is the Messiah, when he is not there."[113] The Church, which had been given only a secondary place in the *missio Dei* concept in the 1960s, was now reaffirmed as "the bearer of a gospel of liberation to others"[114] even though the need for renewal and repentance was acknowledged for the churches to be liberated from "parochial self-absorption."[115]

Beside the evangelicals, the Eastern Orthodox Churches also began to exercise their explicit influence in the 1970s. According to Scherer, a consultation of Orthodox theologians on the subject of "Confessing Christ Today" convened under the auspices of the CWME in Bucharest in 1974 was particularly important. The consultation directly contributed to Section I at the Nairobi Assembly in 1975[116]; the report of the section was also entitled "Confessing Christ Today."[117]

The approach to Christian mission taken by Nairobi 1975 is summarized in the following passage from the report:

> As our high priest, Christ mediates God's new covenant through both salvation and service. . . . As the royal priesthood, Christians are therefore called to engage in both evangelism and social action. We are commissioned to proclaim the gospel of Christ to the ends of the earth. Simultaneously, we are commanded to struggle to realize God's will for peace, justice, and freedom throughout society.[118]

Thus, Nairobi tried to synthesize evangelistic concern and social engagement around the new missiological idea that was later named the "mediatory mission." The basis for this approach was the act of conversion, that is, the act of turning back to Christ the Mediator and confessing him anew as the Savior and Lord in the contemporary situation. The communal nature of confession was also emphasized, and the significance of the Church was recognized anew. A new element in the discussion of the Church was the focus on the Eucharist that had rarely been considered in ecumenical mis-

---

113. "Culture and Identity," 193.
114. "Church Renewed in Mission," 222.
115. Ibid., 217.
116. Scherer, *Gospel, Church, and Kingdom*, 127.
117. Paton, *Breaking Barriers*, 43–57.
118. Ibid., 43.

sion thinking.[119] The report not only affirmed that the Church "finds its primary aim and ultimate purpose in the eucharistic celebration and the glorification of the Triune God," but also that worship centered around the Eucharist has a missionary dimension.[120]

Mission thinking in the ecumenical movement after Nairobi 1975 was mainly characterized by an unresolved tension between the revived Church-centric view of the *missio Dei* and the continuing this-worldly approach now centered on the liberation theme. This tension was clearly revealed at the World Conference on Mission and Evangelism held in Melbourne, Australia, in 1980, and in the document "Mission and Evangelism—An Ecumenical Affirmation" of 1982.[121]

One of the important contributions of Melbourne was the further deepening of the liberation concept. The Kingdom of God—the theme of Melbourne—was understood especially in terms of Jesus' "earthly ministry" that began with the announcement of the Good News to the poor in Luke 4:18.[122] The idea of God's "preferential option for the poor" formulated at the General Conference of Latin American Bishops at Puebla, Mexico, in 1979[123] was introduced. Consequently, the *missio Dei* concept was reformulated at Melbourne as follows:

> God identified with the poor and oppressed by sending his Son Jesus to live and serve as a Galilean speaking directly to the common people; promising to bless those who met the needs of the hungry, the thirsty, the stranger, the naked, the sick and the prisoner; and finally meeting death on a cross as a political offender. The good news handed on to the Church is that God's grace was in Jesus Christ, who "though he was rich, yet for your sake he

---

119. One of few exceptions was written by J. G. Davies who participated in the Western European Working Group on the study "The Missionary Structure of the Congregation" (J. G. Davies, *Worship and Mission* [London: SCM Press, 1966]). In this work, Davies criticized the contemporary disunity of worship and mission and argued that Christians' participation in the *missio Dei* took place both in worship and mission as these were nothing but two different aspects of this divine activity to the world.

120. Paton, *Breaking Barriers*, 48–50.

121. "Mission and Evangelism—An Ecumenical Affirmation," *International Review of Mission* 71 (October 1982): 427–51.

122. *Your Kingdom Come: Mission Perspectives, Report on the World Conference on Mission and Evangelism, Melbourne, Australia, 12–25 May 1980* (Geneva: Commission on World Mission and Evangelism, 1980), 171, 177.

123. John Eagleson and Philip Sharper, eds., *Puebla and Beyond: Documentation and Commentary*, trans. John Drury (Maryknoll, N.Y.: Orbis, 1979), 264–67; Gustavo Gutiérrez, *The Power of the Poor in History*, trans. Robert R. Barr (Maryknoll, N.Y.: Orbis, 1983), 125–65.

became poor, so that by his poverty you might become rich" (II Cor. 8:9).[124]

Thus, Melbourne challenged the churches to be in solidarity with the poor in the world who "are already in mission to change their own situation," and to "join their struggle against the powers of exploitation and impoverishment."[125] It even went on to urge the churches to "be ready to listen to the poor, to hear the Gospel from the poor, to learn about the ways in which they have helped to make them poor."[126]

The implication of this last statement became more explicit in "Mission and Evangelism." The document declared:

> They [i.e., the poor] are both subjects and bearers of the Good News; they have the right and the duty to announce the Gospel not only among themselves, but also to all other sectors of the human family. . . . God is working through the poor of the earth to awaken the consciousness of humanity to his call for repentance, for justice and for love.[127]

This statement is ambiguous as to whether "the poor" means the "churches of the poor" or the poor in general, though it appears that the latter is the case. Despite this ambiguity, ecumenical mission thinking narrowed the locus for God's this-worldly presence to the poor and thereby more or less specifically answered the question of discernment so frequently debated, though the answer could not completely bring the debate to an end.

While strongly concerned for political liberation, Melbourne also displayed the Church-centric tendency quite explicitly. It revived the view expressed by Vicedom in the late 1950s that the Church is "the distinguishing mark of the new age."[128] Under the influence of the Orthodox ecclesiology,[129] the Melbourne report even stated: "The whole church of God . . . is *a sacrament of the kingdom* which came in the person of Jesus Christ and will come in its fulness when he returns in glory."[130] "Mission

---

124. *Your Kingdom Come*, 171.
125. Ibid., 177–78.
126. Ibid., 177.
127. "Mission and Evangelism," 443.
128. Vicedom, *Mission of God*, 44.
129. See, for instance, Alexander Schmemann, "The Problem of the Church's Presence in the World in Orthodox Consciousness," *St. Vladimir's Theological Quarterly* 21 (1977): 10; Ion Bria, *The Sense of Ecumenical Tradition: The Ecumenical Witness and Vision of the Orthodox* (Geneva: WCC, 1991), 35.
130. *Your Kingdom Come*, 193. Emphasis mine.

and Evangelism" also affirmed the centrality of the Church in mission. This document described the mission of the Church as the "mediatory mission" in which the Church manifests God's love for the world in Christ and lifts up to God the suffering, hope, joy, and thanksgiving of the world in its prayer and worship.[131] Certainly, it was acknowledged that the Kingdom was "an inclusive and open reality" that was wider than the Church and found

> in caring and fulfiling [sic] relationships and environments where people are reconciled and liberated to become what God wants them to be.... in the willingness to accept suffering and sacrifices for others. Also in willingness to reflect on and respond to needs and ideas beyond our own community, thus entering into dialogue and service.[132]

A crucial role was, nonetheless, assigned to the Church once more, and "Mission and Evangelism" reaffirmed the old concept of the *plantatio ecclesiae*. Thus, it declared that "the planting of the seed of the Gospel" and the building of a "cell of the Kingdom"—"a church confessing Jesus Christ"—in each human community was "at the heart of Christian mission."[133]

Scherer wrote that the mark which characterized the period after Nairobi 1975 was "the attempt to reconcile 'churchly' and 'worldly' approaches to mission."[134] The fact is, however, that the tension between these two approaches has remained unresolved even in the 1990s. At the CWME Conference at San Antonio in 1989, the tension was revealed especially between Section I and Section II. The report of Section I, "Turning to the Living God," was mainly concerned with the Church in God's mission and asserted: "To receive the message of the kingdom of God is to be incorporated into the body of Christ, the church, the author and sustainer of which is the Holy Spirit."[135] The report of Section II, "Participating in Suffering and Struggle," however, focused on the Holy Spirit acting "as a creative power to lead people to destroy the injustices in society with, as their horizon, the liberation of the whole of humanity."[136] At San Antonio,

---

131. "Mission and Evangelism," 430.
132. *Your Kingdom Come*, 196–97.
133. "Mission and Evangelism," 437–38.
134. Scherer, *Gospel, Church, and Kingdom*, 126.
135. Frederick R. Wilson, ed., *The San Antonio Report: Your Will Be Done, Mission in Christ's Way* (Geneva: WCC Publications, 1990), 33.
136. Ibid., 39.

the difference between the two views of the *missio Dei* was expressed as the one between two different approaches to the relationship between the Holy Spirit, the world, and the Church.

The "creative tension"[137] between the two approaches became an open controversy at the Canberra Assembly of the WCC in 1991, as evidenced in two very contrasting presentations on the theme "Come the Holy Spirit—Renew the Whole Creation." The presentation prepared by Parthenios, the Greek Orthodox Patriarch of Alexandria and All Africa, was highly Trinitarian as well as "churchly." He reminded the audience that "there is no Holy Spirit apart from the Holy Trinity,"[138] and emphasized the centrality of the Church in the work of the Holy Spirit saying: "The holy eucharist, the other sacraments of the church effected by the Holy Spirit, even its symbols, are themselves a manifestation, showing forth, revelation and operation of the Holy Spirit for the blessing of humanity and nature."[139]

Chung Hyun Kyung, a Korean feminist theologian, on the other hand, began her presentation with "an invocation of the spirits of an eclectic collection of martyrs."[140] She called Korea "the land of spirits full of *Han*," and said that the "*Han*-ridden spirits" had been "agents" of the Holy Spirit in Korea's history.[141] The following passage summarizes her entire approach that started from the Holy Spirit directly at work in creation:

> The spirit of this compassionate God has been always with us from the time of creation. . . . The Spirit of God has been teaching us through the "survival wisdom" of the poor, the screams of the *Han*-ridden spirits of our people and the blessings and curses of nature. Only when we can hear this cry for life and can see the signs of liberation are we able to recognize the Holy Spirit's activity in the midst of suffering creation.[142]

The scope of her presentation went far beyond the this-worldly holiness at Melbourne centered in political liberation. As Lee Jae-Won pointed out,

---

137. San Antonio 1989 understood Christian mission as in "creative tension" between "spiritual and material needs, prayer and action, evangelism and social responsibility, dialogue and witness, power and vulnerability, local and universal" (ibid., 20).

138. Michael Kinnamon, ed., *Signs of the Spirit: Official Report, Seventh Assembly, Canberra, Australia, 7–20 February 1991* (Geneva: WCC, 1991; Grand Rapids, Mich.: Eerdmans, 1991), 28.

139. Ibid., 30.

140. Ibid., 15.

141. Ibid., 39.

142. Ibid., 40–41.

Chung's presentation synthesized and integrated the perspectives of liberation theology, feminist theology, Korean *minjung* theology, and ecology.[143] She thus not only addressed the issue of social justice and the integrity of creation; she also challenged the audience with a serious question of the relation between the Gospel and culture, provoking a charge of syncretism and a heated controversy on this issue with her bold use of Korean religious symbols.[144]

Neither Parthenios nor Chung used the term *missio Dei* or God's mission. The difference between them, nonetheless, corresponded to the difference between the Church-centric and the world-centric views of the *missio Dei*. The controversy generated at Canberra on the relation between the Holy Spirit and creation, thus, was a manifestation of the continuing tension in the *missio Dei* theology in the ecumenical movement.

Conclusion

Let us summarize the main observations that have been made in this chapter. The ecumenical movement has been an attempt by a large number of Christians and their leaders to search for wholeness and totality in which they have tried to overcome the historical divisions among them and seek a new Christian identity. In the process, the previously differentiated spheres of Christian life in the West—theology, social engagement, and mission—have gradually been brought together and synthesized.

This process of integration was initiated in the middle of the nineteenth century by the emergence of church planting as a new goal for Protestant foreign missions, resulting in a mutual discovery of the Church and mission. By the middle of the twentieth century, this discovery led mission thinkers to the search for a theological basis for the Church in mission. One of the most important fruits of the theological quest was the concept of *missio Dei*. With its focus on the Triune God as the subject of mission, the concept has served as the guiding symbolism for missiological renewal, providing the ecumenical movement with a theological framework whereby theology, social thinking, and mission thinking could be brought together.

Since its inception, the concept of *missio Dei* has been ambiguous in terms of the relationship between the Church and the world. In the

---

143. Lee Jae-Won, "Spirit and Practice: A Radical Understanding," *Christianity and Crisis* 51 (15 July 1991): 227.

144. Kwok Pui-Lan, "Gospel and Culture," *Christianity and Crisis* 51 (15 July 1991): 223–24.

1950s, the concept was used with a Church-centric emphasis. After New Delhi 1961, ecumenical mission thinking placed an increasing emphasis on world history in the endeavor to respond to the rapidly changing world situations. The concept also came to be used with the primary emphasis on the world as the arena where God is redemptively at work. The new this-worldly orientation resulted in a polarization between the conciliar-ecumenical leaders and their evangelical critics.

The climate surrounding mission thinking, however, shifted in the 1970s again, and a new tendency surfaced at Bangkok 1973. From the early 1970s, liberation and contextual theologies in North America and the Third Word became influential in the ecumenical movement and radicalized its approach to socio-political issues. At the same time, however, the growing involvement of the Orthodox Churches in ecumenism as well as conservative Christians' criticism pressed the ecumenical movement once more towards Church-centrism. As a result, the tension between the Church-centric and the radicalized world-centric positions became characteristic of this period. The tension still exists in ecumenical thinking without being mutually reconciled as the controversy generated by Chung at Canberra displayed. Thus, the dynamic relationship between the two distinct missiological emphases—on the Church and on the world—has constantly characterized the development of mission thinking in the IMC/WCC despite the synthesis of the previously differentiated spheres of Christian life.

In the next chapter, I will focus on the ecumenical movement in Asia in which much of Chung's presentation had its roots. Mission thinking in Asian ecumenism has developed in a constant interaction with mission thinking in the IMC/WCC. Nonetheless, it has its own peculiar characteristics. By tracing its development, I will be able to set both Thomas's and Song's mission thinking in their immediate contexts.

CHAPTER 3

This-Worldly Holiness and the *Missio Dei* Concept in Asian Ecumenical Thinking

THE CHRISTIAN CONFERENCE OF Asia (CCA) is a regional ecumenical body that unites the churches in the region extending from Pakistan to Korea and Japan to New Zealand. The origin of the CCA goes back to the Tambaram meeting of the IMC in 1938 where the possibility of creating the Far Eastern office of the IMC was first discussed. The tangible development of Asian ecumenism, however, began only after the Second World War. In 1949, the Eastern Asia Christian Conference was held at Bangkok, Thailand, under the auspices of the WCC and the IMC. This meeting gathered the representatives of Asian churches for the first time in history to discuss inter-church cooperation. In 1957, the conference held at Prapat, Indonesia, adopted a resolution for the formation of a regional ecumenical body to be called the East Asia Christian Conference (EACC), which was the initial name of the CCA. Two years later, the EACC was formally constituted at its Inaugural Assembly held at Kuala Lumpur, Malaysia.[1]

An important fruit of the activities of the EACC/CCA was the emergence and development of Asian contextual theology with its strong concern for the Asian world. From its beginning, Asian ecumenical thinking did not clearly display the distinction between social and mission thinking

---

1. Bassham, *Mission Theology*, 123–29; Park Sang Jung, "An Ecumenical Understanding of the Mission of the Church in Asia," in *Outcry!: Report of the North-East Asia Church Leaders' Meeting, October 12–16, 1987* (Hong Kong: CCA, 1988), 1–6; Weber, *Asia and the Ecumenical Movement*, 281–88; Hans-Ruedi Weber, "Out of All Continents and Nations: A Review of Regional Developments in the Ecumenical Movement," in *The Ecumenical Advance: A History of the Ecumenical Movement, Volume 2, 1948–1968*, ed. Harold E. Fey, 3d. ed. (Geneva: WCC, 1993), 67–70. The Prapat Conference is usually considered as the first EACC assembly. It is also called the Preparatory Assembly of the EACC. Note that Bangkok 1949 was called the *Eastern* Asia Christian Conference, not the East Asia Christian Conference (Lossky, et al., *Ecumenical Movement*, s.v. "Christian Conference of Asia"; Bassham, *Mission Theology*, 156).

that was so evident in the ecumenical movement in the West. This situation was partly because most Asian churches had rarely been engaged in sending missionaries abroad. Because they traditionally "received" missionaries, they did not fully develop the notion of mission as foreign missions. The absence of a clear distinction between social and mission thinking was also partly because Western missionaries often carried out humanitarian activities in their mission fields and contributed to the modernization of traditional societies of Asia. More significantly, this absence resulted from the deep concern among Asian Christian leaders about the radical social change taking place in their nations in the post-colonial era.

The this-worldly orientation of the EACC was, thus, quite evident in its formative period. Subsequently, it developed as one of the important features of Asian ecumenical thinking as the EACC/CCA continuously struggled to respond to the socio-political realities of Asia. The goal of this chapter is to survey this development and examine the particularities of this-worldly holiness in Asia compared to the ecumenical movement at large.

Christian Witness in the Midst of Rapid Social Changes

The formative period of the EACC coincided with the years of the profound socio-political upheaval in postwar Asia. The Second World War brought about the collapse of the colonialist and imperialist powers in Asia, both Western and Japanese. Many Asian nations achieved independence and embarked on their own programs for rapid modernization and national consolidation. Abject poverty, however, continued to prevail. Nationalism and ideological conflicts increasingly intensified the regional instability, and many parts of Asia were torn apart by the eruption of civil war. The establishment of the Communist state in China in 1949 was symbolic of this profound socio-political turmoil taking place throughout Asia.

During this period, Asian church leaders occupied themselves with the question of how to carry out evangelism in the midst of the radical socio-political changes. At Bangkok 1949, the major concern was evangelism.[2] The participants were, nonetheless, aware that the task of witness had to be carried out "in close relation to the special needs of the human situation" of their time. They discussed various urgent issues, such as the

---

2. P. D. Devanandan, "The Bangkok Conference of East Asia Leaders: An Impression," *International Review of Missions* 39 (1950): 147; W. A. Visser't Hooft, "Asian Churches," *Ecumenical Review* 2 (Spring 1950): 236.

"crisis of culture" brought about by the impact of Western values, the ongoing struggle for political freedom and the awakening of Asian peoples to "a new sense of dignity and historical mission," the ideological conflicts and the victory of Communism in China, and the question of religious freedom. They also recognized that a thorough study of Asian culture and society was essential to their evangelistic task. Bangkok 1949, thus, tackled the question of how Asian churches should face the revolutionary situations of their lands with the message that the Gospel was the only sure foundation for the new quest for human dignity and responsible society.[3]

An important fruit of the Bangkok Conference was that it delineated a basic theological framework for social witness in modernizing Asia. In the report that was drafted by M. M. Thomas and entitled "The Church in Social and Political Life,"[4] the participants stated:

> The gospel proclaims that God's sovereignty includes all realms of life. Christ sitting at the right hand of God reigns, and the Church owes it to the world to remind it constantly that it lives under his judgment and grace. It is not the challenge of any ideology but the knowledge of the love of God in Christ for man that is the basis of the Church's social and political concern. In East Asia, the majority of people both in the rural and urban areas live in conditions of abject poverty and under oppressive systems that cramp their personality; and it is the will of God that the Church should wit-

---

3. *The Christian Prospect in Eastern Asia: Papers and Minutes of the Eastern Asia Christian Conference, Bangkok, December 3–11, 1949* (New York: Friendship Press for the International Missionary Council and the World Council of Churches, 1950), 114–21. In spite of this effort, Visser 't Hooft made a critical comment on the Conference. He reported that, to his disappointment, the defensive attitude of the churches toward the resurgence of traditional religions after independence caused the Conference to articulate very little on "the issue of the relevance of the Christian message to the cultural heritage of Asia." According to him, "Paul Devanandan of India gave a brilliant address on the subject, but the following discussion was meagre." (W. A. Visser 't Hooft, *Memoirs* [Geneva: WCC, 1973], 233).

4. "The Church in Social and Political Life," in *The Christian Prospect in Eastern Asia: Papers and Minutes of the Eastern Asia Christian Conference, Bangkok, December 3–11, 1949* (New York: Friendship Press for the International Missionary Council and the World Council of Churches, 1950), 114–17; M. M. Thomas, *My Ecumenical Journey 1947–1975* (Trivandrum, India: Ecumenical Publishing Centre Private Ltd., 1990), 109–10. This report was given a high credit by Visser 't Hooft, who wrote: "The conference was much more creative in the field of social ethics. The committee on 'The Church in Social and Political Life', ably led by M. M. Thomas of India, produced a remarkable report which contained one of the best statements on the Christian attitude towards communism that had ever been made by an ecumenical meeting." (Visser 't Hooft, *Memoirs*, 233).

ness to his redeeming love through an active concern for human freedom and justice.[5]

Thus, social witness was grounded on the sovereignty of God over the whole world. God's judgment and grace were directed to "all realms of life," including the revolutionary changes taking place in Asia. Christian mission in Asia was to bear witness to this truth. The report declared: "The proclamation of the Word of God, with a profound sense of its relevance to the ideological and political conflicts of the Orient, is therefore the central task of the Church in Asia."[6]

Bangkok 1949 was aware that the efficacy in such a task depended on whether the life of the Church could truly be recognized by people as "a community of persons rooted in the Word of God."[7] The divisions among Christians had seriously hindered their being such a community. The call for a renewed commitment to the Gospel, therefore, required a call for witness *in unity*.[8] While this concern for unity gave Asian ecumenism a strong drive towards the emphasis on wholeness, it also made Bangkok considerably Church-centric. Bangkok was, nonetheless, helped by the vision of God's sovereignty as encompassing peoples and developments beyond the walls of the Church and affirmed explicitly God's this-worldly presence saying: "God has created man in his image; in Christ he is redemptively active in our world."[9]

Such an affirmation inevitably raises the question of discernment. The development of mission thinking in the WCC discussed in the previous chapter clearly revealed this issue. Held in the wake of the Bandung Conference of 1955, Prapat 1957 articulated the concern for discernment as follows: "We have gathered here to seek new insight and strength that will enable us to discern the movement of God's Spirit in the events of our times and to fulfil in Asia and the world God's purpose in our day and generation."[10] Subsequently, the search for the sign of the divine presence was to become one of the central issues continuously discussed among Christian leaders of Asia.

5. "Church in Social and Political Life," 114.
6. Ibid., 115.
7. Ibid.
8. *Christian Prospect in Eastern Asia*, 121.
9. Ibid., 119.
10. *The Common Evangelistic Task of the Churches in East Asia (Papers and Minutes of the East Asia Christian Conference): Prapat, Indonesia, March 17–26, 1957* (N.p.: EACC, [1957?]), 103.

Kuala Lumpur 1959 further elaborated the theological reflections made by Bangkok 1949. The concern for witness became far more tightly intertwined with the concern for social changes. In its message to the member churches, the Assembly declared that the political and social reality of Asia was forcing Asians to ask "searching new questions" about humanity and the world, and that the "only sufficient answer" to such questions was in Jesus Christ. It then went on to claim: "Christian people must go into every part of the life of our peoples, into politics, into social and national service, into the world of art and culture, to work in real partnership with non-Christians, and to be witnesses for Christ in all these realms." In other words, "every Christian must recognise that his primary service to God is the daily work he does in the secular world."[11] The approach to mission advocated by Kuala Lumpur was, thus, that of the Christian presence in the secular world.

The this-worldly orientation demonstrated at Kuala Lumpur was remarkable. The Assembly urged each congregation in Asia to "be chiefly concerned not with itself, but with the world," because it was "put into the world by the Lord as His representative."[12] Kuala Lumpur particularly advocated the type of ministry which Takenaka called "social diakonia,"[13] namely, "Christian action aimed at changing structures of economic and social life to establish a new image of selfhood."[14] This new idea was a manifestation of the unmistakable growth of Asian mission thinking.

The idea of God's this-worldly presence also came to the fore. As noted above, the idea was already expressed at Bangkok 1949. Kuala Lumpur pressed it further and paid far more attention to its missiological implication for Asian churches. Takenaka, for instance, began his background address at the Assembly with the affirmation of God's direct presence in world affairs:

---

11. "A Message from the First Assembly of the East Asia Christian Conference to Its Member Churches and Councils," in *"Witness Together": Being the Official Report of the Inaugural Assembly of the East Asia Christian Conference, Held at Kuala Lumpur, Malaya, May 14–24, 1959*, ed. U Kyaw Than (Rangoon: EACC, [1959?]), v–vi.

12. Ibid., vi.

13. M[asao] Takenaka, "A New Understanding of the World and the Need of Theological Renewal," in *"Witness Together": Being the Official Report of the Inaugural Assembly of the East Asia Christian Conference, Held at Kuala Lumpur, Malaya, May 14–24, 1959*, ed. U Kyaw Than (Rangoon: EACC, [1959?]), 39.

14. Michael Cheng-tek Tai, *In Search of Justice: The Development of the Social Teachings in Asian Churches* (Chilliwack, B.C., Canada: Julia Griffith Insticol of Language Arts Ltd., 1985), 23.

> For all of us who come from the various corners of East Asia, this is an unique opportunity to learn together the concrete social problems of the area in which we have been engaging with the task of Christian mission today. We recognised the importance of this mutual learning process of our situation since we believe God is at work in the midst of rapidly changing Asia today.[15]

Without elaborating the theological basis for this affirmation, Takenaka immediately went on to assert the significance of the task of discernment for Asian churches, saying: "The task of the church is . . . to seriously involve oneself in the common effort with the members of God's people throughout the world to discover what God is doing in the midst of the rapidly changing world."[16] Based on these assertions, he challenged Asian churches to renew their life and theology so that they could discern and interpret the world in the light of biblical understanding of revelation and bear witness to the love of God through the act of social diakonia.

M. M. Thomas also acknowledged the significance of the task of discernment. In his address, he rejected the "pietistic attitude of withdrawing into a shell of retreat" and affirmed that "Christ is the Word through whom this whole creation came into being; He is also the redeemer of this whole creation."[17] He then challenged the churches of Asia, saying:

> If our theological approach is correct, then the question we have to ask is: What is God doing in and through the national movements in Asia? . . . For a Church which acknowledges the Lordship of Christ over the whole world, all history, it is necessary to discern Christ working in the world so that we may witness to what He is doing and be with Him, as He acts.[18]

---

15. Takenaka, "New Understanding of the World," 33.

16. Ibid.

17. M. M. Thomas, "Some Notes on a Christian Interpretation of Nationalism in Asia," *South East Asia Journal of Theology* 2 (October 1960): 19.

18. Ibid., 20. As T. V. Philip pointed out, Takenaka's and Thomas's positive views of the revolution contrasted with Visser't Hooft's rather negative evaluation of the time expressed in his following comparison of 1959 with 1910: "As it looks out upon the world of 1959 the Christian Church does not find, as in 1910, that the stream of world history seems to flow in the same direction as the stream of the history of the Kingdom of God. On the contrary, the two histories seem to enter into a period of conflict with each other" (T. V. Philip, "Christian Conference of Asia: A Historical Overview," *Asia Journal of Theology* 9 [April 1995]: 14; W. A. Visser't Hooft, "The Asian Churches in the Ecumenical Movement," in *A Decisive Hour for the Christian Mission: The East Asia Christian Conference 1959 and the John R. Mott Memorial Lectures,* by Norman Goodall, J. E. Lesslie Newbigin, W. A. Visser't Hooft, and D. T. Niles [London: SCM Press, 1960], 53).

The theological position of the EACC at Kuala Lumpur was well summarized in the report of the Commission on the Witness of the Churches amidst Social Change.[19] In this report, the EACC declared:

> The churches of East Asia are called to be witnesses together to the Gospel of Jesus Christ. What is this Gospel?
>
> Firstly, it is a Gospel of redemption of the whole human race and of the whole created world. By his death and resurrection Jesus Christ has reconciled "all things to himself". His purpose is not to withdraw individual spirits one by one from their involvement with material things and human communities in order to set them in a purely "spiritual" relation to himself. Rather his goal is "to unite all things in Him". Therefore the churches' witness to the redemption of Christ must inevitably include the message of the renewal of society.
>
> Secondly, it is a Gospel of the Kingship of Christ over the world. Therefore the meaning of world history, including that of modern Asian history is to be discovered in that Kingship, which today is hidden and will be revealed at the end of time. The church must endeavour to discern how Christ is at work in the revolutions of contemporary Asia; releasing new creative forces, judging idolatry and false gods, leading peoples to a decision for or against Him and gathering to himself those who respond in faith to Him, in order to send them back into the world to be witnesses to his Kingship. The Church must not only discern Christ in the changing life but be there in it, responding to him and making his presence and lordship known.[20]

This passage reveals the close connection in Asian ecumenism between the search for wholeness and the this-worldly orientation. The entire world now came to be seen as the sphere to which God's redemption in Jesus Christ was directed. As part of the world, Asia was no more a composite of pagan "mission fields" that had to be brought to God through the Western missionary enterprise. Accordingly, Christian mission was given a new definition. The Church's mission was defined as the act of discerning and actively witnessing God's redemptive presence in daily realities of rapidly changing Asian societies. As Bassham observed, taking such an approach to mission, the EACC at Kuala Lumpur pointed to the development in

---

19. The convener of this Commission was M. M. Thomas (Thomas, *Ecumenical Journey*, 207).

20. U Kyaw Than, ed., *"Witness Together": Being the Official Report of the Inaugural Assembly of the East Asia Christian Conference, Held at Kuala Lumpur, Malaya, May 14–24, 1959* (Rangoon: EACC, [1959?]), 60.

mission thinking that was to become widespread throughout the ecumenical movement after New Delhi 1961.[21]

Christian Presence in the Process of Modernization

The concept of Christian presence advocated at Kuala Lumpur became increasingly significant in Asian ecumenical thinking during the 1960s. At the EACC Assembly at Bangkok in 1964 held under the theme, "The Christian Community within the Human Community," an attempt was made to elaborate further the understanding of mission as Christian presence. The Assembly also stressed the importance of the laity as bearers of Christian mission in their daily worship and secular engagement saying: "Whether they are gathered in places of worship on a certain day of the week, or are scattered amidst society pursuing different occupations . . . , Christ is present with them and they represent in the world the presence of Christ."[22]

Bangkok 1964 introduced the concept of "holy living" in this connection. Holy living was a way of life solely grounded on one's acceptance of the holy God. In holy living, two aspects were distinguishable: separation and participation. When one heard the call to such living, one was "set apart from the world to be constantly confronted by the Holiness of God." This setting apart was worship where "true meeting between the sacred and the secular" took place. The call to holy living was at the same time "a call to mirror in life God's relationship with the world." Holy living was a life of a "total commitment to participation in God's purposes in the world." Holiness was not conceived of as "something alien from the secular." It was rather to be sought in the midst of secularity.[23] In other words,

> Whole men . . . are summoned to give their whole being and living to fellowship with the Divine One as He engages in a whole ministry to the whole world. The holy derives from God and His purposes and receives its relevance by its relation to the secular world.[24]

---

21. Bassham, *Mission Theology*, 128.

22. *The Christian Community within the Human Community: Containing Statements from the Bangkok Assembly of the E.A.C.C., Feb–March 1964*, Minutes, Part 2 (Bangalore: C.L.S. Press, 1964), 1.

23. Ibid., 46–47.

24. Ibid., 47.

This-Worldly Holiness and the Missio Dei *Concept in Asian Ecumenical Thinking* 71

Bangkok 1964, thus, maintained that holy living was to be "defined by its purpose that man participate in God's mission in Jesus Christ" to the world.[25]

As this quotation shows, Bangkok 1964 employed the *missio Dei* concept in its reflections. It was the first official appearance of the concept in an EACC Assembly. In its statement entitled "Asian Missions,"[26] the Assembly referred to the *missio Dei* as the basis for Christian mission saying:

> The Church's mission is the result of its involvement in the mission of God to the world in Jesus Christ. Those called to go as missionaries do so under the compulsion of the Holy Spirit. Just as when men turn to God in worship they experience the compulsive power of God's concern for the world, even so it is through worship that the missionary calling is constantly renewed.[27]

As we have already seen, the *missio Dei* concept was initially meant to emphasize the theocentric nature of mission. Mexico City 1963, however, gave it a this-worldly connotation. This new connotation made it easy for Asian Christians to adopt the concept, for they had already been developing their theology with an emphasis on the world. The concept, therefore, obtained a distinctly this-worldly accent in Asia from its initial acceptance, and, subsequently, it continued to be used with the primary focus on world history as the locus of God's redemptive work. Such an accent also linked the concept with the criticism of the tenacious inclination of the churches toward "other-worldly piety" and isolation from the wider society. Bangkok 1964, thus, stated:

> The calling of the churches was to share in God's mission to the nations and to the ends of the earth. This meant mission to the national life of the new nations of Asia and dialogue with men of other faiths; but how content Christians in these lands have been to live the 'religious' life unrelated to the challenges and needs of the secular world, uninformed about the beliefs and practices of those of other faiths and unable to talk with them in mutual openness and in depth.[28]

---

25. Ibid.

26. "Asian Missions," in *The Christian Community within the Human Community: Containing Statements from the Bangkok Assembly of the E.A.C.C., Feb–March 1964*, Minutes, Part 2 (Bangalore: C.L.S. Press, 1964), 59–70.

27. Ibid., 59.

28. *Christian Community within the Human Community*, 52–53.

In the second half of the 1960s, three important ecumenical meetings were held consecutively in Asia. They were the Hong Kong Consultation on Faith and Order in 1966, the Asian Conference on Church and Society in Seoul in 1967, and the Fourth Assembly of the EACC in Bangkok in 1968. These meetings were characterized by a considerably optimistic and affirmative attitude toward modernization. Convened by the EACC under the theme "Confessing the Faith in Asia Today," the Hong Kong Consultation concentrated its attention on the importance of "confessing the faith" for the churches in Asia. The reflections at this meeting were published in a comprehensive report.[29] The Consultation declared that the foundation of the personal and corporate Christian life in Asia was the total act of confessing rather than confessions of the faith, either traditional or new. According to the participants, confessing Jesus Christ as the Lord of the entire world implied seeing both the churches and their sociocultural settings under Christ's Lordship. The churches could not truly be confessing churches as long as they stayed away from "the mainstream and common life of Asian nations."[30] The Consultation also recognized the process of industrialization as "one of the main features of modern society" and affirmed it as "the progressive fulfilment . . . of His command to man to assume lordship and mastery of the world, to till and keep it."[31] The Consultation, accordingly, called the churches in Asia to confess Christ both in their encounter with people of other faiths and in their social and political commitment to the process of modernization.

At Hong Kong 1966, the EACC advocated a "confessing theology," that is, "a theology which is the result of the wrestling of an Asian Church with its Asian environment."[32] It thereby took up the complicated question of the relationship between the unity of the Church and the contextuality of the Christian confession. Confessing theology required Asian Christians to free themselves "from churches which belonged to other cultures and historical experiences"[33] and to start with the conviction that

29. *Confessing the Faith in Asia Today: Statement Issued by the Consultation Convened by the East Asia Christian Conference and Held in Hong Kong, October 26–November 3, 1966* (Redfern, Australia: Epworth Press, 1967).

30. Ibid., 51.

31. Ibid., 69–70.

32. Ibid., 11. The necessity of "confessing theology" distinct from "confessional theology" was first pointed out by the Consultation on Confessional Families and the Churches in Asia held at Kandy, Sri Lanka, in 1965 (Ibid., 10–11; Douglas J. Elwood, ed., *Asian Christian Theology: Emerging Themes* [Philadelphia: Westminster, 1980], 46).

33. Park, "Ecumenical Understanding," 9. The significance of the relationship between the contextuality of the Christian faith and the unity of the Church in connection of the

they all not only belonged to one Christ but also commonly shared the cultures and history of Asia. As a result, Hong Kong 1966 paved the way for the emergence of Asian contextual theology in the 1970s. Such a development can be seen as a manifestation of the maturing awareness among Asian Christians of their identity both as Asians and Christians. Being Christian in Asia did not require their lives to be conditioned by the historical divisions among churches in the West. It rather meant going beyond the confessional identities and confessing the Lordship of one Christ anew while asking the question of how this confession was to relate to the burning issues of the contemporary Asia.

In 1967, Asian Christians gathered at Seoul reaffirmed the significance of modernization as "the central concern and priority in Asia today." According to them, modernization meant the "massive changes" brought about by industrialization, secularization, and "those major transformations of political and social structures and attitudes which will make possible full participation in the life of society." It was considered as "the bearer of 'promise' to Asians" that would release them from the "cyclical 'fate' of nature," "grinding poverty," and "static, outworn or inhibiting social structures."³⁴ This optimism at Seoul was combined by the Bangkok Assembly in the following year with the emphasis on the Christian presence at Bangkok 1964. Thus, Bangkok 1968 declared:

> We recognise the need for dynamic Christian presence in the modernisation and secularisation of the traditional societies in Asia. The Christian presence becomes effective only as the Church participates in the process of transformation of these societies, not only responding to the stimuli of other agencies of modernisation not least the universities [*sic*] but also taking the initiative, wherever possible. The particular area in which the Church must make its presence felt is in the task of eliminating the dehumanising factors inherent in the process of modernisation and secularisation.³⁵

---

identity or 'selfhood' of the churches in Asia was pointed out by D. T. Niles in 1959 in his John R. Mott Memorial Lecture, "A Church and Its 'Selfhood,'" delivered at the Kuala Lumpur Assembly (D. T. Niles, "A Church and Its 'Selfhood,'" in *A Decisive Hour for the Christian Mission: The East Asia Christian Conference 1959 and the John R. Mott Memorial Lectures*, by Norman Goodall, J. E. Lesslie Newbigin, W. A. Visser't Hooft, and D. T. Niles [London: SCM Press, 1960], 72–96).

34. East Asia Christian Conference, *Asian Conference on Church and Society, Seoul, Korea, October 10–16, 1967: Modernization of Asian Societies* (Seoul: EACC, 1967), 49–50.

35. East Asia Christian Conference, Fourth Assembly, 1968, *"In Christ All Things Hold Together": Statement and Findings from the Fourth Assembly of the East Asia Christian* [*sic*]

However, a growing ambivalence in regard to modernization existed in Asian ecumenical thinking of this period. While basically affirming it as the principal project of the time, neither Seoul 1967 nor Bangkok 1968 forgot to call the churches to address themselves to social and political issues, such as the questions of the human rights, the rights of minority groups, the problem of corruption in public life, the concept of law in a rapidly changing society, and the issue of Urban Industrial Mission.[36] Seoul 1967 also mentioned the need for structural changes of political systems by means of mass actions. These were the signs of an emerging new approach to Christian mission and reflected the shift taking place within Asian ecumenical thinking in the late 1960s as to the understanding of modernization. The shift became evident when Bangkok 1968 expressly recognized the necessity of revolutionary changes, that is, of "replacing exploitative institutions and power structures through the people's own efforts and struggles," as an "inesapable [sic] requirement at every stage" in the modernization process of the traditional societies of Asia.[37] This recognition was a clear departure from Bangkok 1964 that chiefly advocated the parliamentary type of liberal democracy and expressed a reservation about people's direct political action.[38]

"Peoples of Asia, People of God"

The shift that the EACC went through in the late 1960s resulted from the growing awareness among Asian Christians of dehumanization and social conflicts intensified by the modernization of Asian societies. As Saral K. Chatterji wrote, the new approach tried to understand the modernization process "not only in terms of the usual categories like economic development or modernization, change in values and social structure, but also in

---

Conference. (N.p.: [East Asia Christian Conference?], [1968?]), 1. The positive approach of Bangkok 1968 towards modernization was articulated particularly in its section report entitled "A Divided Church in a Broken World" (ibid., 1–5).

36. *Modernization of Asian Societies*, 39–40; *All Things Hold Together*, 6–7, 11.

37. *Modernization of Asian Societies*, 43–44; *All Things Hold Together*, 4; Saral K. Chatterji, "Introduction," in *The Asian Meaning of Modernization: East Asia Christian Conference Studies*, ed. Saral K. Chatterji (Delhi: Indian Society for Promoting Christian Knowledge, Christian Literature Society, and Lucknow Publishing House for the E.A.C.C., 1972), 1–2; M. M. Thomas, "Christian Action in the Asian Struggle," in *Christian Action in the Asian Struggle* (Singapore: CCA, [1973?]), 6.

38. *Christian Community within the Human Community*, 18–22; Chatterji, "Introduction," 1; Philip, "Christian Conference of Asia," 16.

terms of the basic conflicts and struggles inherent in any modernization effort in a traditional and oppressive society."[39]

The shift became clearly visible at the EACC Assembly at Singapore in 1973, where the EACC was restructured and its name was changed into the CCA. Its new constitution explicitly set the CCA in the context of the *missio Dei*, stating that one of its functions was "the exploration of opportunities and the promotion of joint action for the fulfilment of the mission of God in Asia and throughout the world."[40] The new approach to modernization also surfaced at Singapore. In his keynote address, M. M. Thomas confirmed the finding of Bangkok 1968 that nationalism had become confined to the elite in many Asian nations as an ideology in their search for power, and he argued that the Asian churches had to participate in the Asian "struggle for social justice." By these words, he meant "the struggle for the transformation of existing power-structures, so as to enable the poor and the oppressed to participate in the exercise of power and in the processes of decision-making."[41] Emerito Nacpil of the Philippines similarly argued in his lecture that the calling of the churches to share in God's mission meant participation in the Asian struggle by action aimed at renewal not *within* but renewal *of* the established order.[42]

Thus, Singapore 1973 placed its major emphasis on the concepts of social justice and liberation instead of modernization and economic development.[43] Its participants recognized the failure of the modernization project to overcome "exploitation of the powerless by the powerful" and declared that justice had to be achieved by the transformation of "all spheres of Asian life." They referred to "the second liberation," namely, the people's gaining of power "to determine what happens in their societies," as the new context of Christian mission.[44] Thus, Singapore challenged the churches in Asia with the call for action saying:

> The era of great statements is over: now is the time for action. Christian Action in the Asian Struggle will take place concretely as

---

39. Chatterji, "Introduction," 1.

40. *Christian Conference of Asia, Fifth Assembly, 6–12 June 1973, Singapore* (Bangkok: CCA, 1973), 10.

41. Thomas, "Christian Action," 7–9.

42. Emerito Nacpil, "Renewing the Church for Christian Action," in *Christian Action in the Asian Struggle* (Singapore: CCA, [1973?]), 33–36.

43. *Christian Conference of Asia, Fifth Assembly*, 55.

44. Ibid., 54.

Christians participate in the struggles of the peoples of Asia for the total liberation and fullness of life promised by God.[45]

To facilitate activities aimed at the liberation of the poor, both in rural and urban regions, the CCA proposed to reorganize its Urban-Industrial Mission (UIM) Committee and rename it the "Urban-Rural Mission (URM) Committee."[46]

Singapore 1973 also recognized the need for contextual theology. The assembly report spoke of the responsibility of the CCA "to discover worthwhile Asian contextual theological works" so that theological education could equip lay people to be "the principle agents" in discerning "the presence and action of Christ's Spirit in concrete situations" in order that they could participate "in this activity."[47] The significance of context was pointed out by Shoki Coe. Missions, he said, took place between a "Text" that was derived from and pointed to the *missio Dei*, on one hand, and the "Context," that is, world history as the locus of the *missio Dei*, on the other hand; therefore, the question constantly had to be raised as to whether the text and operation of missions were relevant to the context.[48] With the distinction between "Text" and "Context," Coe had directly contributed to the formulation of the concept of contextualization by the TEF in the previous year. Adopted also by the CCA, this concept intensified Asian Christians' search for "contextuality," that is, "missiological discernment of the signs of times, seeing where God is at work and calling us to participate in it."[49]

The search for contextuality was naturally inspired by the call at Singapore 1973 for participation in the struggles of peoples of Asia. The notion of people began to emerge gradually as the focal concept in this-worldly holiness of Asian mission thinking. In the years after Singapore, the CCA increasingly became aware of the depth and extent of suffering of the people in the midst of poverty and oppression worsened by the growing concentration of power among the elite in Asian nations. The activities of the UIM in the slums of Asia's cities also contributed to the sharpening of this awareness.[50] In 1977, the CCA Assembly was held in

45. Ibid., 52.
46. Ibid., 55.
47. Ibid., 24.
48. Shoki Coe, "Across the Frontiers: Text and Context of Mission," in *Christian Action in the Asian Struggle* (Singapore: CCA, [1973?]), 71.
49. Coe, "In Search of Renewal," 241.
50. Mackie, "God's People in Asia," 217; Philip, "Christian Conference of Asia," 16–17.

Penang, Malaysia, under the theme "Jesus Christ in Asian Suffering and Hope." The concern for suffering and hope was tightly interwoven with the concern for the people. Preman Niles of Sri Lanka wrote: "When we speak of Asian suffering and hope, these are the peoples we have particularly in mind, so that theologians may seek to clarify the Gospel in relation to the struggles of these peoples."[51]

Theologically, the concern for the people centered in the understanding of the relationship between Asian people and God's redemptive act in Asia. An important contribution to this issue came from C. S. Song. In his 1975 work *Christian Mission in Reconstruction*, Song proposed the doctrine of creation rather than salvation history as the starting point for doing theology in Asia in the framework of the *missio Dei*.[52] Another contribution was made by Preman Niles in his address at a consultation at Hong Kong in 1976. In this address, Niles pointed out that the theological problem in Asia centered on the understanding of "the status of Israel." He observed that "in the Bible the message of hope and salvation is addressed to Israel" and raised the question of which entity in Asia should be considered as "coterminous" with the Israel of the Bible.[53] He then rejected two possible answers as inadequate: the Christian Church as the New Israel and the answer given by Latin American theologians, that is, "the suffering and the poor." The approach he opted for was the view "that God is concerned for all mankind and that this concern is expressed directly and immediately." As for the theological framework for this approach, Niles also adopted the creation motif, thus approving Song's proposal.[54] Niles implicitly asked the question, "Who are the people of God in Asia?"—a question that was to be the major theological focus in the CCA in the following years—and pointed to the emerging idea of the people of Asia as the people of God.

This idea was further developed by a group of Korean Christians. In 1979, a theological consultation was organized in Seoul by the National Council of Churches in Korea under the theme "The People of God and the Mission of the Church." The consultation marked the formal emer-

---

51. Preman Niles, ed., "Report: The Consultation of Theologians, Hong Kong, October 10–15, 1976," in *Asian Theological Reflections on Suffering and Hope*, ed. Yap Kim Hao (Singapore: CCA, 1977), 11.

52. Choan-Seng Song, *Christian Mission in Reconstruction: An Asian Analysis* (Madras: Christian Literature Society, 1975; reprint, Maryknoll, N.Y.: Orbis, 1977); D. Preman Niles, "Christian Mission and the People of Asia," *Missiology* 10 (July 1982): 285–86.

53. Preman Niles, "Towards a Framework of Doing Theology in Asia," in *Asian Theological Reflections on Suffering and Hope*, ed. Yap Kim Hao (Singapore: CCA, 1977), 20.

54. Ibid., 20–22.

gence of Korean *minjung* theology that had been developing in the 1970s. The report of the consultation was later published by the CCA as *Minjung Theology: People as the Subject of History.*[55] This new theology was to have a deep impact on Asian ecumenical thinking with its fresh insight into the notion of people.

Minjung theology had its deeper roots in the feeling of the collective *han* as the ethos of the Korean people as well as the historical experiences of Korean Christians who identified "the people of Israel with the people of Korea as a whole" amid the oppressive rule imposed by the Japanese imperialist regime.[56] The immediate context for this new theological movement was, however, the political experiences of Christians who were actively involved in the UIM and the democratic movement in Korea in the 1970s under the military dictatorship of President Park.[57] In their participation in the people's struggle for justice and freedom, these Korean Christians closely encountered the suffering people, or the *minjung*, and intimately experienced their life, humanity, and power. This encounter led the Christians to see the *minjung* as the authentic subjects of history and prompted them to a fresh re-reading of the Bible and theological re-thinking from the perspective of the *minjung*.[58]

Minjung is one of the Korean terms that signify "people." Particularly, it implies "the people who are oppressed politically, exploited economically, alienated socially, and kept in ignorance."[59] *Minjung* theologians ar-

---

55. Kim Yong Bock, ed., *Minjung Theology: People as the Subject of History* (Singapore: Commission on Theological Concerns, CCA, 1981).

56. David Kwang-sun Suh, "Minjung and Theology in Korea: A Biographical Sketch of an Asian Theological Consultation," in *Minjung Theology: People as the Subjects of History*, ed. Kim Yong Bock (Singapore: Commission on Theological Concerns, CCA, 1981), 32; Kim Yong Bock, "Korean Christianity as a Messianic Movement of the People," in *Minjung Theology: People as the Subjects of History*, ed. Kim Yong Bock (Singapore: Commission on Theological Concerns, CCA, 1981), 94.

57. Suh, "Minjung and Theology in Korea," 18, 39; Younghak Hyun, "Minjung Theology and the Religion of Han," *East Asia Journal of Theology* 3 (1985): 354–55.

58. Hyun, "Minjung Theology and the Religion of Han," 355–56; Y. Kim, "Christian Koinonia in the Struggle and Aspirations of the People of Korea," in *Asian Theological Reflections on Suffering and Hope*, ed. Yap Kim Hao (Singapore: CCA, 1977), 37, 40–41.

59. Chris Hee-Suk Moon, "Culture in the Bible and the Culture of the Minjung," *Ecumenical Review* 39 (1985): 181; Kim, "Christian Koinonia," 37–39. In Korean as well as in Japanese, the term *minjung* (*minshu* in Japanese) is differentiated from both the term *minjok* (*minzoku* in Japanese) and the term *immin* (*jinmin* in Japanese). According to Y. Kim, *minjung* implies both *minjok* and *immin*. More strictly speaking, however, *minjok* particularly denotes "the people as [a] national entity in a nationalist sense" while *immin* means "the people as proletariat in a classical Marxist sense" ("Christian Koinonia," 38). As

gued that the biblical equivalent to this Korean term was *ochlos* rather than *laos,* and that it was the *ochlos* that not only followed Jesus but also were loved by him.[60] The understanding of the *ochlos* as the *minjung* provided the theological basis for their identification as the people of God. The Declaration of Korean Theologians of 1984 affirmed: "The people of that [i.e. God's] kingdom is the Minjung."[61] Such a view was a radical departure from the conventional view that equated the people of God with the *laos* or with the Church, an idea which was also dominant in the EACC in the preceding years.[62]

Significantly, *minjung* theologians did not see the overwhelmingly non-Christian *minjung* in Korea as "pagans" to be converted to Christianity. The *minjung* were their "brothers and sisters," their "most beloved ones."[63] As Chi Myong-Kwan wrote,

> it is *we* who are sharing in a common fate and community with them, whether as a nation or as a people; and it is their cries as a nation or as a people that must form the basis of our thoughts and actions instead of charting ways Christianity can participate in their liberation.[64]

---

for the terms *minjok* and *minjung,* they are associate with the different historical contexts. Kim describes this difference as follows: "Since the modern history of Korea is characterized by the nationalist struggle, the notion of the national people (minjok) against foreign domination has been predominant, but since the end of the Second World War, when the Korean people were 'liberated' from Japanese colonialism, the term minjok has become somewhat ambiguous, for it obscures the internal contradictions of Korean society, that is, between the dictatorial regimes and the people (minjung)" (ibid.). This shift from *minjok* to *minjung* corresponds to the shift that took place in the emphasis of the EACC/CCA in the late 1960s. The EACC that had mainly been concerned with nation-building and modernization in the new Asian nations till the mid-1960s increasingly became aware of and concerned with the internal conflicts inside of the rapidly modernizing nations.

60. Suh, "Minjung and Theology in Korea," 38; Ahn Byung Mu, "Jesus and the Minjung in the Gospel of Mark," in *Minjung Theology: People as the Subjects of History,* ed. Kim Yong Bock (Singapore: Commission on Theological Concerns, CCA, 1981), 136–51.

61. "Declaration of Korean Theologians, October 13, 1984 Seoul, Korea," *East Asia Journal of Theology* 3 (1985): 291.

62. See, for instance, Masao Takenaka, "Christ's Ministry and Ours," *South East Asia Journal of Theology* 3 (January 1962): 11; C. H. Hwang, "God's People in Asia Today," *South East Asia Journal of Theology* 5 (October 1963): 5–17; *Christian Community within the Human Community,* 2.

63. Chi Myong-Kwan, "Theological Development in Korea," *International Review of Mission* 74 (1985): 76.

64. Ibid.

Minjung theology was thus born and developed out of listening to the cries of the suffering people in Korea and trying to respond to their cries. It was "a theology both emerging from non-Christians and directed towards non-Christians. It is also a theology performed with non-Christians."[65] Thus, the concept of *minjung* did not have such ambiguity as the concept of the poor displayed in the documents produced by the WCC meetings during this period. As noted in the previous chapter, the concept of the poor was not clear as to whether it meant "the churches of the poor" or the poor in general. In contrast, the concept of *minjung* was explicitly used to include both Christians and non-Christians. This inclusiveness had a great impact on the theological understanding of people in the ecumenical circles in Asia.

The discovery of the significance of the people's stories was another important contribution made by *minjung* theology. According to one theologian, the *minjung* were "known through their stories" since these stories were their "socio-political biography."[66] In other words,

> The stories of the people become the primary means to reveal the total condition of the minjung, while social science methodologies are instrumental in the understanding of social conditions and contradictions in which the people live, and thus clarify the structural problems. . . . The story that the people bear is the shape that historical consciousness in a given time [sic]. It is through such stories that each new generation mobilizes wisdom from the past traditions throughout human history, and it is through the creation of new stories that the people move into a new future.[67]

This discovery made the people's stories a crucial source for theological reflections. The insight was taken up by Song and Lakshman Wickremesinghe of Sri Lanka at the CCA Assembly held at Bangalore in 1981. Song based his lecture at the Assembly on an ancient Chinese folktale called "The Faithful Lady Meng"—a story of a woman victimized by the powerful emperor of ancient China. Wickremesinghe also delivered a lecture constructed on the interaction with a Puranic story of Hinduism.[68]

65. Ibid., 77.

66. Kim, "Christian Koinonia," 39; Kim Yong Bock, "Messiah and Minjung: Discerning Messianic Politics over against Political Messianism," in *Minjung Theology: People as the Subjects of History*, ed. Kim Yong Bock (Singapore: Commission on Theological Concerns, CCA, 1981), 187.

67. Kim, "Christian Koinonia," 39.

68. C. S. Song, "Political Theology of Living in Christ with People," in *A Call to Vulnerable Discipleship: Living in Christ with People*, by CCA Seventh Assembly, 1981

Song was particularly successful in his theological experiment. He began with an assumption that "*the Story of God*—this is what theology essentially is—is the story of people, not just of Jewish-Christian people, but of millions and tens of millions of people here in Asia."[69] His goal was to read the story of God in the Chinese folktale. According to Song, there were two conflicting political theologies in the folktale. One was that of the people who suffered and hoped and who were represented by the life of Lady Meng. The other was that of the rulers who inflicted suffering and death on them, as the Emperor in the folktale did. For Song, the Incarnation served as the "model" for discerning God in the conflict between these two theologies, for God's redemptive love toward the suffering people was ultimately manifest in Jesus Christ. The story of Jesus was the story of God who kept the world from falling into despair and transformed the people's tears into the power of love and hope. The story of Lady Meng was also the story of the God who worked redemptively in the midst of the people's suffering and hope. Thus, the two stories, Asian and Judeo-Christian, converged in their conviction of the ultimate victory of life over death in the people's history. Song, thus, concluded his reflection saying:

> What makes history history are the people in whom the soul of Lady Meng lives—people humiliated and exploited, but awakened to challenge the power of death with the power of resurrection. . . . But the people bear their history in pain. They carry it forward in suffering, and they create it in anticipation of its fulfilment. Is this not the history of the Cross?
>
> It is into this movement of people's history that we Christians in Asia have become incorporated. We are not writing a "Christian" history of Asia. As far as we are intent on such a history, it becomes a missionary history, a history of confessions and denominations. But as we begin to write history with our fellow Asians, it turns out, to our surprise, to be history of the cross and resurrection in Asia.[70]

The concept of incorporation which appeared in this passage was close to the Korean *minjung* theologian Suh Nam Dong's concept of "confluence"

(Singapore: CCA, 1982), 5–24; Lakshman Wickremesinghe, "Living in Christ with People," in *A Call to Vulnerable Discipleship: Living in Christ with People,* by CCA Seventh Assembly, 1981 (Singapore: CCA, 1982), 25–49. Song's lecture was published also as *The Tears of Lady Meng: A Parable of People's Political Theology* (Geneva: WCC, 1981).

69. Song, *Tears of Lady Meng*, vii.

70. Ibid., 65.

of the *minjung* tradition in Christianity and the Korean *minjung* tradition.[71] Song, as well as Suh, made an important contribution to theological thinking by identifying the people of Asia with the people of God as well as providing a theological interpretation of the people's history and culture.

Both Song and Suh operated with the *missio Dei* concept in their theological reflection on the people of Asia.[72] The connection between the two concepts in Asian contextual theology that rapidly developed from the second half of the 1970s became more explicit toward the end of the following decade. The Asia Mission Conference in Cipanas, Indonesia, in 1989 was particularly important in this development. Held under the theme "The Mission of God in the Context of the Suffering and Struggling Peoples of Asia," the Conference expressly placed the notion of people within the framework of the theology of *missio Dei*. This Conference also explicitly affirmed the identification of the peoples of Asia with the people of God.

At the Conference, the *minjung* theologian Kim Yong-Bock of Korea delivered the keynote address on the theme and declared that the basic theological affirmation that the Asian ecumenical movement had reached was that "the peoples of Asia are the children of God."[73] That is to say, "God the Creator is the God of the suffering and struggling people of Asia, no matter who they are in terms of religion, political ideology, or cultural differences." God hears the cries of these people as God did in the Exodus. God's mission among them is "to restore their life and dignity to the fullest, so that the image of God may be realized among them." In other words,

---

71. Suh Nam Dong, "Historical References for a Theology of Minjung," in *Minjung Theology: People as the Subjects of History*, ed. Kim Yong Bock (Singapore: Commission on Theological Concerns, CCA, 1981), 178; idem, "Hutatsu no monogatari no goryu" [The Confluence of Two Stories], in *Minjun no shingaku* [Minjung Theology], ed. I In-ha and Kida Ken'ichi (Tokyo: Kyo-Bun-Kwan, 1984), 261–320.

72. Choan-Seng Song, "New Frontiers of Theology in Asia: Ten Theological Theses," *South East Asia Journal of Theology* 20 (1979): 28–29; Suh, "Historical References," 156, 178.

73. Kim Yong-Bock, "Keynote Address: The Mission of God in the Context of the Suffering and Struggling Peoples of Asia," in *Peoples of Asia, People of God: A Report of the Asia Mission Conference 1989* (Osaka: CCA, 1990), 12. Obviously, the idea that the people of Asia are the people of God did not mean that only the people of Asia are the people of God. This idea was the answer given to the question, "Who are the people of God *in Asia*?" raised implicitly by Niles in 1976. As noted above, Niles's theological option was the view that God was concerned for all humankind, which implied that all people, whether Asian or not, were the people of God. The identification of the people of Asia as the people of God was the result of the application by the CCA of this all-inclusive idea to Asia.

God is at work among them "for the establishment of God's Sovereign Rule of Justice, in which the people become sovereign."[74] Therefore, "the churches and the ecumenical movement must pursue solidarity with suffering and struggling people," communicating God's solidarity in Jesus Christ with the people of Asia.[75] As Kim pointed out, the ecumenical movement in Asia had gone through a shift from the "ecclesiocentric paradigm" inherited from the West to the "people-centered paradigm" over the years.[76]

The significance of the *missio Dei* concept was obvious in this new paradigm. Kim also pointed out its significance and called the concept "a guiding dynamic for the involvement of Asian Christian communities in the history of their peoples." The *missio Dei* concept released the churches in Asia from their traditional preoccupation with the Church—with their order, confessions, and "evangelistic and social service concerns"—so that they could be "an incarnating community in the life of the people."[77] The *missio Dei* also helped Asian Christians to refocus their concern on the discernment of the living Christ present in the suffering and struggle of the people of Asia.[78] Thus, Kim affirmed that the *missio Dei* was "the central theological theme providing the basis for ecumenical involvement among the people in the world," in Asia in particular.[79] The *missio Dei* was the key concept also in the process of the theological and missiological reorientation of the ecumenical movement in Asia.

Conclusion

In conclusion, I will make several observations that have arisen from this and the preceding chapter regarding the particularities of Asian ecumenism.

The first observation is about this-worldly holiness in Asian ecumenism. Used with a this-worldly emphasis, the *missio Dei* means that God is redemptively at work in world history, and that the mission of the Church is to participate in this redeeming activity of God in the world. This conception of *missio Dei* developed in the 1960s in the West. *In Asian*

---

74. Ibid., 12–13.
75. Ibid., 21, 23.
76. Ibid., 7.
77. Ibid.
78. *Peoples of Asia, People of God: A Report of the Asia Mission Conference 1989* (Osaka: CCA, 1990), 123.
79. Kim, "Keynote Address," 7.

ecumenism, however, the basic thrust of this idea already existed prior to the introduction of the concept from the West and remained central to its thinking and mission approach.

As early as 1949, the participants in the Bangkok Conference conceived of God as the sovereign of all realms of life who was at work in the midst of the Asian revolution, and affirmed that witness to this divine activity was the task of the Church. Bangkok 1949, thus, made the idea of God's this-worldly presence the starting point for Christian mission in Asia.

Among the leading proponents of the idea of God's this-worldly presence were Devanandan, Thomas, and Takenaka. Their conviction of the sovereignty of God over the whole world prompted them to affirm God's active presence in the rapidly changing Asia. Their earnest desire to witness to this divine presence within the socio-political reality of Asia gave their approach to Christian mission a remarkably this-worldly orientation. These Christian leaders had no reason to raise a question of the theological foundation for their this-worldly attitude because their thinking and approach originated in a firm conviction of God's sovereignty over the world. Takenaka's Kuala Lumpur address—one of the earlier expressions of the attitude on an official occasion—clearly shows that God's active presence in world history was taken for granted in their reflections.

Moreover, sending missionaries abroad had rarely been a central missionary concern of the churches in Asia. The Christian leaders of Asia, therefore, had no reason to be troubled with the question of the theological basis for Christian mission, the question that disturbed their Western colleagues for decades. For the Asians, Christian mission had a obvious foundation, that is, the sovereign God who was at work in the Asian revolution. Therefore, the question of the theological basis for mission was not raised even when the term *missio Dei*, a product of the Western response to the question, was introduced to Asia in the 1960s. By that time, even in the West, the concept had already shifted its emphasis from the Triune God as the foundation for mission to the world as the locus for mission.

As a result, God's this-worldly presence has remained as the central theological motif in Asian ecumenical thinking throughout the history of the EACC/CCA. The world-centric approach to mission based on this motif has also remained unchallenged. This consistent this-worldly holiness has made Asian mission thinking distinct from its counterpart in the IMC/WCC that has been characterized by the oscillation and tension between the Church-centric and the world-centric attitudes.

One can observe the same consistency as to the meaning of *missio Dei* too. The second observation is: *ecumenical Asian theologians have almost always used the missio Dei with the world-centric connotation.* They have appropriated this Western term as the symbol that provides a focus around which this-worldly holiness in the Asian churches is given a coherent expression. The significance of the *missio Dei* concept has, however, not been limited to this function. Using the *missio Dei* as their guiding theological concept, theologians, such as Coe, Nacpil, Song, and *minjung* theologians, creatively contributed to the emergence of contextual theology in Asia. In their theological endeavor, the *missio Dei* served as a bridge for bringing together the world-centric attitudes developed in ecumenism in Asia and the West. Furthermore, it helped these theologians to see their own cultures and societies in light of the divine redemption. Through the interactions with the *missio Dei* thinking in the global ecumenical movement, they vigorously elaborated theological interpretations of Asian cultures and societies, thereby making sense of God's sovereignty in the Asian world.

Thirdly, the idea of God's this-worldly presence as the central theological motif has made *the relationship between God and the Asian world with its peoples, cultures, religions, and socio-political life* one of the central theological issues constantly discussed by the Asian theologians. Soon after Bangkok 1949, the leaders of Asian churches began to raise the question of discernment, which became a major concern in Asian ecumenical thinking. Needless to say, the question of the relationship between God and the world is a missiological question. Therefore, theological reflections in Asia came to be characterized by a highly missiological inclination. It is no surprise that, as Preman Niles wrote, "theology and mission have become almost coterminous" in Asia.[80]

Moreover, the question of the relationship between God and the Asian world was inevitably accompanied by a double focus on God and the Asian world. Such a double focus corresponded to the problem of dual identity among Asian Christians that we observed in the first chapter. As already pointed out, the Hong Kong Consultation in 1966 made this duality a conscious agenda for the EACC/CCA search for doing theology in the Asian context.

The problem of dual identity brings us to the fourth point, namely, a question: What is the significance of the shift that took place in Asian ecumenism during the period from the late 1960s through the early 1970s? Prior to this period, the leaders of Asian churches were generally in sup-

---

80. Niles, "Christian Mission," 279–80.

port of the policies of modernization pursued by the political leaders of their countries for the purpose of economic development. From the mid-1960s on, however, the church leaders became more and more disillusioned by modernization, having realized that it had actually increased the concentration of power and widened the gap between the haves and the have-nots. As a result, they became increasingly critical of modernization and shifted their attention towards poverty and oppression in their societies. The major emphasis in Asian ecumenism also shifted from support for and participation in nation-building towards solidarity with the people and participation in their struggle for social justice.[81]

The Asian Christians' rejection of modernization as the economic and political project based on the Western model does not, however, mean that they rejected modernization as the major historical process in the contemporary world. In fact, they remained highly change-oriented, or for that matter modernity-oriented. Their concern for socio-political transformation became even more radical than before. It can be said that their earnest longing for change sustained and deepened by the Christian symbolism pressed them to dissociate themselves from the modernization project.

The shift is rather to be understood in terms of the relationship between these Asian Christians' search for identity and the problem of meaning in their society at large. In the first chapter, the three types of relationship were distinguished: 1) the Christian identification with the traditional identity of their society, 2) the Christian identification with the modernization project, and 3) the Christian identification with "disfavored strata and groups." After the Second World War, the leaders of Asian ecumenism attempted to understand their religious commitment in relation to the second option. In the mid-1960s, however, their disillusionment with the modernization project as well as their growing awareness of internal tensions and conflicts in modern and modernizing societies prompted them toward the third option, which came to be known as "solidarity." Singapore 1973 was the decisive moment for such a reorientation. The emergence of the concept of people or *minjung* as the major theological theme is a telling manifestation of the new way of identification. It also reveals the Asian Christians' discovery that "disfavored strata and groups" in a traditional society have in fact constituted the vast majority of the Asian population throughout history. This discovery prompted many

---

81. This shift corresponded to the shift from developmentalism to liberation that took place in Latin America in the sixties. See Gustavo Gutiérrez, *A Theology of Liberation: History, Politics, and Salvation*, rev. ed. with a New Introduction (Maryknoll, N.Y.: Orbis, 1988), 13–25.

Christian thinkers to do theology out of what Bellah called the "traditional suspicion and hostility" of these people "toward the established authorities and their charisma."[82] Such a reorientation was not confined to Asian ecumenism. As discussed in the second chapter, the development between Uppsala 1968 and Bangkok 1973 displayed a parallel change in the ecumenical movement in general.

This observation reveals an important point regarding the concept of contextualization. Proposed by the TEF in 1972, this concept emerged and developed out of the shift that ecumenical mission thinking went through during this period. In the first chapter, it was pointed out that this concept was primarily oriented toward modernity rather than tradition. The above observation, however, shows that the orientation toward modernity had existed among the Christian leaders in Asia even before the emergence of the concept, and that the concept must rather be seen in connection with the way Christians relate to the search for meaning in their society at large; that is, the concept was associated with the new orientation among Christians toward the "disfavored strata and groups" in modern and modernizing society. In other words, contextualization was the concept that basically implied the third type of Christian identification. As a result, the theologically trained Christians who often came from the most disfavored strata of a society or from minority groups have increasingly become the chief agents of contextualization with whom the entire Church is urged to be in solidarity in its work for mission.[83]

---

82. Bellah, *Beyond Belief*, 71.

83. The meaning of the term "contextualization" has been widened greatly with its gradual acceptance by a wider spectrum of Christian circles. Max L. Stackhouse, for instance, wrote in 1988 that "contextualization of the faith has taken place in the long traditions of the churches in the postbiblical period" ("Contextualization, Contextuality, and Contextualism," in *One Faith, Many Cultures: Inculturation, Indigenization, and Contextualization*, ed. Ruy O. Costa [Maryknoll, N.Y.: Orbis, 1988; Cambridge, Mass.: Boston Theological Institute, 1988] , 4). Whereas his observation is correct, what he means by contextualization here is a historical process that is very different from the initial meaning of the term. As for the evangelicals' response and adoption of the term, see Hesselgrave and Rommen, *Contextualization*, 33–35.

CHAPTER 4

The Theology of God's This-Worldly Presence in M. M. Thomas

IN THE PREVIOUS CHAPTER, I demonstrated that ecumenical mission thinking in Asia has been consistent since the beginning in its strong this-worldly emphasis. This fact contrasts with ecumenical mission thinking in the West that has been characterized by the oscillation and tension between the ecclesiocentric and the this-worldly approaches. In Asia, the idea of God's this-worldly presence was put forward by the EACC/CCA from its inception, and the *missio Dei* concept was an expression of the general tendency towards this-worldliness. The concept appeared in the mid-1960s in Asian mission thinking and subsequently became a key concept in the theological endeavor of the CCA.

In the course of my survey, several references were made to M. M. Thomas. One of the leaders of the ecumenical movement both in Asia as well as in the world, he was also a major advocate of this-worldly holiness in ecumenism. In this chapter, I will review the development of this-worldly holiness in his thinking and examine the role that this spirituality played in his attempt to interpret the world, particularly the Asian world, in light of his Christian faith. My primary focus will be on his mature thinking from 1955 through 1975 because these were the years when his original thought was most creatively developed. His intellectual search, however, began much earlier and continued in a tireless and constant dialogue with his contemporary situations. Much of his thought arose from this continuous dialogue. I will, therefore, approach his thought biographically, beginning with his early life, and attempt to clarify how this-worldly holiness in his mature thinking came into being.

The Context and Early Life of M. M. Thomas

Madathiparampil Mammen Thomas was born on May 15, 1916, in a small village in central Kerala, southwestern India, and passed away on December 3, 1996, near Madras on a train heading for Kerala. At the time of his birth, the village was located in the princely state of Travancore. His family belonged to a local lower middle-class family affiliated with the Mar Thoma Syrian Church.[1]

Kerala, South India

After India gained independence, Travancore was merged with the neighboring princely state of Cochin and the Malabar district of the Madras presidency to form the predominantly Malayalam-speaking state of Kerala in 1956. The current capital of Kerala is Trivandrum or Thiruvananthapuram. This small state, no more than 75 miles in width, stretches for about 360 miles along the Malabar Coast on the western side of the Indian subcontinent facing the Arabian Sea. While bordered by Karnataka to the north and Tamil Nadu to the east, Kerala is separated from the Deccan Plateau by high mountains called the Western Ghats. This geographical isolation has provided the region with an environment favorable to evolve its distinct history and culture under foreign influences.[2]

Kerala is India's most advanced state in education.[3] Its "addiction to education" has contributed to its high literacy rate—the highest in the country reaching 96.17 percent in 1981.[4] The literate public of Kerala have demonstrated a strong political consciousness. T. J. Nossiter describes their politically oriented mindset as follows:

> To a greater degree than in perhaps any other Indian state, public meetings (and elections) are a living ritual of the society, a source of entertainment and prestige to the village and its leaders, as well as the arena of conflict between factions, groups, and classes. Politics is the national sport of Malayalis and the finest orators in

---

1. T. M. Philip, *The Encounter between Theology and Ideology: An Exploration into the Communicative Theology of M. M. Thomas* (Madras: Christian Literature Society for the Newday Publication of India, 1986), 1; "Death of Leading Asian Ecumenist at Age of 80," *ENI Bulletin*, 13 December 1996, 15–16.

2. *New Encyclopaedia Britannica*, 15th ed., s.v. "Kerala," by V. R. Pillai; C. P. Mathew and M. M. Thomas, *The Indian Churches of Saint Thomas* (Delhi: I.S.P.C.K., 1967), 1; Suresh Kumar, *Political Evolution in Kerala: Travancore 1859–1938* (Phoenix Publishing House Pvt. Ltd., [1994?]), xi.

3. *Britannica*, s.v. "Kerala"; Kumar, *Political Evolution in Kerala*, xiv.

4. T. J. Nossiter, *Communism in Kerala: A Study in Political Adaptation* (London: C. Hurst & Co. for the Royal Institute of International Affairs, London, 1982), 33; N. Jose Chander, "Political Culture," in *Dynamics of State Politics: Kerala*, ed. N. Jose Chander (New Delhi: Sterling Publishers Private Ltd., 1986), 15.

a language which lends itself to political rhetoric are an attraction irrespective of party affiliation.⁵

The unique political culture of Kerala is further marked by an exceptional acceptance of Communism after Independence. In 1957, the first election held after the formation of the state made Kerala the first Indian state to vote the Communist Party to power.⁶

As for religion, three major world religions—Hinduism, Christianity, and Islam—have coexisted in Kerala for centuries. According to the latest 1991 census, the majority of the population are Hindus. Their percentage (57.28 percent) is, however, much lower than that in India as a whole (82.41 percent). Christians constitute 19.32 percent of the population and Muslims 23.33 percent; the Muslim population in the entire country counts 11.67 percent while the Christian population only 2.32 percent. The religious outlook of Kerala is thus characterized by a high Christian concentration. Particularly, the former princely states of Cochin and Travancore show an outstanding Christian concentration that reaches about thirty percent of the population.⁷

St. Thomas Christians and the Mar Thoma Syrian Church

Kerala's religious life is marked by yet another uniqueness. It is the existence of the ancient indigenous Christian community known as "St. Thomas Christians."⁸ As their liturgical language is Syriac, they are also

---

5. Nossiter, *Communism in Kerala*, 37–38.

6. C. P. Suresh, "Electoral Politics," in *Dynamics of State Politics: Kerala*, ed. N. Jose Chander (New Delhi: Sterling Publishers Private Ltd., 1986), 152–56; Nossiter, *Communism in Kerala*, 1. According to Antony Kariyil, the Communists' victory in Kerala in 1957 was "the first case of a democratically elected Communist government in the world" with the only exception of the small principality of San Marino in Italy (*Church and Society in Kerala: A Sociological Study* [New Delhi: International Publications, 1995], 136).

7. India, Registrar General and Census Commissioner [M. Vijayanunni], *Religion*, Census of India 1991, Series 1: India, Paper 1 of 1995 (Delhi: Controller of Publications, 1995), xii–xiii. According to a publication in 1968, Christians constituted 34.42 percent of the entire population in the former state of Cochin and 29.24 percent in Travancore (K. G. Krishna Murthy and G. Lakshmana Rao, *Political Preferences in Kerala* [New Delhi: Radha Krishna, 1968], 17; quoted in V. A. Pankratova, *Khristiane Keraly: rol' v sotsial'no-politicheskoy zhizni shtata* [Christians of Kerala: Role in Socio-Political Life of the State] [Moscow: Izdatel'stvo Nauka, 1982], 63).

8. According to Nossiter, St. Thomas Christians constitute more than three-quarters of the Christian population of the state (*Communism in Kerala*, 21).

called "Syrian Christians" though they are racially Indians.[9] According to their oral tradition, the Apostle Thomas founded their Church. He is said to have landed on the Malabar Coast in around A.D. 52 and, after the extensive missionary work, died in A.D. 72 as a martyr at Mylapore near Madras at the hands of hostile Hindus.[10] Scholars are unable to establish any historical facts regarding Thomas's work. However, this tradition has been a source for the unique identity of all Syrian Christians until today.

The history of the Syrian Christians until the end of the fifteenth century is also obscure because of the scarcity of materials. Evidences, however, suggest a connection with the Christian Church in West Asia from the early period—more specifically, their subordination to the Patriarchate of the East in Mesopotamia that became Nestorian at the end of the fifth century.[11] As for their social status in Kerala, Susan Bayly's detailed study points out their "integration" within the wider Hindu society in the pre-colonial Kerala.[12] Syrian Christians long played a key role in Keralan economics through their engagement in maritime trade and commerce. From the fifteenth century on, many of them served the local Hindu rulers as skilled elite warriors and obtained high rankings in the local Hindu society. Religiously, Syrian Christians developed religious rites much in common with their Hindu counterparts. As a result, Syrian Christians were regarded as "persons of clean caste and standing in the Hindu moral order" and even "granted one of the most critical signs of ritual status within the society, the right of access to Hindu temples and sacred precincts," which was denied to low-caste Hindus as well as low-caste converts to Christianity.[13]

The coming of the so-called Vasco da Gama era at the end of fifteenth century resulted in a fundamental change in the life of the Syrian Christian community. The secular and ecclesial politics of the colonial powers created internal conflicts in the community, resulting in many schisms. The

9. Mathew and Thomas, *Indian Churches of Saint Thomas*, 1.

10. Samuel Hugh Moffett, *A History of Christianity in Asia*, vol. 1, *Beginnings to 1500* (San Francisco: HarperCollins Publishers, 1992), 33–35; Mathew and Thomas, *Indian Churches of Saint Thomas*, 7; Cyril Bruce Firth, *An Introduction to Indian Church History*, rev. ed., The Christian Students' Library No. 23 (Madras: Christian Literature Society for the Senate of Serampore College, 1976), 3–4.

11. Firth, *Indian Church History*, 18–33.

12. Susan Bayly, *Saints, Goddesses and Kings: Muslims and Christians in South Indian Society 1700–1900* (Cambridge: Cambridge University Press, 1989), 251. By "integration," Bayly means "a position of high status and acceptance within the region's most prestigious social and religious institutions" (ibid.).

13. Ibid., 244–47, 249–53. See also Firth, *Indian Church History*, 36.

unity of the Syrian Christians was gradually lost. The community eventually came to be divided into several different groups: the Romo-Syrian or Uniate Church, the Jacobite or Orthodox Syrian Church, the evangelical group called the Mar Thoma Church, and other smaller groups.[14]

The fragmentation of the Syrian Christian community was accompanied by the collapse of their integration in the wider Hindu society. The collapse progressed particularly after Travancore and Cochin became tributary states under British colonialism at the end of the eighteenth century. Under colonial rule, Syrian Christians lost their traditional privileged status in society as maritime traders and elite warriors. The frequent interference of the colonial government in ecclesiastical matters, as well as the fierce campaigns of the Church Missionary Society (CMS) to reform the Jacobite Church, deepened the internal fragmentation of the Syrian community and stirred up its clergy into endless succession struggles.[15] The ritual system that had so far sustained the social integration came under harsh attack and increasingly broke down.[16] As a result, the relationship between the Hindus and the Syrians rapidly deteriorated, and the integration began to be replaced with rigid and exclusive religious boundaries, resulting in so-called communalism.[17]

The process of social fragmentation, however, also unleashed the energy for a dynamic social change. This new energy was personified particularly by Abraham Palakunnathu (1769–1845), a Jacobite priest and seminary professor also known as Abraham Malpan, who responded positively to the Western religious impact.[18] Inspired by the missionaries of the CMS, Abraham embarked in 1837 on a revision of the Syrian liturgy "in accordance with the teaching of the Scriptures" and started an evangelical reform movement within the Jacobite Church.[19] When his nephew

---

14. Mathew and Thomas, *Indian Churches of Saint Thomas*, 1–3.

15. According to Bayly, the rites and doctrines of the Jacobite Church condemned by the CMS as "unChristian" included "the offering of prayers for the dead, the 'worship' of the Virgin and the saints with processions, fasts and supplications, prostrations before images of God the Father, [and] the cult veneration of deceased bishops and their tombs" (*Saints, Goddesses and Kings*, 298).

16. Ibid., 281–96.

17. Ibid., 294, 459–61.

18. *Malpan* is a designation for a "Syriac preceptor with the authority to train deacons for the priesthood" (ibid., 301).

19. Mathew and Thomas, *Indian Churches of Saint Thomas*, 74–76. The revision included a removal of prayers for the dead and invocation of saints, the use of Malayalam, and changes in the text for the Holy Communion (ibid., 75–76). Regarding the nature of the reformation of Abraham Malpan and the problems surrounding it, see Mathai John,

Mathew, consecrated as *Metran* (Metropolitan) by the Patriarch of Antioch, came back to Malabar, a long dispute over episcopal legitimacy was ignited between the reformers and their opponents. The Jacobite Church eventually split into two. In 1888, the reformers formed the evangelical wing of St. Thomas Christianity known as the Mar Thoma Syrian Church. They accepted Western evangelicalism in theology while retaining their own Eastern tradition in liturgy and social life, though in a modified form.[20]

Thomas's Early Life

As already noted, M. M.'s family belonged to the Mar Thoma Syrian Church. M. M. himself grew up in its "strong evangelical piety." Its Sunday worship, Sunday school, and prayer and revival meetings, as well as his early education at a school operated by the Church, nurtured in him "a deep loyalty towards the Mar Thoma Church and its evangelical sacramental traditions."[21]

After high school, M. M. spent four years (1931–35) at Science College in Trivandrum to study chemistry.[22] In his first year at college, he had a significant spiritual experience, through which "Jesus Christ became real to . . . [him] as the bearer of divine forgiveness." This evangelical experience led him to a serious involvement in three youth movements.[23] The first movement was the Youth Union of a Mar Thoma parish in Trivandrum, which encouraged students to participate in evangelistic efforts in neighboring villages. The second was the Christian Fellowship

---

"The Reformation of Abraham Malpan: An Assessment," *Indian Church History Review* 24 (June 1990): 31–65; Philip Tovey, "Abraham Malpan and the Amended Syrian Liturgy of CMS," *Indian Church History Review* 29 (June 1995): 38–55.

20. Mathew and Thomas, *Indian Churches of Saint Thomas*, 77–84; Firth, *Indian Church History*, 173–77.

21. Philip, *Theology and Ideology*, 1; T. Jacob Thomas, *Ethics of a World Community: Contributions of Dr. M. M. Thomas Based on India Reality* (Calcutta: Punthi Pustak, 1993), 28. The degree of loyalty thus formed towards the Mar Thoma Church was well expressed much later in his own words: "I fully stand within the evangelical Reformation tradition [of Abraham Malpan] and affirm the positive contribution which it made to the life of the Kerala Churches and to the Kerala culture and society" (M. M. Thomas, *Towards an Evangelical Social Gospel: A New Look at the Reformation of Abraham Malpan* [Madras: Christian Literature Society, 1977], 27).

22. M. M. Thomas, *Ideological Quest within Christian Commitment 1939–1954*, Indian Christian Thought Series No. 16 (Madras: Christian Literature Society for the Christian Institute for the Study of Religion and Society, Bangalore, 1983), iii.

23. M. M. Thomas, "My Pilgrimage in Mission," *International Bulletin of Missionary Research* 13 (January 1989): 28.

Group, an informal prayer fellowship. The third was the interdenominational Student Christian Movement (SCM), which sought under the leadership of K. A. Mathew "to bring students an awareness of the ecumenical and social implications of the gospel."[24] These movements greatly contributed to M. M.'s spiritual formation during the college period. Besides, some devotional classics, such as Thomas à Kempis's *Imitation of Christ* and Brother Lawrence's *Practice of the Presence of God*, served as resources for his spiritual growth.[25] Thomas later wrote: "It is clear to me that I started my life of faith of what may be called an evangelical and sacramental piety. I believe that it still is the foundational structure of my spiritual life."[26]

After college, M. M. joined the Mar Thoma Church Ashram at Perumpavoor. According to T. Jacob Thomas, this ashram was "the center of evangelistic and educational activities of the Mar Thoma Church in North Travancore."[27] There, M. M. worked as a part-time high-school teacher and participated in the evangelistic activities of the ashram in the neighboring parishes.[28] He was also introduced to the Inter-religious Student Fellowship organized by his friend M. A. Thomas. The association with this fellowship brought M. M. into contact with students and leaders of Hinduism and Islam. Also, Gandhian nonviolence confronted him with the problem of "the social implications of religion and the meaning of the cross for politics." M. M. spent hours with M. A. Thomas discussing "the truth and meaning of Christ in the inter-religious setting."[29] This search resulted in the reflections entitled *The Realization of the Cross* (1937).[30] In this writing, he affirmed "the centrality of the crucified Jesus for the movement of the kingdom of God in history, which included God's work in all religions and all urges toward love and justice."[31] Importantly, one of the

---

24. Ibid.; Philip, *Theology and Ideology*, 2; Thomas, *Ethics of a World Community*, 29.

25. Thomas, "My Pilgrimage," 28.

26. M. M. Thomas, "Faith Seeking Understanding and Responsibility," unpublished manuscript, 1971, United Theological College Library, Bangalore, India, 1; quoted in Philip, *Theology and Ideology*, 2.

27. Thomas, *Ethics of a World Community*, 30.

28. Thomas, "My Pilgrimage," 28.

29. Ibid.

30. M. M. Thomas, *The Realization of the Cross (Fifty Thoughts and Prayers Centred on the Cross)* (Madras: Christian Literature Society, 1972).

31. Thomas, "My Pilgrimage," 28.

recurring motifs in the work was the idea of humanity, anticipating the mature Thomas's strong emphasis on anthropology.[32]

In 1937, M. M. left Perumpavoor and joined a Christian institute called the Christavasram at Alleppey. Under the leadership of a Christian *sadhu* named K. I. Mathai, the institute held a "comprehensive vision of the gospel," integrating "evangelization, Bible study, inter-religious dialogue, Christian mysticism and social service activities in its programs."[33] Sadhu Mathai felt that Thomas's "spirituality was too pietistic and subjectivist and not sufficiently world-oriented," and encouraged him to take the social implications of the Christian faith seriously. Responding to the Sadhu's challenge, Thomas returned in 1938 to Trivandrum and began his involvement in social activities "in search of the unity of interiority with active life."[34] He organized an inter-religious home for street children with the help of the SCM. Unfortunately, he was forced to leave the home soon, suspected by non-Christian co-workers as motivated by an evangelistic desire. This experience made him aware of the problem of "communalism" dominant in India preventing inter-religious cooperation. Thomas also organized a beggar relief committee in cooperation with the municipal authorities in Trivandrum. These activities gave him an insight into the dehumanizing reality in which the people of the lowest strata of society lived.[35]

The Early Stage of Thomas's Theological and Ideological Search

The Kerala Youth Christian Council of Action (YCCA) formed at a SCM summer camp in August 1938[36] was a Christian response to the political awakening taking place in Kerala in the late 1930s.[37] Supporting Congress,

---

32. Thomas, *Realization of the Cross*, 3, 10, 11, 15, 28, 29, 43.

33. Thomas, "My Pilgrimage," 28; Thomas, *Ethics of a World Community*, 31.

34. Thomas, "My Pilgrimage," 28; Philip, *Theology and Ideology*, 5.

35. Thomas, "My Pilgrimage," 28; Thomas, *Ethics of a World Community*, 31–32; Philip, *Theology and Ideology*, 6.

36. George M. John, *Youth Christian Council of Action 1938–1954: The Story of a Dynamic Movement of Christian Youth*, C.I.S.R.S. Social Research Series No. 10 (Madras: C.L.S. for the Christian Institute for the Study of Religion and Society, Bangalore, 1972), 1–2. This camp was the ninth South Kerala Camp of the SCM of India held in the Sivagiri School Buildings at Varkala from August 11 to 14, 1938, under the theme "God Speaks to This Generation." It was attended by about 110 delegates from the colleges of Trivandrum, Kottayam, and Changanacherry (ibid.).

37. At the end of 1929, the Indian National Congress under the leadership of Mahatma

the YCCA encouraged young Christians to take part in its freedom movement, to study political and social ideologies in the light of the Christian faith, and to define Christian tasks in relation to the social, economic, and political problems of Kerala.[38]

Thomas participated in the YCCA as secretary from its beginning and was deeply involved in its activities in the following years.[39] This commitment provided him with the first opportunity for an intense theological and ideological reflection on the unfolding socio-political reality in India as well as the world. He thus began his career as a Christian thinker with no formal theological education. T. M. Philip says that this fact gave Thomas's writings "the character of developing his own explorations in understanding the meaning of the Christian faith and relating it to his own context."[40]

In the 1930s, Socialism and Communism also grew influential in Kerala besides Gandhism.[41] As a result, the YCCA suffered the ideologi-

---

Gandhi adopted *purna swaraj* or complete independence from the British rule as the ultimate goal of their political struggle. The following decade became the most decisive period in the freedom movement of Congress. The impact of such a political development was also felt in Kerala, first in the British Malabar and later in Travancore and Cochin too. According to Mathew and Thomas, the princely state of Travancore became the major battlefield for the nationalist campaign in Kerala during this period (*Indian Churches of Saint Thomas*, 145). As early as in 1924, a *satyagraha* campaign started at Vaikkom seeking the *avarnas'* right to enter Hindu temples. Supported by Gandhi, this struggle resulted in the Temple Entry Proclamation of the *maharaja* of Travancore in 1936. In 1932, All Travancore Joint Political Congress was formed by various political organizations of low-caste Hindus, Muslims, and Christians and soon embarked on a joint agitation against the constitutional reform of 1932. In 1938, Congress abandoned its policy of non-interference in the princely states, declaring: "The purna swaraj is for the whole of India, inclusive of the states." The Travancore State Congress was thereby set up for "the achievement of responsible government" and launched a civil disobedience movement in August 1938, which was, according to Suresh Kumar, "the first political struggle of the entire people cutting across communal, sectional and regional interests" in Kerala (Stanley Wolpert, *A New History of India*, 3d ed. [New York: Oxford University Press, 1989], 310–11, 314–15; Kumar, *Political Evolution in Kerala*, 120–21, 135–44, 147–51, 156–59; Tatsuro Yamamoto, ed., *Indo shi* [A History of India], Sekai kakkoku shi 10 [Tokyo: Yamakawa Shuppan Sha, 1960], 437–38).

38. Thomas, *Ethics of a World Community*, 32–33; Mathew and Thomas, *Indian Churches of Saint Thomas*, 148.

39. Thomas, "My Pilgrimage," 30.

40. Philip, *Theology and Ideology*, 19.

41. The Communist Party of India was organized in the early 1920s. In Kerala, however, the influence of Marxism began to be felt at the beginning of the 1930s. According to Nossiter, the "first proto-marxist organization" in Kerala was a "tiny Trivandrum-based Communist League" formed in 1931. In 1934, the Kerala unit of the Congress Socialist

cal tension from its beginning between "Christian Gandhiites" and the "Trivandrum group" inclined towards Marxism. The former espoused "the liberal theological tradition which saw the Kingdom of God as a goal to be reached through a social programme based on Non-violence" whereas the latter "sought to combine the Christian realism of Neo-orthodoxy with Gandhian and Marxian social insights."[42] This tension ended up with the split of the YCCA in 1943. Thomas, who belonged to the Trivandrum group, withdrew from the YCCA and organized a new but short-lived body called the National Christian Youth Council. The Council expressly accepted "Marxist Scientific Socialism" and sought to combine it with the "Catholic Christian Faith." It also tried to cooperate with Communists.[43] Its activity, however, came to an end when Thomas became the Youth Secretary of the Mar Thoma Church in 1945.[44]

The thinking and ethos of the YCCA was remarkably this-worldly. The statement issued at its first meeting affirmed God's active presence in history as follows: "God is ever actively working in this world and calls all men and especially the youth of this generation to venture forth with Him and risk life and all in the service of truth, justice and love."[45] The statement also advocated a holistic view of human life and redemption saying: "The gospel of Christ offers redemption to the whole of human life. We fail because we try to draw a line between personal and social, and attempt to spiritualise the individual apart from his social relationships. All life is one."[46] These were the ideas, though in their seminal forms, that became central to the thinking at Kuala Lumpur 1959 and came to be known in the 1960s as the world-centric view of *missio Dei*. They were repeated in a document called "A Social Manifesto for the Church" adopted by the Mar Thoma Students' Conference in 1943 summarizing the YCCA thinking built up through the years.[47] As Thomas was "primarily responsible"

Party was formed and was transformed into the Communist Party in 1940 (Nossiter, *Communism in Kerala*, 65, 72, 84).

42. John, *Youth Christian Council*, 57, 59, 62; Mathew and Thomas, *Indian Churches of Saint Thomas*, 148–49.

43. Thomas, *Ideological Quest*, 75; Philip, *Theology and Ideology*, 9.

44. John, *Youth Christian Council*, 67.

45. Ibid., 4.

46. Ibid. For the Kuala Lumpur emphasis on God's this-worldly presence as well as wholeness, see p. 69 above.

47. "A Social Manifesto of the Church" is found in Thomas, *Ideological Quest*, 61–74. In it, Thomas wrote: "Not that the Gospel of Christ can be divided into a social and an individual gospel. Human life is one indivisible whole and the Gospel offers redemption to the whole of that life. To compartmentalise life into self-sufficient and mutually exclusive

for the "corporate thinking" expressed in it as well as "putting it down in writing," the manifesto reveals the extent to which the YCCA owed him intellectually.[48]

Drawing on these ideas, the YCCA criticized the communal exclusiveness and "ethical indifference" of the Christian churches in Kerala. It was also critical of the one-sided emphasis on the individual in the evangelical tradition brought by the CMS to Kerala. The YCCA thus urged the churches to make the impact of the Christian witness "bear upon the national social life of India."[49]

In Thomas's thinking during this period, the notion of God's this-worldly presence was not the leading motif. Much of his later intellectual development, nonetheless, had its roots in the central concerns of the YCCA and its theological emphasis on the world and wholeness. The period of his involvement in the YCCA and the National Christian Youth Council can be seen as the formative stage for his thinking.

Initially, Thomas was inclined toward a liberal approach. In the summer of 1939, Thomas read a paper entitled "Gandhism and the Principles of Jesus"[50] at the first annual Vacation Study Courses of the YCCA.[51] Focusing on similarities in Jesus' and Gandhi's ethics, he presented a Christian interpretation of the Gandhian *satyagraha*.[52]

Thomas, however, swiftly abandoned this attempt to combine liberal theology with Gandhian ideology.[53] A sign of the shift was already notice-

---

component parts, as individual and social, material and spiritual, is what is called dualism, which is the bane of our Christianity today" (Thomas, *Ideological Quest*, 62–63); "We believe that the Spirit of Christ is active in this world working out His loving purpose of creating a divine community of persons in free, loving and Holy communion with one another and with the Father" (ibid., 67). *Ideological Quest* is a collection of Thomas's major works written from 1939 through 1954. It was compiled with intent "to indicate . . . [his] early struggles in the search for a historically relevant social and political ideology within the framework of . . . [his] commitment to the Christian faith" (ibid., iii). See also John, *Youth Christian Council*, 54.

48. Thomas, *Ideological Quest*, 61.

49. John, *Youth Christian Council*, 45.

50. Thomas, *Ideological Quest*, 1–17.

51. As for the details of the Vacation Courses of the YCCA, see John, *Youth Christian Council*, 14–20.

52. Thomas writes: "God meets evil with a 'transcendent satyagraha'. And this is the fundamental basis of the Christian concept of non-violence" (*Ideological Quest*, 2). The concept of "transcendent *satyagraha*" was taken from A. G. Hogg's Christmas sermon at Tambaram 1938 (ibid.).

53. Thomas later wrote that "Gandhism and the Principles of Jesus," as well as the earlier *The Realization of the Cross*, had pointed to his early attempt at "a combination

able in a paper he read the same summer at a Mar Thoma youth retreat at Trivandrum.[54] In this paper, he presented a highly Church-centric position affirming the Church as the "primary," if not "the only," means "of extending Christ's Kingdom on earth and redeeming the world."[55] He was, however, sharply critical of the actual condition of the churches of Kerala. Rejecting their tendency to "divide the gospel into 'personal' and 'social' gospels,"[56] he argued that "the spiritual has to be realised and expressed in and through the material."[57] He was highly this-worldly when he asserted social justice as his primary ecclesiological concern, declaring:

> Man is so brutish that it is time that we forsake all faith in ourselves to bring in the Kingdom, and depend solely on God. But if such a triumphant faith degenerates into a callous indifference about society, if it diminishes our craving for a just social, economic and political order, based on reverence for human personality and organised to meet human need, and if it takes away the eyes of the Church from this world, to the skies, I would desire to forsake the eschatological faith, to make the Church *earth-centred* rather than *sky-centred*—for, what is most important is the task of the Church to establish the Kingdom of God on earth.[58]

He held that the Church could be moral only when it came to recognize "economics as a potent factor in guiding and influencing human life" and rose "above the present evil economic system."[59] Subsequently, he came to accept Marx's historical materialism under the influence of Father Leonard Schiff, a Christian Marxist, and urged the churches also to embrace the

---

of Liberal Theology and Gandhian Ideology as informing my social work and thought" (*Ideological Quest*, iv.). T. M. Philip, therefore, calls the period of Thomas's life from 1937 till 1939 "the liberal phase" in Thomas's theological development (*Theology and Ideology*, 19–22).

54. M. M. Thomas, "The Church: What I Owe to It; and My Complaint against It," TMs [photocopy], December 1939, United Theological College Archives, Bangalore, India. This paper was published with the title "Marxism—Its Challenge to the Church Youth" in Thomas, *Ideological Quest*, 18–32.

55. Thomas, "The Church," 1.

56. Thomas, "The Church," 7. Thomas rejected this tendency because of his conviction that "all life is one and the Church's attempt at establishing peace and goodwill have [sic] failed because she has sought to divide life into compartments and so save the individual apart from his environment" (ibid.). His holistic approach to anthropology and redemption was consistent with the views of the YCCA. See p. 98 above.

57. Ibid., 8.

58. Ibid. Emphasis mine.

59. Ibid., 7.

Marxist philosophy to interpret social history and economic conditions of India.[60]

While Thomas abandoned his earlier commitment to Gandhism, his critical dialogue with it remained an essential part of the source and context for his theological and ideological search. In "Gandhism and the Principles of Jesus," Thomas had raised a question whether Gandhi's "belief in the inherent goodness of man and in the immanence of God, [sic] results in any 'shallow view of evil' or any 'minimising of the scope and effects of sin.'"[61] In the early 1940s, he came back to the question and dealt with it extensively in his long essay entitled "Christianity and the Indian Situation: Nicolas Berdyaev and Gandhism" (1941–42).[62] Later, he defined his approach from 1940 until 1948 retrospectively "as seeking to redefine the dialectics of Karl Marx within the Neo-orthodox theology of Karl Barth, Reinhold Niebuhr and Nicolas Berdyaev."[63] The Russian philosopher Berdyaev's impact was particularly significant. His notion of history as "tragic destiny" came to play a crucial role in Thomas's theological and ideological search in the 1940s. As we will discuss later in this chapter, Berdyaev's personalism also had a tremendous impact on Thomas's thinking.

Gandhi's doctrine of *ahimsa* or nonviolence was grounded on the religious tradition of India as well as the Russian writer Leo Tolstoy's interpretation of Christianity.[64] With a careful examination of Hinduism,

---

60. Thomas, *Ethics of a World Community*, 34. As for Leonard Schiff, see also John, *Youth Christian Council*, 15, 17. This Anglican priest was remembered by M. M. as a man who "made a tremendous contribution" to the "spirits and minds" of the young Christians in the YCCA with his "combination of Anglo-Catholicism, Niebuhrian Neo-Orthodoxy, and Marxism" (Thomas, "My Pilgrimage," 30).

61. Thomas, *Ideological Quest*, 4.

62. M. M. Thomas, "Christianity and the Indian Situation: Nicolas Berdyaev and Gandhism," TMs [photocopy], 1941–42, United Theological College Archives, Bangalore, India. Part of this essay was published in Thomas, *Ideological Quest*, 39–60 under the title "Gandhi, Marx and Nicholas Berdyaev's Neo-Orthodox Critique of Modern Civilization."

63. Thomas, *Ideological Quest*, iv.

64. According to Dennis Dalton, Gandhi took the idea of *ahimsa* "from the Indian tradition, and particularly the Jain religion," and fused it with Tolstoy's Christian pacifism and the Sermon on the Mount (*Mahatma Gandhi: Nonviolent Power in Action* [New York: Columbia University Press, 1993], 14). Among the Indian religions, Jainism places a special emphasis on *ahimsa*; the idea is, however, also very important in both Hinduism and Buddhism (Keith Crim, Roger A. Bullard, and Larry D. Shinn, eds., *The Perennial Dictionary of World Religions*, 1st Harper & Row paperback ed. [Nashville, Tenn.: Abingdon, 1981; reprint, San Francisco: HarperCollins Publishers, 1989] s.v. "Ahimsa,"

Gandhism, and Tolstoy's "Liberalism," Thomas concluded that they all shared a faith in the "inherent goodness" of human nature.[65] He could not accept this faith and found an ally in Berdyaev, who was also critical of such optimism while sharing with Gandhi a convinced opposition to modern Western civilization.[66]

Thomas noted that Berdyaev's thought was grounded on the conception of the fall of humankind and its redemption by the incarnation of the "God-man." Berdyaev's view of human history was "characterized by a pessimissim [sic], . . . conscious of the tragic depths of man and his social destiny" and, unlike Hinduism and Liberal Christianity, had "no faith in the inherent goodness of human nature."[67] Thomas observed that the idea of "the free creativity" of human beings rooted in their divine origin was central to Berdyaev. According to Thomas, while this idea led the Russian philosopher to exalt human life as "a participation with God in the unfinished task of moral creation," it introduced "a strong tragic element" to his thought, for, to Berdyaev, there could be no authentic freedom nor moral life "without freedom in evil." The liberal belief in progress was deceptive because "there is only progress in the tragic sense . . . of the good-evil, divine-demonic antithesis, of the principles of good and evil in collaboration." Redemption was to be found beyond any moral law; it was a liberation from the moral antithesis in the grace of Jesus Christ.[68]

---

by G. R. Welbon).

65. Thomas, "Berdyaev and Gandhism," 32; idem, *Ideological Quest*, 141.

66. Thomas, "Berdyaev and Gandhism," 2.

67. Ibid., 33.

68. Ibid., 37, 41–42. Note that, discussing Berdyaev's thought, Thomas talks here of human beings' "participation with God in the unfinished task of moral creation." Obviously, he means by it Berdyaev's idea of "creative co-operation." In his *The Destiny of Man*, Berdyaev writes: "As the image and likeness of the Creator, man is a creator too and is called to creative co-operation in the work of God. Man is not merely a sinful being expiating his sin, is not merely a rational, developing and social being, not merely a being sick with the conflict between his consciousness and the unconscious, but, first and foremost, *he is a creative being*" (Nicolas Berdyaev, *The Destiny of Man*, tr. from the Russian by Natalie Duddington [London: Geoffrey Bles, 1937], 53). The idea of "creative co-operation" in Berdyaev is based on the Eastern Orthodox notion of "participation" in God which, according to John Meyendorff, is the ground for anthropology and soteriology in the Christian East (John Meyendorff, *Byzantine Theology: Historical Trends and Doctrinal Themes* [New York: Fordham University Press, 1979], 138–40, 171). For Thomas, the notion of "participation" later evolves into a key concept in his mission thinking; it also becomes cardinal to the concept of the *missio Dei* in ecumenical mission thinking. The impact of the Christian East on Thomas as well as the *missio Dei* concept in terms of the notion of participation deserves a further survey.

Thomas pointed out that Freud, Marx, and Nietzsche also disclosed the "lie" of the liberal belief.[69]

In an address at a SCM meeting in 1943, Thomas elaborated the concept of tragic destiny in his own words, criticizing the evolutionary view of progress:

> The Liberals thought that with the increase of good, evil decreased; ... But the Christian doctrines give a different picture. Whatever be the good, when infected with the original sin or pride, becomes evil. The greater the goodness in the world, the greater the evil also becomes.... So in history, we cannot see a progress from evil to good; the only progress is in the increase of good along with the increase of evil, and therefore there is progress only in the intensity of the good-evil conflict.... The good of man is unable to destroy the evil in him, because in the very assertion of good over evil, the good turns into evil. When one good has destroyed one evil, the very good itself appears as evil.[70]

This pessimism made Thomas deeply suspicious of utopianism. The fundamental problem of Gandhism and Liberal Christianity was that both the Gandhian *ahimsa* and the liberal belief in progress—and also the Christian pacifism—were "utopian," and that they ignored the fundamental dilemma of the destiny of humankind. The lack of "social realism" was the "great weakness" of Gandhism.[71]

To Thomas, as to Berdyaev, the fallenness of social history meant that a society was primarily "a place of conflicts and violences."[72] The tragic nature of human history was "nowhere more real than in the problem of social power." Drawing on Reinhold Niebuhr, Thomas argued that power as "a structural principle of all organisms" fulfilled the meaning of historical groups and yet also betrayed it, turning such groups into demons.[73] Amid the world where Fascism, Stalinism, and imperialism were violently crushing each other, this "tragic realism" convinced Thomas of his option for the Marxist analysis of social history as "a necessary ideological basis for political action for social justice in India."[74]

---

69. Thomas, "Berdyaev and Gandhism," 33.
70. Thomas, *Ideological Quest*, 100.
71. Thomas, "Berdyaev and Gandhism," 50–51.
72. Ibid., 45.
73. Thomas, *Ideological Quest*, 101–3.
74. Thomas, "My Pilgrimage," 30.

Despite this option, Thomas was aware of the utopian tendency in Marxism which as a "source of tyranny" could turn its aspiration for justice into totalitarianism.[75] To him, establishing the Kingdom on earth did not mean "identifying the Kingdom of God with some social order," no matter how perfect it would be. He warned of an inherent danger of a this-worldly emphasis saying: "just as other-worldliness is an escape of human life and social realities, this-worldliness can also be an escape through compromise with an order very much less than Christian." A Christian quest for political action was, therefore, to be pursued in the context of the "worship of the Holiness of God" which could sustain the dialectic between a "worldliness" and an "unworldliness."[76] The Christian mission was thus seen as witnessing to the transcendent forgiveness in Christ within the framework of political commitment to the Marxist struggle for social justice.[77]

While Thomas later shifted his ideological position, this dialectical approach to mission, as well as the concept of human history as tragic destiny, continued to characterize Thomas's thinking. Almost fifty years later, he repeated the same thought saying: "my tragic sense of history prevents me from identifying any historical movement of human creativity or political liberation as totally continuous with the movement of the kingdom."[78]

An Emergence of the Motif of God's This-Worldly Presence in Thomas's Thinking

The Ideological and Theological Shift in 1948

In 1947, Thomas was invited by the WSCF to join its staff in Geneva and moved from Travancore to Switzerland, marking the beginning of his "ecumenical journey."[79] He served the WSCF from 1947 till 1953,

---

75. Thomas, *Ideological Quest*, 123–24; idem, "My Pilgrimage," 30.

76. Thomas, *Ideological Quest*, 66–67.

77. Because of this conviction, Thomas applied in 1943 for the ordination in the Mar Thoma Church and the membership in the Communist Party. He was, however, rejected by the Church due to his association with the Communist Party and by the Party due to his commitment to the Christian faith (Philip, *Theology and Ideology*, 8; Hielke T. Wolters, *Theology of Prophetic Participation: M. M. Thomas' Concept of Salvation and the Collective Struggle for Fuller Humanity in India*, with a foreword by K. C. Abraham [Delhi: ISPCK/UTC, 1996], 28).

78. Thomas, "My Pilgrimage," 31.

79. Thomas's autobiography *My Ecumenical Journey* begins with a letter of August 28,

first as full-time secretary and then as an officer.[80] On arriving in Geneva, Thomas became involved in the WSCF Political Commission and participated in the making of the new Asian policy of the WSCF. The next year, he organized the first WSCF Asian Leaders' Conference in Kandy. He also attended various ecumenical meetings, including Bangkok 1949, where he represented the WSCF as vice-chairperson. Besides, he was appointed a member—the only non-Western—of the Study Commission on "The Church and the Disorder of Society" for the WCC Amsterdam Assembly in 1948.[81] These activities brought him into contact with many Christian leaders and theologians in the West and Asia.

As noted above, Thomas's central concern in the 1940s was a Christian witness within a critical commitment to the Marxist ideology. In 1948, however, two incidents led him to "rethink furiously" his pro-Communist stance. The first incident was the adoption by the Indian Communists of a new policy to confront Jawaharlal Nehru whom the new Communist leadership considered "as the betrayer of Indian independence." The second was the news of the Stalinist *coup d'état* and destruction of other socialist parties in Czechoslovakia. In these incidents, he saw his fear of the tyrannical nature inherent in Communism come true. His involvement in the discussions in the WCC Commission on the responsible society also influenced his political thinking.[82] As a result, his ideological position began to move away from Communism.

Thomas's paper written in 1947 in the preparation for Amsterdam 1948 still expressed his sympathy for Communism.[83] His paper written in 1949 as the report of Kandy 1948, however, revealed a clear ideological shift.[84] In the tyranny of Stalinism, he saw the corruption of Communism caused by its utopianism, resulting in self-righteousness and a search for power to control the future of human history.[85] His option was now for

---

1946, from Robert Mackie, the then General Secretary of the WSCF, that invited Thomas to join its staff in Geneva, Switzerland (*Ecumenical Journey*, 1).

80. Thomas, "My Pilgrimage," 30.

81. Thomas, *Ecumenical Journey*, 20–24, 61–87, 105–12.

82. Ibid., 59–60; Thomas, *Ideological Quest*, 203.

83. This paper is included in *Ideological Quest*, 190–202, with the title "Man, Machine and Society—An Asian View." Its abridged version was published with the title "The Situation in Asia—II" in *Man's Disorder and God's Design: The Amsterdam Assembly Series*, vol. 3, *The Church and the Disorder of Society: An Ecumenical Study Prepared under the Auspices of the World Council of Churches* (New York: Harper & Row, 1948), 71–79.

84. Thomas, *Ideological Quest*, 203.

85. M. M. Thomas, *Towards a Theology of Contemporary Ecumenism: A Collection of Addresses to Ecumenical Gatherings (1947–1975)* (Madras: Christian Literature Society,

"social democracy." He realized that "liberal social democratic" values in social democracy, unlike Communism, embodied "the recognition . . . that man has a dignity in society arising from his moral nature and his destiny beyond society and State."[86] He thus became "appreciative of the political insights of Liberal Democracy" and "committed to the democratic path to the social Revolution in India."[87]

With this change, Thomas began to reassess Gandhism. In a paper he wrote during self-study at Union Theological Seminary in New York from 1953 till 1954, he praised Gandhism as "the one political and social ideology" that took seriously "the primacy of the human person in politics and economics."[88] This paper was his new attempt to rescue Gandhism from its utopianism by redefining it with the help of the Neo-orthodox view of humanity and society.[89]

Thomas's ideological shift was, naturally, accompanied by a shift in his theological emphasis, though the theological shift took place within the framework of Neo-orthodoxy. His earlier preference for Marxism was theologically based on the doctrine of the Fall. He thought that power inevitably developed into tyranny because of the "Original Sin at work" in history. A destruction of the inevitable tyranny by another power—revolution—was God's judgment in history, and the Christian task was to proclaim this divine judgment. That is why he opted for the cooperation with Communists in their struggle to overthrow the corrupt Western colonial power. There, history was seen as "the story of man's sin and God's judgment" while its ultimate meaning as "a suprahistorical reality, that could not be comprehended within the historical process."[90]

With his ideological shift, Thomas began to think that the question of ultimate meaning had to be asked even within history. Having realized that the concept of judgment was inadequate for this purpose due to its negative implication, he proposed the idea of redemption as a new theological emphasis. He wrote:

> Can Christ only judge politics? Can He not also in some measure redeem it here and now? Cannot forgiveness be realized as power

---

1978), 32–33.

  86. Thomas, *Ideological Quest*, 210–11.

  87. Ibid., v.

  88. Ibid., 238. For Thomas's stay at Union, see Thomas, *Ecumenical Journey*, 155, 159–63.

  89. Thomas, *Ideological Quest*, 236–52.

  90. Ibid., 100–104.

in the structures of the collective and institutional life of man in society? . . . I believe that it is possible for politics itself to be redeemed from its extreme perversions and be made more or less human, if it recognizes and receives into itself the power of the Gospel.[91]

The Christian task was now defined as "redeeming" ideologies and movements to build a secular liberal democratic society, that is, presenting the gospel "as the power which can redeem them from their 'most terrible perversion' and re-establish them in such a way that they do not betray, but realize, their true human ends."[92] Thus, "a redefinition of Marxism, Gandhism and Liberalism within the framework of the theology and realistic anthropology of Christian Neo-orthodoxy" became Thomas's new goal.[93]

The Emergence of the Idea "God in Christ at Work in History"

Thomas's new ideological and theological approach was given its first clear formulation in two official documents in 1949 for which he was primarily responsible in thought and writing. The first was the WSCF Commission report on the "Christian in the World Struggle,"[94] which was expanded later into a WSCF Grey Book entitled *The Christian in the World Struggle* by him and his British colleague Davis McCaughey.[95] The second was the statement "The Church in Social and Political Life" adopted by Bangkok 1949.[96] Endorsed officially, these two documents served as Thomas's guide to his interpretation of Indian social and political reality for the following years.[97] Significantly, the new approach indicated the resurfacing of the two main theological emphases in the statement of the first YCCA meeting as well as the document "A Social Manifesto of the Church" almost a decade earlier. These emphases were the idea of God's active presence in the world and the holistic view of humanity and redemption.

---

91. Thomas, *Theology of Contemporary Ecumenism*, 36.

92. Ibid., 37.

93. Thomas, *Ideological Quest*, v.

94. Ibid., 217–23.

95. M. M. Thomas and J. D. McCaughey, *The Christian in the World Struggle: A Grey Book of the World's Student Christian Federation* (Geneva: World's Student Christian Federation, [1951?]).

96. We mentioned this statement in our discussion of Bangkok 1949 in Chapter 3. See pp. 65–66 above. The statement was also included in Thomas, *Ideological Quest*, 223–26.

97. Ibid., 217.

The WSCF report was to formulate a common approach of the diverse national SCMs to the social and political reality of the contemporary world. To define the ongoing worldwide struggle, Thomas introduced the concept of revolution in the report and elaborated it in the Grey Book.[98] Johannes Aagaard saw the significance of this book in that it introduced the term "revolution" as a theological concept and prepared for the theological development in the 1960s.[99] As we have already seen, this concept was in fact not new for Thomas. In the report, however, he defined it much more broadly than before as "the rise of submerged classes, nations, races, demanding not simply amelioration of their lot, but participation in the total life of society."[100] The revolution thus defined was called a "social revolution" and distinguished from a Marxian "political revolution," that is, "the overthrow within the state of one political power by another."[101] According to Thomas and McCaughey, the social revolution as a global phenomenon in the postwar world was a profound and comprehensive process that was not confined to the economic or political dimension of social life. It was essentially "the demand of the people . . . for *power as the bearer of dignity* and for significant and *responsible participation in society and social history.*"[102]

Interpreted this way, the revolution was no longer considered merely as a vehicle of God's judgment; rather, it was now understood in terms of God's redemption as "an instrument of social justice" that pointed to God's righteousness, that is, "a justice which God wills for men but which is not yet openly revealed." Thomas, therefore, argued with McCaughey that Christians must say "yes" to the revolution.[103] In this connection, the concept of participation—the concept that he mentioned in his study on Berdyaev in the early 1940s—surfaced in Thomas's thinking; that is, the Christian task in the context of the social revolution was "to work together humbly with God as Sovereign Lord" in God's righteous activity, bearing witness to God's love and concern for all people.[104] Furthermore, while acknowledging Marx's contribution to the concept of revolution, Thomas

---

98. Ibid., 218; Thomas and McCaughey, *Christian in the World Struggle*, 15–37.

99. Aagaard, "Trends during the Sixties," 23–24. Based on this assessment, he called *The Christian in the World Struggle* "a most important piece of study for the historian who wants to understand the ecumenical development in the sixties" (23).

100. Thomas, *Ideological Quest*, 218.

101. Thomas and McCaughey, *Christian in the World Struggle*, 17–18.

102. Ibid., 19.

103. Ibid., 25–26; Thomas, *Ideological Quest*, 220; idem, *Ecumenical Journey*, 97.

104. Thomas, *Ideological Quest*, 220.

did not forget to repeat his warning that Christians could not share the Utopian vision of history with Marxists. While welcoming revolution, Christians also had to "be sensitive to those points at which the potentiality and inner significance of the revolution is betrayed."[105]

As the theological basis for the Christian participation in the revolution, Thomas suggested "the universal Lordship of Jesus Christ" and "Christ's concern for humanity as such." The WSCF report, the Bangkok statement, and the Grey Book were all explicit in this approach.[106] As the authors of the Grey Book wrote, the Gospel was "the good news of the kingly rule of Christ over all realms of life," and, therefore, there was "no 'order' outside Jesus Christ and his control."[107] God's redeeming activity embraced the entire cosmos. As Paul wrote in II Cor. 5:19: "God was in Christ reconciling the kosmos unto himself,"[108] God's love and judgment were directed not merely towards the personal life of individuals or a certain segment of humanity but towards the total human world. The socio-political dimension of human life was not outside the scope of redemption. God's redemption was thus both cosmic and social. The ongoing revolution in the world was, therefore, also under God's active rule restoring in Christ humankind and the created order to a right, responsible relationship with God and one another.[109] Affirming thus God's presence in the contemporary historical process, the Grey Book declared:

> Behind and within the social revolution of our day, . . . the Christian sees by faith the righteous hand of God. Even in the worst human situation God's creative and redeeming will is active, waiting to be grasped by faith, seeking to bring men into responsible relation to Him and to one another.[110]

---

105. Thomas and McCaughey, *Christian in the World Struggle*, 23–26.

106. Thomas, *Ideological Quest*, 218; Thomas and McCaughey, *Christian in the World Struggle*, 14; "Church in Social and Political Life," 114; M. M. Thomas, "The Churches in the Political Struggles of Our Day," *Ecumenical Review* 3 (January 1951): 122. The Bangkok statement expressed this theological staring point as follows: "The gospel proclaims that *God's sovereignty includes all realms of life* . . . . It is not the challenge of any ideology but the knowledge of *the love of God in Christ for man* that is the basis of Church's social and political concern" ("Church in Social and Political Life," 114. Emphasis mine.).

107. Thomas and McCaughey, *Christian in the World Struggle*, 4–5.

108. Thomas and McCaughey quoted this verse with the original Greek word *kosmos* for the world (ibid., 39).

109. Ibid., 12, 39–40; M. M. Thomas and Paul E. Converse, *Revolution and Redemption* (New York: Friendship Press, 1955), 52; Thomas, *Theology of Contemporary Ecumenism*, 45.

110. Thomas and McCaughey, *Christian in the World Struggle*, 40.

To the authors of the Grey Book, the ideals of social justice bore witness to "a dim recognition" on the side of humankind of such a this-worldly activity of God in every social situation for restoring the responsible relationship or "responsible society."[111] Thus, the political concern of Christians was nothing but the proclamation to the world of the fact that it lived under God's judgment and grace in Christ.

In this connection, the Grey Book recognized the significance of faith in the act of discerning God's activity in history, saying:

> Faith when living is *the substance of things hoped for*, and therefore if we wait in hope for the open disclosure of Christ's judgment and redemption of the collective life of man, this waiting in faith should mean that in the political order we shall see, however partially, perversely and provisionally it may be, the judging and the redeeming hand of God to which we have to witness in political thinking and action. Faith always works in man some act of the will and brings some new insight or knowledge about God's dealing with the world.[112]

For Thomas, the centrality of faith in the act of understanding and discernment remained a basic conviction. Faith was seen also as a basis for political participation. Grounded on the knowledge in faith, any political conversations among Christians were, "explicitly or implicitly, directly or indirectly," a proclamation of God's judgement and grace. Thomas and McCaughey thus emphasized the missiological significance of the Christian concern for politics, affirming it was essentially "evangelistic."[113]

As already noted, a biblical basis for the idea of cosmic and social redemption in the Grey Book was II Cor. 5:19. After his one-year study at Union, Thomas published a book entitled *Revolution and Redemption* with his friend Paul E. Converse in 1955. There, the verse was expanded into a brilliant articulation of the *missio Dei* concept as follows:

---

111. Thomas and McCaughey interpreted the Amsterdam 1948 concept of responsible society theologically as the "social righteousness" of God, that is, "a given divine fact of every historical situation, the datum of life, waiting to manifest itself only for man's act of 'humbling recognition' of the givenness of it and the giver." The task of Christians within the revolutionary situation was then to see such "social righteousness" as "the essential truth of the struggle" and witness to it. In other words, Christians were thought to be called to point "not to what *ought* to be but to what *is*" (ibid., 39; Thomas, "Churches in the Political Struggles," 122).

112. Thomas and McCaughey, *Christian in the World Struggle*, 6.

113. Ibid.

> For God was and is at work in Christ reconciling this world to himself. And God calls men to become actively involved with him in the world for its redemption.
>
> God is at work in Christ reconciling this world—torn by social revolution, political division, and oppression of many kinds—to himself. It is in this context that we must rethink the mission of the church to the world.[114]

This idea became the kernel of the EACC theology at Kuala Lumpur 1959. In the Introduction to its official document "The Witness of the Churches amidst Social Change," Thomas formulated the idea as follows:

> Christ is at work in the revolutions of contemporary Asia, releasing new creative forces, judging idolatry and false gods, leading peoples to a decision for or against Him and gathering to Himself those who respond in faith to Him, in order to send them back into the world to be witness to His Kingship. The Church must not only discern Christ in the changing life but be there in it, responding to Him and making His presence and lordship known.[115]

Thus, the Christian mission was defined as "a participation in Christ's mission" at Kuala Lumpur.[116] This refined formulation of the idea of God's this-worldly presence raised the question of discernment more seriously than ever. In his address at the same assembly, Thomas asked directly: "If our theological approach is correct, then the question we have to ask is: What is God doing in and through the national movements in Asia?"[117] The same year, he published an essay entitled "Indian Nationalism: A Christian Interpretation" and attempted to discern "the living presence of God-in-Christ active in the very centre of national life" of independent

---

114. Thomas and Converse, *Revolution and Redemption*, 42.

115. "The Witness of the Churches amidst Social Change (An EACC Study Document)," *Religion and Society* 6 (June 1959): 27. At an interview held by the author with Thomas on January 10, 1995, at Princeton Theological Seminary, Princeton, NJ, Thomas said that he had written the introduction to this document. In this interview, he said that the idea "God is at work in history (or in the world)" had originated in the EACC, and answered affirmatively the author's question whether it meant that the idea, which later became popular in the ecumenical movement, had first emerged in Asia and then influenced the West, and not vice versa. In this connection, he particularly referred to the "preamble for the Church and Society document" at the Kuala Lumpur conference as an important source, and added that he himself wrote it. By "preamble," he meant the introduction to "The Witness of the Churches amidst Social Change."

116. Thomas, *Christian Response*, 28.

117. Thomas, "Christian Interpretation of Nationalism," 20.

India.[118] In the following years, his major concern was a response to the question of discernment.

Discerning the Signs of God in Christ at Work in History

After the one-year study at Union, Thomas participated in Evanston 1954 and then returned to India. The next year, he was appointed as part-time Asian staff consultant to the WCC study project on Rapid Social Change.[119] After his return to India, Thomas's life was marked by a fruitful collaboration with Paul D. Devanandan (1901–1962). This collaboration began in 1952 when the NCC of India created the Committee for Literature on Social Concerns with Devanandan as chairperson and Thomas as secretary. In 1957, Devanandan's conviction that a study of religion could not be separated from that of society in India led to the formation of the Christian Institute for the Study of Religion and Society (CISRS), Bangalore, with Devanandan himself as director and Thomas as full-time associate director.[120] Their collaboration continued until 1962 when Devanandan died and was succeeded by Thomas as director of the CISRS. They worked very closely. Stanley Samartha later wrote of Thomas as the man who had "had more intimate contact than any one else with Devanandan's mind."[121]

This collaboration had a profound intellectual impact on the younger Thomas. Affinities between their ways of thinking helped him to incorporate many of his colleague's ideas into his own thought.[122] One of such

---

118. M. M. Thomas, "Indian Nationalism: A Christian Interpretation," *Religion and Society* 6 (June 1959): 5.

119. Thomas, *Ecumenical Journey*, 164, 167–68. Evanston 1954 was the first WCC General Assembly that Thomas attended.

120. Thomas, *Ecumenical Journey*, 187.

121. S. J. Samartha, "Paul David Devanandan (1901–1962): A Biographical Introduction," in P. D. Devanandan, *I Will Lift Up Mine Eyes unto the Hills: Sermons and Bible Studies*, ed. S. J. Samartha and Nalini Devanandan (Bangalore, India: Christian Institute for the Study of Religion and Society, 1963), 6.

122. Samartha summarized Devanandan's thought into three basic affirmations: 1) the all-inclusive character of the redeeming work of God in Jesus Christ, 2) that God's redeeming work in the world is not of the world, and 3) "the ongoing work of contemporary Christ bringing healing and wholeness to broken humanity'" (ibid., 11). These affirmations were in fact not very different from the position toward which Thomas had already been moving after his theological and ideological shift in 1948. We already saw that this shift was toward the emphasis on the idea of God at work in world history and the holistic vision of redemption. At the end of the 1950s, Thomas affirmed his position again

ideas was the concept of new creation and new humanity. Thomas also learned from his colleague to appreciate the significance of religion in society.[123] With Devanandan's death, Thomas's life entered the most creative and productive period. With its highly this-worldly approach to mission, his address at Mexico City 1963 ignited a controversy in the mission circles in the West. He chaired the controversial Geneva Conference in 1966 that marked a culmination of this-worldly spirituality in the 1960s with its focus on the revolution. At Uppsala 1968, he was elected as moderator of the WCC Central Committee—the position he held until Nairobi 1975.

The Centrality of Humanity

Thomas's thought was characterized by an emphasis on humanity. He called his anthropological approach "a post-Kraemer theological framework."[124] His theology stressed less the theocentric nature of the Gospel— "the Gospel is 'from God'"—than its anthropocentric nature—"the Gospel is 'for man.'"[125] Devanandan's concept of new creation and new humanity greatly contributed to the refinement of his theological anthropology.

The emphasis on humanity was evident from Thomas's early years. One must turn to this period to understand the significance of this concept in his thought. As already noted, humanity was a recurring motif in *The Realization of the Cross*. He began the work with a reflection that portended his future intellectual development: "God's purpose is to create

---

saying: "Jesus Christ is Lord of the World, and His salvation is both social and cosmic. This is a basic affirmation which is the Church's starting point for a Christian interpretation of national development" (Thomas, "Indian Nationalism," 5). Besides, both Thomas and Devanandan shared a concern for the cooperation between Christians and non-Christians in independent India to overcome communalism and work for a secular Indian state. It is quite likely that their similar intellectual orientations made their intimate collaboration over years possible.

123. At the beginning of his collaboration with Devanandan, Thomas was suspicious of the partner's emphasis on religion. He later recalled the collaboration at the CISRS and wrote: "At the beginning I had my doubt whether an over-emphasis on the study of religion would weaken that of society." The collaboration, however, changed Thomas, and he started to appreciate the significance of religion in society. In his recollection, he also wrote: "It was in his [Devanandan's] comradeship that I became aware of the Hindu religious dimension of social issues in India in a new way, and got involved in dialogue between Christianity and Renascent Religions, especially Neo-Hinduism, in the context of the common struggle for a new society" (Thomas, *Ecumenical Journey*, 187–90).

124. M. M. Thomas, "A Rewarding Correspondence with the Late Dr. Hendrik Kraemer," *Religion and Society* 13 (June 1966): 13.[5–14]

125. M. M. Thomas, "Christ-Centred Syncretism," *Religion and Society* 26 (March 1979): 29–30.

a family of men and women who reflect the glory of the true humanity that lives in him alone."[126]

After Thomas studied Berdyaev, this emphasis was further strengthened by the Russian philosopher's personalism.[127] As mentioned above, the concept of "free creativity of man" was central to Berdyaev. According to him, personality was "the image and likeness of God" in human beings and, therefore, "*the* moral principle"; the essence of personality was free creativity because human beings were the Creator's image and likeness.[128] Berdyaev distinguished two kinds of freedom: the "freedom of choice" and the "freedom of creation." To him, the former was the freedom only to accept or reject given moral values, and he did not believe it as real freedom because its teleological determinism was a negation of creativity that cramped humankind "with life within a necessity." He argued that human freedom had to be the freedom to create values, that is, to "create for oneself the end which one may realise."[129] The highest moral imperative was, "be thyself, to thine own self be true," and every moral activity had to be "individual and unique in the highest sense."[130] In other words: "To be a personality to the end, and not to betray it, to be individual in all one's action, is an absolute moral imperative, paradoxical as it sounds."[131]

Berdyaev's influence was obvious in Thomas's 1944 essay entitled "The Human Person."[132] Thomas argued in it that the human being as created by God was essentially the "person" characterized by freedom, and that the essence of freedom did not consist "in the formal freedom of choice, but in the end which it freely chooses."[133] He stated his basic understanding of freedom as follows:

---

126. Thomas, *Realization of the Cross*, 3.

127. It is noteworthy that Thomas was led to the reassessment of Gandhism in the early 1950s precisely because he considered it as "the one political and social ideology which has taken seriously the *primacy of the human person* in politics and economics" (Thomas, *Ideological Quest*, 238. Emphasis mine.).

128. Berdyaev, *Destiny of Man*, 53, 55.

129. Thomas, "Berdyaev and Gandhism," 39; Berdyaev, *Destiny of Man*, 79–80, 132–33.

130. Berdyaev, *Destiny of Man*, 134; Thomas, "Berdyaev and Gandhism," 40. The phrase "to thine own self be true" is taken from *Hamlet* 1.3.78.

131. Berdyaev, *Destiny of Man*, 134. Thomas quoted the entirety of this sentence in "Berdyaev and Gandhism," 40.

132. This essay is found in Thomas, *Ideological Quest*, 107–26.

133. Thomas, *Ideological Quest*, 107–10.

We should choose the true end. In other words, *real human freedom consists in choosing that end which is really and truly man's own*, so that the exercise of freedom means the spontaneous expression of his original and essential nature. We are free only when we spontaneously express what we essentially are by our original nature. . . . We are free, when the end we follow corresponds with the end we have. As freedom is the essence of personality, we may put the same truth differently thus: *We are persons when we are what we are in fact*.[134]

As for the "true end" of human beings, Thomas drew on the doctrine of Creation and defined it as the "communion with God and community with neighbour."[135] That is, "worship of and obedience to God, and reverence of and community with neighbour are correlatives of personality, and are of the very essence of personal being." In other words, dependence and relatedness marked personality. Contrary to God's, human freedom and creativity were finite and obtained their true meaning as long as they were exercised in the responsible relationship with God and neighbors.[136]

To Thomas, however, personality in the actual life of human beings was disintegrated as a result of their refusal to accept finiteness and dependence; consequently, they lived in self-alienation, conflicts, and tyranny. This situation was what the Bible called the Fall. In their rebellion against God and neighbors, any effort of human beings to be good was doomed to frustration and failure. It was God that had taken the initiative in restoring the original relationship and indeed restored it in the Incarnation in Jesus Christ. Redemption was thus the restoration of human beings to their original personality, that is, to their true end.[137] Redemption was also the restoration of their creative freedom as the essence of personality within their finiteness and dependence.

In the mid-1940s, Thomas identified such restoration with the "rebirth" into the Church as the "Community of Persons in the world," and called the Church "the destiny of man."[138] By the late 1950s, however, he became aware of the ambiguity of the Church and the world as he wrote:

> In the present, the powers of the old (alienated) and the new (reconciled) orders operate together. The distinction is not between the

---

134. Ibid., 110–11.
135. Cf. Berdyaev, *Destiny of Man*, 57–58.
136. Thomas, *Ideological Quest*, 111.
137. Ibid., 111, 114–15.
138. Ibid., 111–12.

Church and the society outside it, for, in the Church and in the world outside, the forces of sin and salvation interpenetrate.[139]

This shift from the ecclesiocentric position corresponded to his increasing conviction of God's this-worldly presence. Significantly, however, Thomas's basic conviction of human nature survived his ideological and theological shift in the late 1940s to become a basic component of his mature thought.[140] It is also noteworthy that the concept of human personality as the highest moral value provided him with the principle that pointed to the ultimate which transcended the historical process of the world, making him capable of judging the contemporary socio-political developments.[141]

The New Creation in Christ

As the emphasis on humanity, the concept of new creation was not unfamiliar to the early Thomas long before his collaboration with Devanandan. As early as in 1939, he wrote: "Christianity is not a new system of religion; it is not a new community; . . . it is essentially and fundamentally a new creation with a new spirit realising Christ and His life in the old organisations and in the old nations."[142] Subsequently, however, the concept did not play a major role in his intellectual development.

In the mid-1950s, the concept resurfaced in Thomas's thinking. His theological and ideological shift from 1948 drove him to a search for an adequate religious understanding of human beings, society, and the world in the age of dynamic social change. In 1958, he wrote an essay on the doctrine of Creation and critically evaluated "two important religious doctrines of Creation . . . current in India": the "mystic apprehension of Creation" in Vedantic monism and "the doctrine of the order of Creation" implied in the idea of *karma* and *dharma*. Rejecting them as inadequate,

---

139. M. M. Thomas, "Persons and Social Institutions: A Biblical Approach," in *Human Person, Society and State*, ed. P. D. Devanandan and M. M. Thomas (Bangalore, India: Committee for Literature on Social Concerns, 1957), 134.

140. See Thomas, "Persons and Social Institutions."

141. The transcendental nature of Thomas's conception of personality was clearly displayed in the following statement: "The social institutions should recognise man's personality as the criterion of right social ordering, *i.e.*, of justice. . . . In other words, in the organisation of its functions, society should recognise that man has ends and loyalties beyond society and a personal dignity that transcends social justice. Society is truly just only when it embodies within its structures, the fundamental right of freedom for the human person" (ibid., 136).

142. Thomas, "The Church," 10; idem, *Ideological Quest*, 31.

Thomas proposed "a doctrine of Creation derived from the doctrine of Redemption." This doctrine was "the New Creation in Christ."[143]

The idea of new creation was central to Devanandan's thought. As Thomas pointed out, Devanandan tirelessly presented the Gospel as the good news of new creation in Jesus Christ.[144] While accepting the basic premises of Neo-orthodoxy, he tried to go beyond it. The idea of new creation served this purpose well, providing him with a dynamic understanding of God's internal working within history, which Neo-orthodoxy tended to ignore because of its strong emphasis on God's otherness.

According to Devanandan, creation was not a finished act. He considered it as an ongoing cosmic process in which God was continuously working throughout history, bringing the entire creation into its wholeness and ultimate transformation at the end of history into "a new heaven and a new earth." Devanandan, however, also held that this eschatological reality had already become a present one in Jesus Christ. As "in Jesus Christ God was reconciling the world to Himself," Jesus Christ was the "New Humanity," and one would become a new creation in the "here and now" through commitment to him. The new creation was "the one determining factor in world history which gives it significance and meaning." The Church was the community that was partaking in this eschatological reality and was called to witness to it amid the present concerns of both secular and religious life.[145]

Thomas accepted Devanandan's insight and further worked out its social implications, interpreting it in light of his own anthropology. He viewed the New Humanity in Christ as the offer of a new human nature restored into the original personality as created by God. He wrote: "Man

143. M. M. Thomas, "Towards an Adequate Doctrine of Creation," *Religion and Society* 5, no. 1 (1958): 37, 38, 43, 44, 49.[37–50]

144. M. M. Thomas, "The Significance of the Thought of Paul D. Devanandan for a Theology of Dialogue," in *Inter-religious Dialogue*, ed. Herbert Jai Singh, Devanandan Memorial Volume No. 3 (Bangalore, India: Christian Institute for the Study of Religion and Society, 1967), 7[1–37]; M. M. Thomas, *Risking Christ for Christ's Sake: Towards an Ecumenical Theology of Pluralism* (Geneva: WCC, 1987), 91.

145. P. D. Devanandan, *Christian Concern in Hinduism*, with a foreword by S. Radhakrishnan (Bangalore, India: Christian Institute for the Study of Religion and Society, 1961), 119-20; idem, *I Will Lift Up Mine Eyes unto the Hills: Sermons and Bible Studies*, ed. S. J. Samartha and Nalini Devanandan (Bangalore, India: Christian Institute for the Study of Religion and Society, 1963), 22, 65-69, 128, 153; idem, *Preparation for Dialogue: A Collection of Essays on Hinduism and Christianity in New India*, ed. Nalini Devanandan and M. M. Thomas, Devanandan Memorial Volume No. 2 (Bangalore, India: Christian Institute for the Study of Religion and Society, 1964), 180–81, 186–89; Boyd, *Indian Christian Theology*, 191.

is born again to personality and into community, not through contemplation or effort, but by the 'humbling recognition' of the gift of God's new creation in Christ."[146] This renewal of human nature was the restoration of "divine-human community" as well—the community that would transcend all hostilities and divisions in human communities. In other words, the New Humanity in Christ was the offer of a renewed human relation or the "new human fellowship in Christ," and we had in Christ "the renewal of society and social relations."[147] To Thomas, such a renewal "is not confined to the Church, but transforms also social relations outside the Church, and brings into being the idea and reality of a new society, based on the common humanity of all men in the light of God's act in Jesus Christ."[148] Thomas thus considered the new awareness of human dignity and freedom emerging in the dynamic change of traditional society as relevant to his attempt to discern God at work in the contemporary world.

The renewal of human nature, moreover, meant to Thomas the redemption of human freedom and creativity from their subversive distortion into their original context of the communion between God and humans. In Christ, humans were restored as God's partners who were capable of creative cooperation with God in the divine work for the renewal of the universe. The concept of new creation thus helped Thomas from the late 1950s on to talk of human freedom dynamically as a source for creative participation of humans in God's redemptive act in history. He wrote:

> In the creative process, man has been called to share and to cooperate. Of course, not on the basis of equality between God and man, for God is infinite freedom, and human freedom is finite. Nevertheless, the creativity of human freedom, man's capacity to create new orders of existence, new values of life, in short, new civilizations, must be considered as [an] essential part of the nature of man.[149]

Moreover, Thomas also did not hesitate to accept Devanandan's emphasis on the cosmic character of the new creation because Thomas himself had constantly been insisting on the holistic nature of redemption. Devanandan's view that the new humanity in Christ embraced the whole cosmos meant to Thomas that even the material and subhuman creation,

---

146. Thomas, "Person and Social Institutions," 133.

147. M. M. Thomas, *New Creation in Christ: Twelve Selected Sermons Given on Various Occasions*, with a foreword by S. J. Sadiq (Delhi: I.S.P.C.K., 1976), 3–5.

148. Ibid., 5.

149. Thomas, "Adequate Doctrine of Creation," 48.

including science and technology, constituted part of the wholeness of humanity and was not outside the scope of the divine renewal.[150]

Thus, the new humanity in Christ was, for Thomas, the restoration of the human person in Christ as God's free creative agent in the divine act of new creation to restore the wholeness of the entire universe throughout history. As he believed this reality transcended the institutional Church, he formulated his search within the revolutionary situations in Asian nations as an attempt to discern in faith

> the signs of God's new creation in Christ, not only in the transformed lives of individuals, but also in the struggles and purposes of men to renew structures of society, culture, and religion and to transform earth and heaven in the name of the dignity and destiny of man.[151]

The Meaning of Social Revolution in Asian Nations

With the doctrine of new creation in Christ, Thomas came to define the central meaning of social revolution in Asia as the radical renewal of society emancipating human beings from the bondage of traditional living into a "fuller humanity," or a greater creative freedom and a richer realization of human person in social life. At the WSCF conference at Strasbourg in 1960, he spoke of the revolution as the primary context for Christian mission in the postwar world and presented his new thesis: "Under the creative providence of God, the revolution of our time has within it the promise of Christ for a fuller and richer human life for men and societies."[152] Subsequently, he reiterated and elaborated this thesis on various occasions, including Mexico City 1963 and Geneva 1966. Geneva 1966 was particularly important because, chaired by Thomas himself, it not only took up the revolution as its main theme but also used his interpretation of it as the official framework for the discussions at the plenary sessions.

Thomas's understanding of modern social revolution consisted of three major observations. The first observation was that the revolution was characterized by a tremendous development of science and technology. According to Thomas, this development was accompanied by an equally tremendous change of the world view, freeing human beings from the

---

150. Thomas, *New Creation in Christ*, 7.

151. M. M. Thomas, "Toward an Indigenous Christian Theology," in *Asian Voices in Christian Theology*, ed. Gerald H. Anderson (Maryknoll, N.Y.: Orbis, 1976), 32.

152. M. M. Thomas, "Christ's Promise within the Revolution: The Meaning of Evangelism and Service in the Post-War World," *Religion and Society* 8 (April 1961): 20.

static traditional conceptions of cosmos and nature characteristic of premodern society. Science and technology thus unleashed human creativity suppressed so far by religious sanctions, leading to a high increase of mobility and dynamism as well as a growing sense of powerlessness and alienation. The scientific and technological development also resulted in a significant change of the nature of national and international relationships and had an enormous impact on the political life of humankind.[153]

Thomas's second observation was that the revolution was further marked by "the self-awakening of the hitherto submerged and suppressed peoples of the world and their demand for full participation in the life of society where power is exercised."[154] As the Grey Book pointed out a decade earlier, this "revolutionary ferment" was in essence the people's awakening towards human dignity that expressed itself in their struggles against poverty, inequality, and oppression. To Thomas, this modern quest for just society and fundamental human rights implied a "discovery of individual personality and its freedom" in social and political life.[155]

Thirdly, Thomas pointed out that such a quest for "a new pattern of society" was accompanied by a "more searching" question of a "new cultural ethos" that would provide the newly emerging social pattern with an adequate cultural and spiritual foundation. This quest for a new ethos was a spiritual search for a social ideology that could relate the ideals of economic development, social justice, and personal freedom "to the ultimate nature and destiny of man and an ultimate interpretation of history." In other words, it was a search for the legitimation that would make rapidly changing societies in Asia truly open while providing them with coherence and identity. At Mexico City 1963, he emphasized the missiological significance of the second and third points of his observation saying: "The search for a new pattern of human society and for an adequate spiritual dynamic for this pattern are realities of the contemporary world which are relevant to the task of defining missions today."[156]

At Geneva 1966, Thomas spoke of the search for a new cultural ethos as characterized by the "transition from a traditional ethos to a spirit of

---

153. M. M. Thomas, "The World in Which We Preach Christ," in *Witness in Six Continents: Records on World Mission and Evangelism of the World Council of Churches Held in Mexico City, December 8th to 19th, 1963*, ed. Ronald K. Orchard (Edinburgh: Edinburgh House Press for the Division of World Mission and Evangelism of the World Council of Churches, 1964), 11–13[11–19]; Thomas, "Christ's Promise," 16–17.

154. Thomas, *Theology of Contemporary Ecumenism*, 147.

155. Thomas, "The World in Which We Preach Christ," 13–14.

156. Ibid., 14.

modernity" and delineated its three aspects. The first aspect was the shift from "an undifferentiated emotional continuum" of traditional society toward "a differentiated individualism" of modern society. The second was the shift from the concept of "world-as-nature" dominated by the cyclical view of history as well as the sense of harmony to the concept of "world-as-history" characterized by the positive attitude toward creativity and freedom. The third was the movement of secularization, namely, the shift from a sacred ethos to a secular one. While the sacred ethos was stamped by the integration of religion, society, and state, the secular ethos was characterized by the autonomy of the political and social realms of life from religious authority and an emphasis on scientific rationality, personal freedom, and social justice in these realms. According to Thomas, these shifts were bringing to the traditional ethos "a new awareness of responsible selfhood and interpersonal relations, a new sense of history, historical mission and human creativity, and a new emphasis on empirical science and its secular rationality as paths to truth"—the newness that could be seen as a whole "as symbolic of the awakening of traditional cultures to a new dimension of human existence, which may be termed personal, i.e., man as freedom in responsibility."[157]

In Thomas's view, the search for a new cultural ethos was embodied by three distinct modern movements.[158] The first movement was secularism in the sense of secular humanist ideologies as well as the separation of the state and social institutions from religious authority as it was found in independent India.

The second was the resurgence and renaissance of traditional religions. It could take a form of that self-defensive religious reaction against secularization which tried to reassert traditional values and religious authority. The religious resurgence could also express itself in a movement that sought a break with the traditional authority to redefine ancient values and provide the struggle for a new society with a valid cultural and spiritual foundation. Thomas learned from Devanandan the significance of the latter type of religious renaissance for the contemporary social renewal. His largest publication entitled *The Acknowledged Christ of the Indian Renaissance* in 1969 was a survey dedicated to this subject, covering the major figures of the "renascent Hinduism" in India, such as Ram Mohan Roy, Vivekananda, Radhakrishnan, and Mahatma Gandhi.[159]

157. Thomas, *Theology of Contemporary Ecumenism*, 125–31.
158. Ibid., 103, 137; Thomas, *Christian Response*, 79–90.
159. M. M. Thomas, *The Acknowledged Christ of the Indian Renaissance* (London: SCM Press, 1969).

The third embodiment of the search for a new ethos was Western Christian missions and indigenous churches. Thomas positively appreciated the significance of the Western missionary movement and wrote that it had "played no mean part in awakening of the people of the non-Western world to a new human dignity and a spirit of humanism" through Western education as well as Western liberalism and socialism often associated with Christianity.[160] In fact, the renaissance of traditional religions often emerged under the direct impact of Christianity. As Thomas wrote many years later,

> The figure of Christ and the principle of agape love the cross represents, and the ideas of human community symbolized by Christian fellowship have played a part in the awakening that led independent India to commit itself to the new ideals embodied in the constitution formulated by the Constituent Assembly: fundamental rights of personhood; justice to the untouchables, tribals, women, workers and other weaker sections; and fraternity which recognizes and transcends religious and ethnic identities. This has also set in motion a nationwide search for a new concept of what it means to be human. The quest is for a new humanism able to serve as a spiritual inspiration and as a criterion to reinforce and adjudicate issues concerning the national commitment.[161]

In this connection, it is noteworthy that Thomas interpreted Abraham Malpan's reformation as a movement of the second type although it was a Christian movement. According to Thomas, Malpan's reform movement represented a break in the Syrian Christian community with its traditional rigidities under the impact of evangelical CMS missionaries and the opening of the community to liberal democratic values of the West. The Mar Thoma Church that had resulted from this reformation was, therefore, "the embodiment and bearer of this evangelical reform of Syrian Christian religion and democratic renewal of the Syrian Christian culture in Kerala."[162]

---

160. Thomas, *Christian Response*, 87–88.

161. M. M. Thomas, "A Christ-Centered Humanist Approach to Other Religions in the Indian Pluralistic Context," in *Christian Uniqueness Reconsidered: the Myth of a Pluralistic Theology of Religions*, ed. Gavin D'Costa (Maryknoll, N.Y.: Orbis, 1990), 54.

162. Thomas, *Towards an Evangelical Social Gospel*, 10–11, 13.

Theological Implications of the Revolution

Regarding the modern resurgence of traditional religions as well as secular ideologies, Devanandan left a searching question:

> Can Christian faith discern in such renewal the inner working of the Spirit of God, guiding men of other faiths than ours, as well as men of no faith, into a new understanding of God's ways with the world of men today? If all "New Creation" can only be of God where else could these 'new' aspects of other beliefs in the thinking and living of people have sprung from?[163]

Devanandan himself answered the question affirmatively, but it was of a tentative nature. Thomas's answer was, however, categorical; he asserted the presence of Christ's promise for a fuller and richer human life within the radical renewal of society. He interpreted the newness emerging through the Asian revolution—the unleashing of human creativity, the recognition of human dignity and freedom, and the search for the new cultural ethos—as "the signs of God's new creation in Christ" or the dynamic working of the New Humanity in Christ in the contemporary world. Through the revolution, God was "creating in Asia the basic condition of greater human dignity, enhanced human creativity and maturer human living" and thereby offering Asian peoples the vision of a fuller human existence as a divine gift.[164] A greater freedom of human beings implied a greater possibility for them to respond with greater creativity and responsibility to God's call for cooperation in the divine work for the new creation. For Thomas, therefore, the revolution had both theological and missiological significance.[165]

---

163. Devanandan, *Preparation for Dialogue*, 177.

164. Thomas, *Christian Response*, 29–31.

165. In 1966, the Barthian theologian H. H. Wolf criticized Thomas's view of God at work in history in reference to the Barmen Declaration. Whereas he admitted that Thomas's view was nothing to do with German Christians', he, nonetheless, critically pointed out the existence of some "similarities" between them in their ways of "equating" a particular historical process with God's revelation and/or will. Wolf insisted that God's act was uniquely disclosed in the Incarnation of Christ, and that "*how* He acts within the particular events of history remains hidden, even from faith" (M. M. Thomas, *Some Theological Dialogues* [Madras: Christian Literature Society for the Christian Institute for the Study of Religion and Society, Bangalore, 1977], 62). To him, while Christ was certainly at work in history, one could "never take certain phenomena or situations as norms or manifestations of his work" (ibid., 63). It was actually Wolf's misunderstanding that Thomas tried to equate God's revelation with a particular historical process, for the latter was in fact always critical of such an identification as our survey reveals. Responding to Wolf, Thomas himself wrote: "Even after reading Dr. Wolf, I must confess I cannot see

As earlier, however, his awareness of the tragic nature of human destiny kept him from becoming overly optimistic about the revolution. He wrote: "the revolution has inherent in it evil powers of both individual and collective egoism, self-righteousness and idolatry which are likely to betray its promise of the fuller human life."[166] A greater creativity and maturity as God's gift in the revolution also implied the increase of the good-evil conflict as Thomas argued:

> Civilization meant greater maturity but also greater knowledge of good and evil. I would say the same thing about the larger Asian revolution. A new personal self-awareness has made new levels of interpersonal relations and community possible, but it has also opened the way for new alienations and conflicts. The sense of national unity and vocation is a means of higher creativity, but it produces messianic complexes and international conflicts.[167]

Therefore, the revolution could create in human life not only the greater freedom and creativity but "new anxieties, tragedies and hell" as well, setting up a nation, a class, or a race as a false "New Messiah" to save humankind.[168] According to Thomas, humankind could avoid this false Messiah

---

where in this formulation [in his address at New Delhi 1961], either explicitly or implicitly, I have identified the Afro-Asian revolutions or its [*sic*] ideologies with the revelation of God in Jesus Christ or with the movement of redemption or the Kingdom of God" (ibid., 66–67). While Wolf put emphasis on the Church's unique role as the witness to God's saving work in the rebellious human world, Thomas disagree with such Church-centrism and wrote: "the Church and the world have the same centre, Jesus Christ; it is impossible therefore to confine the work of Christ in or through the Church" (ibid., 63, 68). Thomas disagreed with Wolf also in the latter's view of the hiddenness of Christ's work. He argued that such hiddenness would deprive Christians of any guidance in secular life, leaving "the time between the first coming of Christ and His second coming really meaningless without any pattern of God's action." The Church was not only responsible in theology, but also had a "theologically based responsibility in politics" (ibid., 69). Therefore, said Thomas, "a Christian's responsible participation in the secular political realm requires discrimination between the creaturely and the idolatrous in the secular, leading to an affirmation of the creaturely (the human) and resistance to the idolatrous (which is the source of the inhuman) in the power of the Holy Spirit" (ibid., 71). After Uppsala 1968, he also criticized Peter Beyerhaus of Tübingen for a similar reason (M. M. Thomas, *Salvation and Humanisation: Some Crucial Issues of the Theology of Mission in Contemporary India* [Madras: C.L.S. for the Christian Institute for the Study of Religion and Society, 1971], 7). It is evident from this debate that Thomas's principal theological interest was not of an epistemological nature but a missiological one.

166. Thomas, "Christ's Promise," 22.
167. Thomas, *Christian Response*, 30.
168. Ibid.; Thomas, "Christ's Promise," 22.

only through turning to Jesus Christ present in the revolution as the only source for true humanity. He wrote:

> Jesus Christ is also at work in the revolution as victor over these evil powers through His Cross and Resurrection; and His Kingdom and His New Humanity are offered within the revolution as the fulfilment of its promises. Therefore, the promise of Christ for a richer human life for men will be fulfilled only if the revolution receives within it Christ's Gospel of Redemption and the New Creation of which the Church is witness.[169]

Thomas thus made a clear distinction between the *signs* of God's new creation in Christ, that is, the radical renewal of society created by the revolution, on one hand, and *Christ* himself judgingly and redeemingly at work in the Asian revolution, bringing it to the fulfillment of its divine vocation, on the other hand.

This distinction leads us further to Thomas's conception of the revolution as the *preparatio evangelica* for Asia. This view was that "through the Asian revolution God is preparing the Asian peoples to face up to the challenge of deciding for or against Jesus Christ."[170]

The idea of *preparatio evangelica* was initially introduced into the Christian discourse of India by Western missionaries, such as Alexander Duff (1806–78) and William Miller (1838–1923), to refer to the significance of Western culture, particularly education, in preparing Hindus for conversion. Later, however, the missionary Charles F. Andrews (1871–1940) and Indian Christians, such as H. C. Zacharias and K. T. Paul (1876–1931), interpreted India's cultural awakening under the Western impact as the *preparatio evangelica*.[171]

Thomas followed this second tradition in his conception of *preparatio evangelica*. According to him, through the profound social and cultural change introduced by the revolution, Asian nations were confronted for the first time in history by "fundamental questions about freedom and responsibility, the human person and his destiny, the relation between law and love in community."[172] In his address at Kuala Lumpur 1959, he expressed a view that "the whole of Asia" was being drawn through this radi-

---

169. Thomas, "Christ's Promise," 22.
170. Thomas, *Christian Response*, 31.
171. Thomas, *Acknowledged Christ*, 245–53.
172. Thomas, "Christ's Promise," 24.

cal change "into a situation in which Jesus Christ cannot be ignored but has to be accepted or militantly opposed."[173] That is to say:

> In every national movement and pattern of social change and in the cultural transformation of every country, people are led to a decision for or against Jesus Christ, because the situation raises fundamental questions of God, man and the world in more or less Christian terms. This does not mean that the people will accept the salvation of Christ. It may mean a greater militancy of anti-Christian forces. But the national movement is beginning to ask questions which really should either end in Christ or lead to Antichrist.[174]

This new situation was produced by the impact of Western culture which, despite its ambiguities, introduced Asian nations with new ideas of "man as free person, of society as community of justice and love, history as purposive movement towards a goal, world as real and meaningful."[175] Nationalism was the fruit of this Western impact on Asia. Due to the tragedy inherent in human nature, these new ideas inevitably confronted Asian nations with questions regarding the foundation of freedom, the purpose of history, and their redemption from the tragedy. These questions were ultimately the question of deciding for or against Christ present in the revolution as the only source for the authentic renewal of humanity. In this sense, the national awakening, produced under the impact of Western colonialism, served as the divine vessel that brought Asian peoples to the fundamental question of God's creation and redemption in Jesus Christ. Therefore, the Asian revolution was a "preparation of Asia for the gospel."[176]

Later in his study of human faiths published in the mid-1970s,[177] Thomas paraphrased this thought and wrote that the radical newness introduced by the revolution—the "spirit of modernity"—had arisen from the cultural and spiritual climate created by what he called the "messianic faiths," following Berdyaev once again. An important consequence of

---

173. Thomas, "Christian Interpretation of Nationalism," 25.

174. Ibid.

175. Thomas, "Indian Nationalism," 10.

176. Ibid., 7–8; Thomas, "Christian Interpretation of Nationalism," 26.

177. M. M. Thomas, *Man and the Universe of Faiths*, Inter-religious Dialogue Series No. 7 (Madras: Christian Literature Society for the Christian Institute for the Study of Religion and Society, 1975). See also M. M. Thomas, "Two Kinds of Messianism: Report of the Chairman of the Executive Committee," *Ecumenical Review* 26 (October 1974): 546–62.

this revolution was, said Thomas, that the traditional "universe of unitive faiths" in Asia had been brought into "the 'anthropological' and 'theological' circle of messianic faiths in a radical way," either reviving "the seeds of messianism" present in the unitive traditions themselves or interpreting them within the theological framework of messianism. At the same time, however, the unitive universe was also brought into the historic conflict between two kinds of messianism inherent in the messianic faiths, namely, "the national messianism of the conquering king" and "the universal messianism of the suffering servant." For Thomas, the increase of the good-evil conflicts in modernizing Asia meant that Asian nations were being drawn into the tragedy of this spiritual dialectics between the Suffering Messiah and the Conquering Messiah.[178] Asia was now pressed to choose between the ideology and spirituality of the Suffering Messiah and those of the Conquering Messiah. Thomas also pointed out the presence in this new situation of a "growing sense about the significance of the unitive vision or of an indigenous synthesis of it with the idea of the Crucified Messiah to check the unlimited dynamism of the Conquering Messiah."[179]

The Mission of Salvation
Seeking the Christ-Centered Koinonia

As already mentioned, Thomas was elected as moderator of the WCC Central Committee at Uppsala 1968. Significantly, this Assembly became an important landmark in the history of the interaction between ecumenical mission thinking of the West and that of Asia. The Uppsala report on "Renewal on Mission" defined Christian mission as follows: "There is a burning relevance today in describing the mission of God, in which we participate, as the gift of a new creation which is a radical renewal of the old and the invitation to men to grow up into their full humanity in the new man, Jesus Christ."[180] Thus, the definition officially merged the two lines of Christian mission thinking into one. They were the *missio Dei* thinking originating in the missiological debate in the West and the idea of new creation developed by Devanandan and Thomas.

According to Thomas's study on Indian Christian theology, Devanandan's idea of new creation and new humanity belonged to the

---

178. Thomas, "Two Kinds of Messianism," 558–60; idem, *Man and the Universe of Faiths*, 35–37, 45. For the discussion of messianism, Thomas relied on Nicolas Berdyaev, *The Beginning and the End* (London: Geoffrey Bles, 1953), 200–205.

179. Thomas, *Man and the Universe of Faiths*, 46.

180. Goodall, *Uppsala Report*, 28.

trend that had "emerged as an indigenous tradition in India." Thomas traced this tradition back to the emphasis on humanity in the thought of Keshub Chunder Sen (1838–1884), C. F. Andrews, and Surjit Singh. This emphasis was further developed by Pandippedi Chenchiah (1886–1959) and Devanandan.[181] Thus, the encounter of the *missio Dei* theology and the idea of new creation was in fact an aspect of the encounter between Western Christianity and Indian Christianity. In this junction, Thomas approvingly mentioned Chenchiah's criticism of both Barthian theology and Shankara's Advaita philosophy for their common preoccupation with the Absolute that hindered them from taking seriously the historical process, and for that matter, the new creation working in world history.[182]

As we have seen, Thomas's principal interest throughout his career was the search for an adequate Christian response to the ongoing revolution in Asia. This interest gave a distinctly missiological character to his entire theological endeavor that was generally geared to society and politics. In fact, he had addressed himself to the question of Christian mission in various occasions. After Uppsala 1968, however, he turned to the issues of the theology of mission more specifically in response to the post-Uppsala controversy on mission. In 1970, he delivered a series of lectures on this subject in Bangalore and published them next year with the title *Salvation and Humanisation*.[183] Built on the above quoted Uppsala formulation of Christian mission, his argument was an attempt to explicate the missiological implications of the modern quest for fuller humanity, or, as Thomas expressed it, "the relation between Mission and Humanisation."[184]

Although the term "God's mission" was widely accepted in the ecumenical movement in the 1960s, Thomas did not adopt it in his own discourse despite the fact that he was a leading proponent of the world-cen-

---

181. Thomas, "Indigenous Christian Theology," 29. The British Anglican missionary C. F. Andrews was Gandhi's close friend. Because of this association, Thomas regarded Andrews as a Christian belonging to "the inner circle of Gandhi's friends" and did not hesitate to count him among those who contributed to the indigenous Christian tradition in India (Thomas, *Acknowledged Christ*, 225).

182. M. M. Thomas, "Some Trends in Contemporary Indian Christian Theology," *Religion and Society* 24, no. 4 (1977): 14; idem, "Indigenous Christian Theology," 30; idem, *Acknowledged Christ*, 161–62. See also Boyd, *Indian Christian Theology*, 319.

183. For the bibliographical information of Thomas, *Salvation and Humanisation*, see n. 165 above. Thomas began this work with a critical response to Peter Beyerhaus (*Salvation and Humanisation*, 6–11), who criticized the Uppsala approach to mission as a "radical shift of the centre from God to man, and accordingly the replacement of Theology by Anthropology" (ibid., 6).

184. Ibid., 2.

tric idea of *missio Dei*. The theocentric conception of *missio Dei* was also not alien to Thomas who wrote: "God sent His Son into the world that the world through Him might be saved (Jn. 3:17). That in the life, death and resurrection of Jesus of Nazareth God has acted to save the world is the core of the Christian gospel."[185] He, nonetheless, seldom used the term "God's mission" or the like in his own speeches and writings unlike many other Third World theologians, including even Devanandan.[186] Nor did he use the term "mission" in the broad sense of *missio Dei*. Instead, he defined mission in a narrow, evangelistic sense to designate "the communication of this message of salvation through Jesus Christ to the end that men may respond in faith and be saved" and called it the "mission of salvation."[187] Thus defined, Christian mission in the context of the modern search for fuller humanity was "the invitation to man to put on the New Humanity offered to all men by God in the New Man, 'Jesus Christ incarnate, crucified and risen.'"[188]

In Thomas's view, the concept of salvation was not identical with that of humanization, that is, the struggle for a fuller human life in state, society, and culture. These two were, nonetheless, closely related to each other. According to him, salvation was the "ultimate destiny" of humankind—the new creation in Christ—while humanization was their "historical destiny."[189] Human society could not be the Kingdom of God because every society was bound to sin and death, however perfect it might be. Salvation was the eschatological reality in which the victory of Christ over

---

185. Ibid.

186. Devanandan, for instance, wrote: "The last quarter of a century of Christian thinking has contributed a great deal towards a fuller understanding of the nature of the Church.... In consequence we have come to accept in our generation that the Church of Christ is of God's design and not of man's making, the people of God, the community of forgiven sinners who have been entrusted with a mission. It is this mission which gives the Church its main reason to exist, to carry forward till the end of time the *Mission of God* Himself. So we no longer talk of missions, but of Mission; and we believe that this mission is the *Mission of God in Christ* reconciling the world to Himself" (*Christian Concern in Hinduism*, 116–17. Emphasis mine. See also Devanandan, *Preparation for Dialogue*, 183–84). Thomas shared this thought but did not follow Devanandan in the latter's use of the term "God's mission."

187. Thomas, *Salvation and Humanisation*, 2. Similarly, in *The Christian Response to the Asian Revolution* of 1966, Thomas defined mission "to mean communicating the gospel of the crucified and risen Jesus Christ to all men, to the end that they may accept him as Lord and Saviour, and enter into the fellowship of his Body the Church which is the bearer of witness to him" (93).

188. Thomas, *Salvation and Humanisation*, 3.

189. Ibid., 20.

the dehumanizing forces would be ultimately manifest both in personal and corporate life of humankind.[190] Because the final destiny of humankind was the restoration of true humanity in their original relationship with God and neighbors, salvation was humanization "in a total and eschatological sense." Because Jesus Christ was the New Humanity, salvation was the ultimate "incorporation [of humankind] into Christ's glorified humanity."[191]

This eschatological view of salvation, however, did not mean that salvation was a reality that utterly transcended the earthly life as some Barthian theologians insisted.[192] To the contrary, Thomas held that salvation began and was "partially realised here and now, within the dimension of a history facing death and disintegration."[193] Here was the significance of the modern quest for a fuller human life. Therefore,

> the historical responsibility within the eschatological framework cannot but include the task of humanisation of the world in secular history. The mission of salvation and the task of humanisation are integrally related to each other, even if they cannot be considered identical.[194]

For Thomas, moreover, humanization was a *sign* of Christ's saving presence in history. Although humanization was a human struggle on earth for the "fragmentary realisation" of true humanity, this struggle still pointed to the "eschatological humanisation as . . . [its] judgment and fulfilment."[195] The Christian who participated in this struggle had to discern and witness in faith the crucified and risen Christ in it as "the source and foundation of true humanisation." Thus, Thomas said: "Our mission is to make clear that salvation is the spiritual inwardness of true humanisation, and that humanisation is inherent in the message of salvation in Christ."[196]

In this connection, Thomas introduced a concept of *koinonia* or "new human fellowship" in Christ to denote the social dimension of the New Humanity in Christ.[197] Observing the impact of the Western missionary

190. Ibid., 8.
191. Ibid., 18.
192. See n. 165 above.
193. Thomas, *Salvation and Humanisation*, 9.
194. Ibid., 8.
195. Ibid., 18.
196. Ibid., 10.
197. See p. 118 above.

enterprise on Indian society, he acknowledged the significance for salvation and humanization of the Church as the religious community centered on worship and the Eucharist. In India, salvation in Christ first became the source of *koinonia* in this religious community, striking "a blow to the spiritual rigidities of an unequal social structure." Salvation, however, transcended the natural and historical divisions of humankind and, for that matter, the division between the spheres inside and outside the Church.[198] The "idea of religious fellowship in Christ" in the Christian community gradually spilt over its walls, giving a rise to "the idea of a secular fellowship in the total village or the total college community." Humanization was, thus, initiated in the wider society.[199]

To speak of humanization at work in society, Thomas suggested the concept of "a Christ-centered fellowship outside the Church," or the "*koinonia*-in-Christ" that transcended the institutionalized Christian community.[200] He maintained that the Church was the "structured nucleus" of this *koinonia* while there was a need to recognize a "larger unstructured stream of a *koinonia*-in-Christ" that was "spiritually continuous" with the nucleus.[201] According to him, the task of the Christian community was to enter an open dialogue in all realms of life, both religious and secular, with this larger stream, that is, religious and secular movements struggling for a fuller human society, so that they might also acknowledge Jesus Christ, the New Humanity, "as the bearer of both true human life and salvation."[202] Criticizing the prevalent fear of syncretism among Christians,[203] Thomas

---

198. M. M. Thomas and Lesslie Newbigin, "Salvation and Humanization: A Discussion," in *Mission Trends No. 1: Crucial Issues in Mission Today*, ed. Gerald Anderson and Thomas F. Stransky (New York: Paulist Press, 1974; Grand Rapids, Mich.: Eerdmans, 1974), 217.

199. Thomas, *Salvation and Humanisation*, 12.

200. Ibid., 13, 40; idem, *Man and the Universe of Faiths*, 137.

201. Ibid.

202. Thomas, *Salvation and Humanisation*, 41.

203. In the 1960s, Thomas's stance toward "syncretism" was still negative. In his *Christian Response to the Asian Revolution*, he made a distinction between religious "syncretism" and cultural "synthesis" and affirmed the latter alone as the goal of dialogue in the common search for the new cultural ethos (*Christian Response*, 92, 95). By the mid-1970s, however, he changed his position towards "syncretism" because he had realized that "the negative connotation of the word 'syncretism' remains a continuing hindrance for Christians to enter into dialogue with other religions, and deal creatively with the plurality of cultures and religions." As a consequence, he accepted the term and suggested to use it with a neutral definition as History of Religions did to designate "any interpenetration between religions and between cultures," and to make a distinction "between a wrong and right kind of syncretism" rather than rejecting syncretism as a whole. Furthermore,

also suggested that the Church in India, taking such dialogue seriously, should be ready to take a form of a "Christ-centred Hindu Church of Christ," not only "expressing Christ in terms of the contemporary Hindu thought and life patterns" but also transforming them "from within."[204]

Conclusion

While Thomas's view of revolution as the self-awakening of the submerged peoples remained consistent, his position regarding the specific locus for such an awakening gradually shifted after the mid-1960s. Until then, Thomas talked of the revolution in terms of the nationalist revolts in the Third World *against* the Western domination and the subsequent modernization projects in new independent nations. At Bangkok 1964, however, he showed a sign of change, warning that nationalism was betraying the Asian revolution by dissociating itself from the concern for human freedom and social justice and confining itself to the elite sectors of society.[205] After Geneva 1966, he began to emphasize the significance of the revolution defined as radical change in the existing power structure and its ideological and religious sanction *within* a national society and in international life.[206] Becoming critical of liberal democracy and moving toward the liberation movement, he called in 1968 the struggle of the poor in the Third World against poverty "the most important expression of the new awakening of the people."[207] At Singapore 1973, he urged Asian Christians to regard the "struggle for the transformation of all spheres of Asian life," *both* traditional *and* modernized, as the locus for the Christian witness. He particularly pointed to the significance of the people's mass struggle

---

he observed that Western Christianity itself was a product of syncretism with Christ at its center, and proposed a "Christ-centered syncretism" as the goal of Christian mission in Asia (Thomas, *Man and the Universe of Faiths*, 157; idem, *Some Theological Dialogues*, 156; idem, "Christ-centred Syncretism").

204. Thomas, *Salvation and Humanisation*, 40.

205. Thomas, *Theology of Contemporary Ecumenism*, 105–21.

206. Ibid., 147, 152. This shift is also observed by Philip, who writes: "The writings of Thomas since 1966 reflect a great deal of change with regard to the understanding of the nature of social revolution in India." Philip also observes the influence on Thomas in this period of several Indians, such as the then editor of the *Guardian* E. V. Mathew, the socialist Saral. K. Chatterji, and the economists Samuel Parmar and C. T. Kurian (Philip, *Theology and Ideology*, 14).

207. Thomas, *Theology of Contemporary Ecumenism*, 149.

for a transformation of the existing power structure to achieve their full participation in the decision-making process.[208]

This change was the second shift that occurred in Thomas's primordial identification as Christian. Opting for the Marxist ideology, Thomas initially identified himself with "disfavored strata and groups" in the land ruled by the colonial power. After Independence, he shifted his identification toward that with the modernization project led by the newly emerged elite of the new nation. Now, however, he moved back toward the identification with "disfavored strata and groups," realizing that nationalism led by the elite had degenerated in many parts of Asia. Despite these changes, his principal concern remained with the dialectical participation of the Church in the "permanent revolution" in a search for just society and fuller humanity. Even after the second shift, his tragic conception of human history kept him from an "idolatry of the people," that is, identifying "the people's movement of liberation with the movement of the revelation of God and the Kingdom in history."[209]

Thomas's principal concern has its roots in the social evangelical piety of the Mar Thoma Church and in his involvement in political activism of the young Keralan Christians at the end of Western colonialism. Before Independence, Kerala was divided into various caste and religious groups interacting with each other dynamically in a search for a new form of social and political life under the dominant influence of two political ideologies, Gandhian and Communist. Thomas's career as a Christian thinker began in response to this dynamic reality as a quest for a coherent ideological and theological foundation for an effective Christian participation in political life of the rapidly changing Indian society. His option was initially for the Marxist politics. He also came under the influence of Neo-orthodox theology in his attempt to refute the Gandhian and, for that matter, Hindu anthropology as well as Christian liberalism. He relied, *inter alia*, on Berdyaev, a philosopher of the Christian East, who was also critical of the West and kept a dialectical position towards Marxism.

---

208. Ibid., 199, 201–2. This radical stance remained unchanged in the 1980s. See, for instance, M. M. Thomas, "Spiritual Penetration: Revolts of the Poor and the Oppressed," *Religion and Society* 27 (March 1980): 10–20. In this article, he wrote about "liquidation of extreme poverty" through "total revolution, i.e. revolution in the totality of the economic, social and cultural patterns" (ibid., 18). In his "Theological Aspects of the Relationships Between Social Action Groups and Churches" (*Religion and Society* 31 [June 1984]: 17–23), he urged the Church to move from "prophetic theology" for protest to "political theology" for transformation (ibid., 20).

209. Thomas, *Theology of Contemporary Ecumenism*, 203.

Having joined the WSCF staff in Geneva in 1947, his scope was widened to include the West as well as Asia. He began his career as a leading ecumenist both in Asia and in the international scene. Kerala, India, Asia, and the world became the four principal concentric contexts for his reflections and activities. In 1948, the degeneration of Communism into Stalinism led him to a rethinking of his ideological stance, which was accompanied with a major shift of his theological emphasis. This shift was characterized with a move from the Barthian-Kraemerian emphasis on transcendence to a post-Barthian-Kraemerian emphasis on the immanence. Thomas thus embarked on a search for a theologically grounded political ideology to distinguish the creaturely and the demonic in the ongoing social revolution of Asia.

While Thomas had displayed a remarkable this-worldly orientation from his earlier stage, the idea of God's this-worldly presence arose from this renewed search from the late 1940s. Indeed, the idea was not necessarily unique to Thomas; it was expressed by those young Keralan Christians who gathered to form the YCCA at the end of the 1930s. However, Thomas's endeavor from 1948 on to develop a relevant ecumenical theology of revolution greatly contributed to the momentum that the idea gained in the ecumenical movement, first in Asia and then in the West, from the late 1950s.

Once the idea was given an elaborated formulation at Kuala Lumpur 1959, Thomas pressed himself on to answer the question of discernment of God's presence in the world. Here, the emphasis on the human person and the concept of new creation in Christ played a central role. Both had already existed in the early Thomas's reflection. However, only with the theological shift in 1948 did they grow central to his thought. In this connection, the impact of Berdyaev's personalism on the early Thomas and the influence of Devanandan in the 1950s were crucial. Thomas reinterpreted Devanandan's idea of new creation and new humanity through his own understanding of humanity built on Berdyaev's anthropology and applied it to the interpretation of the Asian revolution. As a result, he came to place a special emphasis on the newness, both material and spiritual, that the revolution was creating in traditional societies and cultures of Asia, bringing about a possibility of a fuller realization of human freedom and creativity.

Thomas's conception of human history as tragic destiny also came from Berdyaev. This dialectical concept became crucial not only to Thomas's anthropology but also to his theology of mission. The awareness of human tragedy kept him from identifying the newness, or the modern movements in search of a fuller realization of humanity, with God's reign in Christ in world history. The newness constituted the "signs" of Christ's promise in the revolution and not Christ himself who was the only source of true humanity. For Thomas, Christian mission was to witness to this Christ, the New Humanity, in the midst of active and yet critical participation in the revolution.

Thus, once given a clear formulation, the idea of God's this-worldly presence became the starting point for Thomas to develop creatively his theology of critical discernment and participation in the revolution.

CHAPTER 5

The Theology of God's Mission of Incarnation in C. S. Song

As we have seen in the third chapter, when the CCA was developing its people-centered approach, C. S. Song made significant contributions to this-worldly holiness in Asian ecumenical thinking in the 1970s and 1980s. This chapter focuses on understanding Song's missiological and theological thinking in detail and surveys the significance of the idea of God's this-worldly presence in his thought. Special attention will be paid to the problems that confronted Song in his early theological career and to the question of how he strove to overcome them and develop the idea of God's this-worldly presence in this process.

Unlike Thomas's, Song's theological style is non-biographical, meaning that he does not usually speak in his writing about those events and interactions in his life that have had important impacts on the formation of his thought. He usually, so to speak, hides himself behind generalized theological discourse. Our discussion in this chapter will, therefore, focus more on the development of Song's theology itself than the theological interactions he had with his context.

Taiwan and C. S. Song's Earlier Life

Choan-Seng Song was born in Tainan, the old cultural and political center in the south of Taiwan, on October 19, 1929, when the island was under the Japanese colonial rule. His parents, committed members of the Presbyterian Church,[1] belonged ethnically to the Taiwanese Chinese whose

---

1. Choan-Seng Song, "Curriculum Vitae," in "The Relation of Divine Revelation and Man's Religion in the Theologies of Karl Barth and Paul Tillich" (Th.D. diss., Union Theological Seminary, New York, 1965), 299; Karl H. Federschmidt, *Theologie aus asiatischen Quellen: Der theologische Weg Choan-Seng Songs vor dem Hintergrund der asiatischen ökumenischen Diskussion*, with a foreword by Konrad Raiser (Münster, Germany: Lit, 1994), 63.

ancestors immigrated from the mainland prior to the Japanese period and who today compose about 85 percent of Taiwan's population.[2]

The island of Taiwan is located in the western Pacific rim, separated from the Chinese mainland by the Taiwan Straits that are about 80 to 140 miles wide. The island, crossed by the Tropic of Cancer, is approximately 250 miles long and 80 miles wide at the central part. Taiwan's capital Taipei extends its jurisdiction not only to the Island of Taiwan but also to many surrounding islands, including the Pescadore (Penghu) Islands in the Taiwan Straits as well as Quemoy Islands and Matsu Islands situated near the mainland.[3] All these territories are officially known as the Republic of China (ROC).

Religiously, Christians constitute only about seven percent of Taiwan's entire population. The great majority of the residents today adhere to two major conventional religions of the island: Mahayana Buddhism and Chinese folk religion also called Taiwanese popular religion. The latter is "a combination of magic, ancestor-veneration and devotion to divinities, with influences from Taoism, Buddhism and Confucianism as well as traditional animistic beliefs and practices."[4]

The History of Taiwan and the Presbyterian Church

Although the People's Republic of China in Beijing also claims its sovereignty over the territories under the Taipei jurisdiction, the island of Taiwan and its people have their own distinct history. Some knowledge of this history would help us to understand Song's theology better.

Out of about 20 million residents of today's Taiwan, 1.5 percent is composed by people generally called aborigines or Native Taiwanese. These people of Malayo-Polynesian origins, divided into nine distinct tribal groups, were the oldest inhabitants of the island whose ancestors came there long before the arrival of Chinese immigrants.[5] By A.D. 1000, some

---

2. John F. Copper, *Taiwan: Nation-State or Province?* (Boulder, Colo.: Westview Press, 1990), 8.

3. Copper, *Taiwan*, 1–2; Republic of China Government Information Office, "Geography," in *The Republic of China Yearbook 1998* [yearbook on-line], available from http://www.gio.gov.tw/ info/yb97/html/ ch1.htm, Internet, accessed 16 October 1998.

4. David B. Barrett, ed., *World Christian Encyclopedia: A Comparative Study of Churches and Religions in the Modern World, AD 1900–2000* (Oxford: Oxford University Press, 1982), 235.

5. Kiyoshi Ito, *Taiwan* (Tokyo: Chuokoron Sha, Chuko Shinsho, 1993), 4–5; Tai Kuo Fei [Tai Kuo-hui], *Taiwan* (Tokyo: Iwanami Shoten, Iwanami Shinsho, 1988), 6–8; Copper, *Taiwan*, 8. In 1997, Taiwan's entire population was 21.74 million while the total

Chinese immigrants settled down in Taiwan. During the Ming dynasty (1368–1644), the number of Chinese immigrants significantly increased, mostly coming directly from Fukien Province across the Taiwan Straits.[6] The history of Taiwan is, however, usually considered to begin with the arrival of the Dutch in 1622 at the Piscadores because they were the first to establish rule over Taiwan.[7] The Dutch colonial rule was brief and ended in 1662 when a pirate leader of Ming named Cheng Ch'eng-kung (also known as Koxinga), refusing the submission to the new Ch'ing dynasty (1644–1911) in the mainland, conquered Taiwan and established his Ming-style government there. Cheng was accompanied by about 30,000 followers. Their move to Taiwan marked the first mass immigration from the mainland to the island.[8]

In this period, Christianity was also brought to Taiwan for the first time. The first missionary who came to Taiwan was Georgius Candidius (1597–1647), a minister of the Dutch Reformed Church. He arrived there in 1627. He not only took care of the Dutch in Zeelandia, today's Tainan, but also worked among the native inhabitants.[9] The activity of the Dutch Reformed mission came to an end when Cheng occupied Taiwan. When the next missionaries, this time British Presbyterian, came back to Taiwan two hundred years later, they "found almost no traces of Christianity left."[10]

The Cheng government was plagued by internal conflicts and did not last long. After the death of Cheng's son, the Ch'ing troops destroyed the

---

aborigine population was 389,974 (Republic of China Government Information Office, "People," in *The Republic of China Yearbook 1998* [yearbook on-line], available from http://www.gio. gov.tw/info/yb97/html/ch2.htm, Internet, accessed 19 October 1998).

6. Copper, *Taiwan*, 8.

7. Ibid., 18; Ito, *Taiwa*n, 7–9, 11–13; O Ikutoku [Wang Yü-te] and Takayuki Munakata, *Atarashii Taiwan: Dokuritsu e no rekishi to mirai-zu* [The New Taiwan: A History towards Independence and Its Future] (Tokyo: Kobundo, 1990), 26–28; Shi Mei (Shih Ming), *Taiwan wa Chugoku no ichibu ni arazu: Taiwan shakai hatten 400 nen shi* [Taiwan is not part of China: The 400 Year History of Taiwan's Social Development], tr. Masaru Shiga into Japanese (Tokyo: Gendaikikakushitsu, 1991), 36–37. These books treat the history prior to the arrival of the Dutch as Taiwan's prehistory in their introductory sections.

8. Ito, *Taiwan*, 25–29; Copper, *Taiwan*, 19–20. According to Ito, the population in the final years of the Dutch rule was about 100,000, including both aborigines and immigrants from the mainland (Ito, *Taiwan*, 29). It is, therefore, not difficult to imagine how massive the immigration that followed Cheng's move to Taiwan was.

9. J. J. A. M. Kuepers, *The Dutch Reformed Church in Formosa 1627–1662: Mission in a Colonial Context*, Schriftenreihe der Neuen Zeitschrift für Missionswissenschaft (Immensee, Switzerland: Neue Zeitschrift für Missionswissenschaft, 1978), 10–16.

10. Ibid., 42–43.

fleet of the Cheng government and occupied Taiwan in 1683. Next year, the Ch'ing government in Beijing declared Taiwan as part of the Chinese territory, thereby marking the beginning the 212-year Chinese rule over the island.[11] Ch'ing, however, did not have much interest in Taiwan. Ch'ing regarded the island as a "frontier area" and generally ignored its local problems.[12] Finally, in 1885 Ch'ing upgraded the status of Taiwan to a province, recognizing its strategic significance under the growing threat from Japanese and Western colonialism.[13]

In 1895, Taiwan came under the Japanese colonial rule as a result of the Sino-Japanese War. Abandoned by the Ch'ing government, the Taiwanese declared the independence of the "Republic of Taiwan"—the unrecognized and yet first republic in Asia. Their courageous resistance against the Japanese troops was, however, soon suppressed.[14] During the Japanese period, Taiwan experienced modernization for the first time in its history: agricultural productivity rapidly increased; economic infrastructure was built and organized; and a modern education system was introduced though it was accompanied with the forced use of the Japanese language.[15] In the first half of this period, the Taiwanese frequently organized armed resistance against the Japanese authorities. In the second decade of the twentieth century, their struggles became political, aiming at Taiwan's autonomy under the Japanese rule. These struggles and the resulting suppressions helped the Taiwanese to strengthen their political awareness and

11. Copper, *Taiwan*, 20–21; Ito, *Taiwan*, 34–40.

12. Copper, *Taiwan*, 21.

13. Ito, *Taiwan*, 40, 60. The Taiwanese historian Shih Ming considers the Cheng and Ch'ing periods as the period of Chinese colonialism in the history of Taiwan in which the colonial relationship was thoroughly maintained between the mainland and Taiwan (Shi, *Taiwan wa Chugoku no ichibu ni arazu*, 58).

14. O and Munakata, *Atarashii Taiwan*, 100; Ito, *Taiwan*, 69. For the details of this anti-Japanese resistance, see Harry J. Lamley, "The 1895 Taiwan Republic: A Significant Episode in Modern Chinese History," *Journal of Asian Studies* 27 (August 1968): 739–62; idem, "The 1895 Taiwan War of Resistance: Local Chinese Efforts against a Foreign Power," in *Taiwan: Studies in Chinese Local History*, ed. Leonard H. D. Gordon (New York: Columbia University Press, 1970), 23–77.

15. Copper, *Taiwan*, 22–24. O Ikutoku (Wang Yü-te, 1924–85) called Japan's "successful" colonial rule on Taiwan "a near perfection of capitalist colonialism" (O and Munakata, *Atarashii Taiwan*, 114). Located in Japan, O was a leading activist for Taiwan's independence. He left Taiwan after the February 28 Incident and taught at Meiji University in Tokyo. As for Taiwan's education system under the Japanese rule, see E. Patricia Tsurumi, "Colonial Education in Korea and Taiwan," in *The Japanese Colonial Empire, 1895–1945*, ed. Ramon H. Myers and Mark R. Peattie (Princeton, N.J.: Princeton University Press, 1984), 279–94.

the national identity as Taiwanese that had gradually emerged in the previous periods.[16]

During the final decades of the Ch'ing period, the first Protestant missionaries after the collapse of the Dutch Reformed mission arrived at Taiwan. In 1865, the British Presbyterian missionary James L. Maxwell began his work in Tainan and was followed by the Canadian Presbyterian missionary George L. Mackay who landed at Tamsui near Taipei in 1872 and worked mainly in the northern part of the island.[17] Their work became the foundation of the Church now known as the Presbyterian Church in Taiwan (PCT), with which Song is affiliated.

After Taiwan became Japan's colony, the rulers did not allow other Protestant denominations to enter the island. This policy was in effect for thirty years and helped the Presbyterians to prosper as the only Protestant denomination in Taiwan.[18] As war broke out between China and Japan in 1937 and between Japan and the Allies in 1941, the Taiwanese Christians increasingly came under the pressures of the Japanese wartime regime and experienced persecutions.[19] A movement for church union also developed among the churches in Taiwan in correspondence to the formation of the

---

16. According to Ito, the resistance of the Republic of Taiwan against Japan contributed to the emergence of the common Taiwanese identity among Taiwan's inhabitants of different origins. This new identity was, subsequently, strengthened by the discrimination against them by the Japanese and their political struggle against the Japanese colonial rule (Ito, *Taiwan*, 75–76, 82, 106). Shih, however, holds that the colonial relationship between China and Taiwan during the Ch'ing period contributed to the formation of the distinct identity of the Taiwanese as a nation (Shi, *Taiwan wa Chugoku no ichibu ni arazu*, 58–60).

17. Hollington K. Tong, *Christianity in Taiwan: A History* (Taipei: China Post, 1961), 21–25, 46–51; Murray A. Rubinstein, *The Protestant Community on Modern Taiwan: Mission, Seminary, and Church, Taiwan in the Modern World* (Armonk, N.Y.: M.E. Sharpe, 1991), 19.

18. Ibid., 20–21. As for Roman Catholicism in Taiwan, the first missionaries were Spanish Dominicans led by Farther Martines. They came to the Keelung and Tamsui area in northern Taiwan in 1626 when the Spanish troops occupied this area. In 1642, however, the Spaniards were driven out of Taiwan by the Dutch, and their missionary work came to an end. In 1859, the Spanish Dominicans Fernando Sainz and Angel Bofurull came to Kaoshiung in the south and built the first Roman Catholic church there. They later expanded their work to the Tainan and Pintung areas. Thus, the Catholic mission in Taiwan was dominated by the Dominicans from the beginning (Republic of China Government Information Office, "Religion," in *The Republic of China Yearbook 1998* [yearbook online], available from http://www.gio.gov.tw/info/ yb97/html/ch25.htm, Internet, accessed 12 October 1998; Ito, Taiwan. 19–21).

19. Tong, *Christianity*, 76–83.

United Church of Christ in Japan (the Kyodan) in Japan.[20] A result of the movement was the merger of two Presbyterian Churches, southern and northern, which in turn formed a union with the Anglicans and the Taiwan District of the Kyodan next year.[21] This union was, however, short-lived and dissolved in 1945 when the Japanese rule came to an end. The indigenization of church administration was another important impact of the war as the Presbyterian missionaries were forced to evacuate from Taiwan in 1940.[22]

After the Second World War, Taiwan was "restored" to Nationalist China under Chiang Kai-shek, and the Nationalist authorities assumed political control over the island in October 1945. The Taiwanese initially welcomed the restoration to China. To their disillusionment, however,

> Taiwan was not made a province of China as had been expected, nor were the Taiwanese treated as compatriots. No efforts were made to establish a democratic government; instead the island was placed under military rule. Chaing Kai-shek appointed Ch'en Yi governor-general and supreme commander and gave him the same kind of near-absolute power the Japanese governors had enjoyed.[23]

The complaints among the Taiwanese erupted into an island-wide uprising at the end of February 1947. The leaders of the uprising "proposed democratic elections for county chiefs and city mayors; the abolition of government monopolies; government guarantees for human life and property; and protection of the freedom of speech, publication, and assembly."[24] The Nationalist administration, however, mobilized troops on a large scale from the mainland and suppressed the uprising thoroughly. Killing the intellectuals, including journalists, doctors, lawyers, and businessmen, the Nationalist troops "systematically wiped out an entire generation of the Taiwanese elite." Randomly, many ordinary urban and rural

---

20. Nihon Kirisuto Kyodan Taiwan Kankei Iinkai, ed., *Tomo ni nayami tomo ni yorokobu: Nihon Kirisuto Kyodan to Taiwan Choro Kyokai no kyoyaku teiketsu no tame ni* [Suffering Together, Rejoicing Together: Towards the Agreement between the United Church of Christ in Japan and the Presbyterian Church in Taiwan] (Tokyo: Nihon Kirisuto Kyodan, 1984), 85–109.

21. Ibid., 94, 99, 164–67.

22. Ibid., 161–62.

23. Copper, *Taiwan*, 26.

24. Republic of China Government Information Office, "History," in *The Republic of China Yearbook 1998* [yearbook on-line], available from http://www.gio.gov.tw/info/yb97/html/ch4.htm, Internet, accessed 12 October 1998.

people were also massacred.[25] This incident is known as the "February 28 Incident." More than 28,000 Taiwanese were killed and executed by the Nationalists in the course of this incident and the subsequent suppression.[26] The Taiwanese community, as a result, lost its political leaders, and the effect of the loss was felt for the coming decades.[27]

In 1949, the entire government of the Republic of China under Chiang Kai-shek moved to Taiwan from the mainland, having lost their war against the Communists. A large portion of the Nationalist army also followed Chiang, and the island was forced to absorb more than a million and a half people in a short period, marking the second mass Chinese immigration from the mainland. The same year, the Nationalist government with its claim to be the only legitimate representative for the whole China imposed martial law over Taiwan—the longest martial law in world history that remained in effect until 1987—with an explicit goal of recovering the entire mainland from the Communists.[28] Thus, it became obvious for the people of Taiwan that the Nationalist government was yet another foreign ruler who denied their right for self-determination. Today, the mainlander Chinese who came to Taiwan with the Nationalist government compose around 14 percent of the island's total population.[29] The February 28 Incident resulted in a deep-seated animosity and mistrust among the Taiwanese towards these mainlanders. Escaping Chiang's dictatorship, many politically-minded Taiwanese left their homeland for the following decades and organized the movement for Taiwan independence abroad.[30] The Taiwanese who remained in Taiwan were forced to keep the political silence, which was not broken until 1971 when the PCT issued a statement called "Public Statement on Our National Fate." Later, I will examine this political development more.

25. Mark J. Cohen, *Taiwan at the Crossroads: Human Rights, Political Development and Social Change on the Beautiful Island* (Washington, D.C.: Asia Resource Center, 1991), 12; Alan M. Wachman, *Taiwan: National Identity and Democratization*, Taiwan in the Modern World (Armonk, N.Y.: M.E. Sharpe, 1994), 99.

26. Ito, *Taiwan*, 159. According to Ito, this number is based on the official release made by the Nationalist government. The February 28 Incident was under taboo in Taiwan for almost four decades. However, under the Taiwanese president Lee Teng-hui, the Nationalist government formally apologized to the Taiwanese population in 1993, acknowledging the Nationalists' role in the incident (Wachman, *Taiwan*, 99).

27. Copper, *Taiwan*, 27; Ito, *Taiwan*, 159.

28. Ito, *Taiwan*, 163–66; Copper, *Taiwan*, 27–28; Cohen, *Taiwan at the Crossroads*, 13–14.

29. Copper, *Taiwan*, 8.

30. Ito, *Taiwan*, 160–61.

In the 1920s, Japan permitted non-Presbyterian denominations to enter Taiwan.[31] The foundation of Communist China in 1948 resulted in the "missionary invasion" of Taiwan bringing a number of mission boards from the mainland. The Presbyterians survived these new situations and grew prosperous, even doubling its membership between 1955–65.[32] In 1951, the two Presbyterian Churches, southern and northern, merged again to form the PCT and joined the WCC the next year.[33] The distinct feature of the PCT among many denominations was its special tie with the indigenous Taiwanese community, both aborigines and Taiwanese Chinese. This tie arose from the fact that the Presbyterians were Taiwan's only Protestant Church for almost sixty years after the beginning of their missionary work. Unlike other churches, they did not regard themselves as a Chinese Church but a Taiwanese Church. They identified themselves with the aspirations of the Taiwanese, and their leaders "outspokenly opposed" the Nationalist regime, even after the February 28 Incident.[34] This Taiwanese identity and political stance of the PCT greatly contributed to the development and shape of Song's theology, even though he rarely discussed these issues explicitly in his work.

Song's Early Life and Theological Formation

Choan-Seng received his early education during the Japanese period; he attended primary school (1936–42) and middle school (1942–45) under the Japanese educational system.[35] These years coincided with the time when Japan rapidly built up the wartime regime following the outbreak of the Sino-Japanese War in 1937. Japan intensified the policy of assimilation, destroying the cultural heritage of the Taiwanese to "integrate" them into the ultranationalist Imperialist regime. Education was a primary means to carry out the integration policy.[36] After the Second World War, Song continued his middle school education under the new Chinese education system.[37] This change gave him a chance to become conver-

31. Rubinstein, *Protestant Community*, 20–27. As a result, the True Jesus Church operating from the mainland and the Holiness Church operating from Japan established themselves in the island in the 1920s as the competitors of the Presbyterians (ibid.).

32. Ibid., 33–44.

33. Nihon Kirisuto Kyodan Taiwan Kankei Iinkai, *Tomo ni nayami tomo ni yorokobu*, 124, 196.

34. Rubinstein, *Protestant Community*, 21, 29.

35. Song, "Curriculum Vitae."

36. Ito, *Taiwan*, 125–35.

37. Song, "Curriculum Vitae."

sant in three languages: Taiwanese, which he spoke at home, Japanese, and Mandarin Chinese.[38] After graduating from middle school, he desired to attend Tainan Theological College (TTC), a Presbyterian seminary in Tainan. Shoki Coe, then principal of the seminary and the Song family's friend, however, advised Choan-Seng to study philosophy first and then go to the West for theological education. Thus, Song entered National Taiwan University in Taipei in 1950 and studied with the Chinese philosopher Thomé H. Fang (Fang Tung-mei, 1899–1977).[39]

After graduating from the university in 1954, Song served the military for a year and then left for Europe with Coe's recommendation to receive theological training. First, he spent three years at New College, the University of Edinburgh, from which he received his B.D. degree in 1958. At Edinburgh, the theologian Thomas F. Torrance had a particularly important impact on Song, introducing him to the theology of Karl Barth.[40] Upon completion of the B.D. program, he went to New York to study the Old Testament with James Barr at Union Theological Seminary for one year as a PARS Fellow, and then went back to Europe to make his "theological dream come true," that is, "to sit at the feet of that great master in Basel"—Karl Barth.[41]

After he spent one year at Basel, he taught the Old Testament courses as lecturer at TTC for two years. In 1962, he returned to New York and worked for his doctorate at Union with the systematic theologian Daniel D. Williams as his supervisor.[42] In 1965, Song received a Th.D. degree with an ambitious dissertation entitled "The Relation of Divine Revelation and Man's Religion in the Theologies of Karl Barth and Paul Tillich,"[43] in which he tried to harmonize Barth and Tillich.[44]

Having completed his theological education, Song served as principal for TTC from 1965 on. In 1970, he moved again to the United States with his family to serve as Secretary for Asian Ministries of the Reformed Church in America. In 1973, he joined the Secretariat of the Faith and Order Commission of the WCC in Geneva. As we will see later, the change

38. Federschmidt, *Theologie*, 71.
39. Song, "Curriculum Vitae"; Federschmidt, *Theologie*, 71–77.
40. Song, "Curriculum Vitae"; Federschmidt, *Theologie*, 77–80.
41. Ibid., 80–81.
42. Ibid., 92.
43. Choan-Seng Song, "The Relation of Divine Revelation and Man's Religion in the Theologies of Karl Barth and Paul Tillich" (Th.D. diss., Union Theological Seminary, New York, 1965).
44. Federschmidt, *Theologie*, 96–102.

in the international environments surrounding Taiwan drove the PCT into political engagement in the 1970s, and Song became deeply involved in this development as a leader of the overseas Taiwanese Christian community. In 1982, he accepted the position of "Regional Professor of Theology" at the South East Asia Graduate School of Theology in Singapore and Hong Kong. Since 1985, he has also been teaching at the Pacific School of Religion in Berkeley, California, as the professor of Theology and Asian Cultures.[45]

Primary Questions: The Churches in Asia and the West

As Michael S. Moore pointed out, Song's theological concerns were "intensely personal."[46] As noted at the beginning, however, Song's writings rarely inform the reader of the events and interactions in his personal life; they usually present his thought with no references to such events and interactions. It is, therefore, not very easy to see from his writings the immediate circumstances that affected the course of his theological development.

Despite such difficulty, obviously, Song's theological education at some of the best theological schools in the West made him quite conversant with Western theology, particularly with Neo-orthodoxy. This exclusively Western theological training, however, profoundly hampered his mind as he started his career as a professional theologian in Taiwan. Song's frustration also arose from his observation that his fellow theological students in Asia were often incapacitated, by their intellectual captivity to the West, from responding creatively to urgent issues in their own world.

The Problem of Theology in the Christian Churches in Asia

In 1960, that is, the year when Song began teaching at TTC, he published a paper entitled "The Obedience of Theology in Asia." Under the influence of Neo-orthodoxy, he expressed a suspicion about "Asian theology" associated with the Asian revolution, nationalism, and political independence of Asian nations, and said that theological thinking in Asia was not to set itself "over against Western Theology" but "to learn from it first" because "a

---

45. Yoichi Kishimoto, postface ("Kaisetsu—Atogaki ni kaete") to Choan-Seng Song, *Minwa no shingaku* [Theology of Folktale], trans. Yoichi Kishimoto and Keiichi Kaneko into Japanese (Tokyo: Shinkyo Shuppan Sha, 1984), 203–204; Federschmidt, *Theologie*, 271.

46. Michael S. Moore, "A Critical Profile of Choan-Seng Song's Theology," *Missiology* 10 (October 1982): 463.

distinction between West and East" was "arbitrary and questionable."[47] Yet he was also critical of Asian theologians who merely repeated the teachings of Western theology, ignoring the difference in the historical contexts between Asia and the West. Song insisted on the need to examine "the contents of the Christian faith in the light of the life and thought with which they [i.e. Asian Christians] are organically bound."[48]

According to Song, a true theological response to the divine revelation had not yet emerged out of the Asian soil. He summarized the causes for this situation into six points. First, theological students in Asia were unable to develop a critical reasoning ability because they were "not trained to think theologically and philosophically." Secondly, Asian Christians had a tendency to see Western theology as the only theology. Thirdly, theological students inclined to be interested in systematic theology under the influence of the major theological figures of the West, ignoring biblical studies. Fourthly, Western missionaries' traditional emphasis on "a clean break from the pagan past" as well as their uncritical acceptance of Western culture as the criterion of value judgment resulted in the general ignorance among Asian Christians of their own cultures. Fifthly, Asian theologians often had to rely on English as the means of communication and expression because of the lack of a common Asian language. Finally, having "received the whole or at least part of their theological training in the West," many theological students in Asia felt unable to get rid of the influence of Western theology to become creative in the encounter with their own people.[49]

Whether or not these points truly reflected the historical reality of the churches in Asia, the core of Song's observation was their theological, cultural, linguistic, and psychological dependence on the Western churches. The other side of this dependence was isolation: Asian Christians were

---

47. Choan-Seng Song, "The Obedience of Theology in Asia," *South East Asia Journal of Theology* 2 (October 1960): 7. Song's suspicion of the theology inspired by nationalism apparently originated partly in his observation of the experience of Japanese Christians during the Second World War as he wrote: "Here he [the Asian theologian] has a great deal to learn from the vicissitudes of the Churches in Japan and Germany during the last World War" (ibid., 8). Regretfully, he has never developed this important observation despite the fact that the Taiwanese churches closely witnessed the development of so-called *Nippon-teki kirisutokyo* or "Japanese Christianity" that syncretically mixed Christianity and the Shinto ideology of the Imperial Japan under the wartime regime. As for "Japanese Christianity," see Yasuo Furuya, ed. and trans., *A History of Japanese Theology* (Grand Rapids, Mich.: Eerdmans, 1997), 56–58.

48. Song, "Obedience of Theology," 9.

49. Ibid., 10–12.

"strangers in their own lands" and "have little in common with their neighbours who have a totally different set of spiritual and religious values."[50] Thus, Asian Christians were unable to respond to the ongoing cultural and religious development in their societies. For Song, this inability was evidently displayed in 1962 when the prominent Chinese modernist Hu Shih (1891–1962) passed away. Reacting to this pragmatic atheist's death, many Christians in Taiwan praised him as "a model of the moral man and a hero of religious tolerance"; some even wrote that he must have been saved and was in heaven because of his moral stature. Song's indictment was that "Chinese Christians in Taiwan" lacked "the right sense of judgment based upon the correct understanding of the Gospel."[51]

In Song's observation, the social isolation of Christians was sharpened by the socio-cultural complexity caused by internal conflicts in the contemporary society and the popular Chinese religiosity. The intellectuals in Taiwan were divided by Hu Shih's followers who advocated the total Westernization of Chinese society and the "neo-Neo-Confucianist school" who argued for the reconstruction of Chinese society based on the Confucian values. As for the common people, the "confusion of value and truth" was prevalent both among non-Christians and Christians because of the practical nature of Chinese religiosity. To Song, this confusion made it impossible for Christians and non-Christians "to communicate with each other understandingly and sympathetically."[52]

As a cause for Christians' isolation, Song also pointed out the emphasis on the individualistic piety that the churches in Asia inherited from

---

50. Choan-Seng Song, "Whither Protestantism in Asia Today?" *South East Asia Journal of Theology* 11 (Spring 1970): 67.

51. Choan-Seng Song, "An Analysis of Contemporary Chinese Culture and Its Implication for the Task of Theology," *South East Asia Journal of Theology* 4 (April 1963): 9–10. In the 1960s, Song regularly called Christians in Taiwan "Chinese Christians in Taiwan." Similarly, he referred to Taiwan's society as "Chinese society in Taiwan." Judging from his usage of the term, he did not then intend to mean by "Chinese" only the Chinese mainlanders as opposed to the Taiwanese. In Song's vocabulary, the clear differentiation between "Chinese" and "Taiwanese" emerged later through his political engagement in the movement for Taiwan's self-determination in the 1970s. In 1989, Song answered Karl Federschmidt's question regarding his ethnic identity saying: "Ethnically I am Chinese, and I do not deny the strong Chinese cultural influence. But politically I'm a Taiwanese" (Federschmidt, *Theologie*, 64). The author of the current study himself had a chance to ask Song personally whether he was Chinese or Taiwanese when Song visited Princeton Theological Seminary to attend the annual conference of the International Concilium Foundation held from May 22, 1994, through May 25, 1994. Song's answer to the author was basically the same as the one Federschmidt recorded.

52. Song, "Analysis of Chinese Culture," 10–15.

the missionaries. This emphasis ended up treating individual Christian converts "as if their cultural heritage and historical inevitability mattered little."[53] To make the situation even worse, Christians in Asia were often content with their social isolation. Song thought that such contentment was caused by the security and comfort they enjoyed in the status quo of the institutional Church. This observation made him highly critical of the established forms of the churches in Asia, in particular their denominationalism and institutionalism rooted in the history of Western churches. He also welcomed the effort by some Asian Christians to respond to rapid social change as "a sign of hope."[54]

As a consequence of such dependence on the West and isolation in society, Song wrote, "a theology of history and culture that . . . [took] into full consideration the particular historical and cultural contexts" of Asia had "not come into being" despite the considerable degree of indigenization that the churches in Asia had achieved on the organizational level. In other words, "the Gospel did not truly become incarnate because the Christian presence in China had failed to bring both judgement and forgiveness, death and resurrection, to the culture of China."[55]

Song was thus convinced that Asian Christians' incapacity for theological response had its roots in their past: the Western missionary movement and the resultant formation of the church establishments in Asia in accordance with the patterns of Western Christianity. To change the situation of theological stagnation, he argued for the need of "radical re-formation" in the entire life of the churches, including theology, church structure, and the relationship of the Church to the world. Without such re-formation, the churches in Asia would "cease to be the vessel of God's reconciling love," making Christianity "a mere religion finding its comfortable place among other religions." He thus considered the issue of the structural and theological re-formation as "the problem of life and death for Christianity as a religion in Asia."[56]

---

53. Choan-Seng Song, "Taiwan: Theology of Incarnation," in *Asian Voices in Christian Theology*, ed. Gerald H. Anderson (Maryknoll, N.Y.: Orbis, 1976), 148.

54. Choan-Seng Song, "Confessing the Faith in Today's World," *South East Asia Journal of Theology* 8 (July–October 1966): 98; idem, "Whither Protestantism?" 67, 70, 71; idem, "Analysis of Chinese Culture," 11.

55. Song, "Theology of Incarnation," 148.

56. Song, "Whither Protestantism?" 66–69.

A Search for a True Theological Response in Asia

In his essay "Confessing the Faith in Today's World" written for the Hong Kong Consultation on Faith and Order in 1966, Song made a distinction between confessing the faith and a confession of the faith. To him, the act of confessing the faith was an event that happens when a believer is confronted by God in a particular historical setting. A confession of the faith arose from the act of confessing the faith, and its content was determined by this act. He held that a theological reflection in Asia had to be done as the act of confessing the faith and not as the mere repetition of historic confessions produced by the churches in the different historical contexts.[57]

In a series of articles published by the beginning of the 1970s, Song tried to outline the approach to a constructive theology in Asia. His proposal in this period became the basis for his own theological construction in the coming decades.

THE IMPORTANCE OF METHODOLOGY

First, Song emphasized the importance of methodology, endorsing the Chinese philosopher Fung Yu-lan's words: "It is the method, and not the ready-made conclusion of Western philosophy, that is important."[58] To Song, it was a "duty" for theological students in Asia to "unlearn" the content of theology they had learned at the seminaries in order to theologize truthfully out of their own cultural and social background. He thought, however, that methodology was unlike the content of theology and had a universal character. Thus, he suggested that the students should learn the theological method of the West in order that they could build the ability

---

57. Song, "Confessing the Faith," 105.

58. Fung Yu-lan, *A Short History of Chinese Philosophy*, ed. Derk Bodde (New York: Free Press, 1948; Free Press Paperback, 1966), 330; Song, "Analysis of Chinese Culture," 18. According to Fung, "the permanent contribution of Western philosophy to Chinese philosophy" was "the method of logical analysis." He wrote that Taoism and Buddhism in China both used the "negative method" and tried to "eliminate distinctions and to tell what its object is not." In contrast, the analytical method of the West, which Fung also called the "positive method," tried to "make distinctions and tell what its object *is*." Fung considered that the introduction of this new method to China was "a matter of the greatest importance" because it gave "the Chinese a new way of thinking, and a change in their whole mentality" (*Short History of Chinese Philosophy*, 329–30). Apparently, Fung's favorable attitude towards the method of Western philosophy had an influence on Song's critical and yet affirmative stance toward the method of Western theology. Song even wrote: "There is even a universal character in [theological] methodology" ("Obedience of Theology," 12). He was, thus, able to urge theological students in Asia to learn methodology rather than content from Western theology.

to analyze the religious and philosophical statements of their compatriots and critically discern truth and falsehood in their arguments.[59]

Biblical as Well as Theological

Song felt that the lack of interest in biblical studies among theological students in Asia would be disastrous because an indigenous theology could be developed only by listening to what God spoke to them through the Bible. Song thus emphasized the importance of the Bible. He particularly pointed out the significance of the Old Testament often ignored by Asian Christians as a mere "supplement to the New Testament." In his view, the Old Testament would be able to assist Asian Christians because it was "essentially an oriental book" and contained "thought-forms, social structure and psychology of the people . . . so much akin to" East Asians.[60]

Song also pointed out a tendency among Chinese Christians to be "biblical" in a narrow sense—a tendency to take interest only in facts about the Bible and fail to apprehend the fundamentally "theological" nature of the Bible and its "theological" implications for the contemporary world. In Song's mind, this tendency arose out of the traditional Chinese emphasis on memory that encouraged the Chinese intellectuals "to learn their religious or classical texts by heart without understanding them at all." He countered this problem with the argument that Christian thinking in Asia had to be both biblical and theological.[61]

Not Indigenization but Incarnation

Critical of the common tendency of the Chinese churches to neglect their own culture, Song urged Asian Christians not to dismiss the studies of their cultural heritage. Importantly, Song was suspicious of the concept of indigenization. In his opinion, the concept had come "to take on different shades of meaning," reflecting different interests of different Christian groups.[62] He was disturbed by the observation that the concept was too often used to imply merely a nationalization of the church organizations without breaking away from the structure and theology inherited from the West. As noted above, such indigenization was a cause for the social isola-

---

59. Song, "Obedience of Theology," 12; idem, "Analysis of Chinese Culture," 18–19.
60. Song, "Obedience of Theology," 12–14.
61. Song, "Analysis of Chinese Culture," 16.
62. Ibid., 21.

tion of Asian Christians, discouraging them from searching the implication of the Christian faith for their culture and society.[63]

More importantly, Song felt that the concept of indigenization as the goal of the work of the churches was theologically inadequate. In his view, the Gospel was not something one could make indigenous.[64] Its essential character was "foreignness and strangeness." The problem of the churches in Asia consisted in the fact that the strangeness and foreignness which they inherited from the Western churches tended "to obscure the foreignness and strangeness of the kerygma." To him, the churches in Asia had to recover the foreignness and strangeness of the kerygma through a true response to God in their own settings.[65] Thus, indigenization was, for Song, not only the negation of the fundamental character of the Gospel but the negation of this urgent task confronting the churches in Asia.

Song's proposal was to replace indigenization as the criterion of Christian mission with the concept of incarnation. Song wrote:

> No matter what you do in the areas of literature, art, music, architecture, liturgy, and theology, the ultimate thing is not whether it has a native or indigenous touch or flavour or not. The ultimate criterion is whether it is a humble and obedient instrument which serves to manifest the pain and love of God incarnate in Christ our Redeemer. Our eyes should be directed to what Christ has done for us in His love in the Incarnation and not to what we can salvage out of our own resources. Our discipleship should be turned to the discovery of what the incarnating love of God in Christ is saying to this or that particular form of culture, philosophy, or religion, and not to how much or how little we can make use of them in our communication of the Gospel.[66]

To Song, the incarnation as the criterion of mission meant responding to the saving act of God who became human in Jesus Christ. In the 1970s, Song developed this idea more in his missiological reflection. Subsequently, the incarnation became the central theme of his theology to which he constantly came back; the scriptural phrase, "And the Word became flesh and dwelt among us, full of grace and truth" (John 1:14 RSV), also became the key passage for his theological reflection.

63. Song, *Christian Mission in Reconstruction*, 56.
64. Song, "Analysis of Chinese Culture," 21.
65. Song, "Confessing the Faith," 98–99.
66. Song, "Analysis of Chinese Culture," 21–22. This passage shows that Song's approach to human culture and religion was fundamentally "theological" in contrast to Thomas's anthropological approach.

The Centrality of Christology

The emphasis on the incarnation brings us to another important point in Song's thinking, namely, the emphasis on Christology. According to Karl Federschmidt, Song learned the centrality of Christology to Christian theology from Torrance at Edinburgh.[67] Concluding his dissertation on Barth and Tillich, Song accepted their distinction between Jesus Christ and Christianity as a religion and wrote that Christ was "the criterion of the truth of religion and religions."[68]

In his 1964 article entitled "The Role of Christology in the Christian Encounter with Eastern Religions," Song examined some modern reactions, Indian and Chinese, to Christianity and concluded: "All religious problems seem to boil down in the end to one single focal point, namely, the person and work of the Christian Saviour Jesus Christ."[69] He was particularly critical of the separation of Jesus' work and person observed in some Christian and non-Christian thinkers, such as Radhakrishnan, Keshub Chunder Sen, Gandhi, Hu Shih, Lin Yu-tang, and Francis Wei. In Song's judgment, the very unity of the person of Jesus Christ and his work—the unity that together formed "an inseparable totality in the redemptive love of God"—was at stake among these thinkers. To him, God was "reconciling the world to Himself" in the person and work of Jesus Christ, who was the Word become flesh.[70] The divorce of the person of Jesus from his work would obscure the redemptive power of God's incarnating love in Christ and cause Asians to "see in Jesus Christ either an incarnation among numerous incarnations or appearances of the Absolute, or an ethical teacher who has fulfilled his human nature through his moral

---

67. Federschmidt, *Theologie*, 77.

68. Song, "Divine Revelation and Man's Religion," 254, 262–65.

69. Choan-Seng Song, "The Role of Christology in the Christian Encounter with Eastern Religions," *South East Asia Journal of Theology* 5 (January 1964): 15.

70. Song, "Role of Christology," 23–24. Here, Song linked his favorite John 1:14 with 2 Cor. 5:19 and wrote: "'The Word became flesh and dwelt among us.' . . . This action on the part of the Word of moving out from Himself and of settling down in the world leads us to the dynamic synthesis which embodies in itself the purpose and goal of that action, namely, 'God was in Christ reconciling the world to Himself' (2 Cor. 5.19). This is the act of God's redemption realized and actualized in the 'becoming' and 'dwelling' of the Word among men" (ibid., 23). As we have seen in the previous chapter, 2 Cor. 5:19 was crucial to the idea of God's this-worldly presence. Linking these two verses together, therefore, displays the centrality of the incarnation in Song's understanding of God's this-worldly presence.

perfection."[71] Song was thus opposed to the separation of the person and work of Jesus Christ.

In this emphasis on Christology, Song was, as usual, critical of repeating the Western teachings and argued that mere repetitions of traditional Christological formula would fail to make the "incarnating Love of God" have a real bearing on the people living in a Asian religious tradition. Christology, therefore, had "to break its narrow confinement in order that the light of Jesus Christ may shine in the darkness of man's understanding of God, of himself, and of the world." What Song envisaged was not a transformation of Asian societies and religions by means of Christian humanism and Western science and technology, but their "Christological transformation," that is, the transformation by the "redeeming process of death and resurrection" through a confrontation with the person and work of Jesus Christ.[72]

The Significance of Mission in Theology and the Church

In the mid-1960s, Song defined the Christian Church as a "kerygmatic community" centered on Kerygma.[73] His thinking thus revealed a clear missiological nature from the early period. By the beginning of the 1970s, this tendency became even more explicit. In 1970, he affirmed mission as the key to the reformation of the Protestant churches in Asia and wrote:

> The church is mission. That is to say, mission constitutes the ontological ground of its being. . . . That the church is mission means that the church lives for mission, subsists in mission, and derives her strength from mission. Mission is the heart of the church. The church is mission, mission, mission . . . She is nothing but mission. . . . This means, and implies, a radical re-formation of the theology of the Christian faith concerning the church. This demands a radical re-formation of the structure of the church in the light of missionary out-reach. This means the reconciliation of the world to God. The church which is not mission is not the church at all, in the true sense of the word.[74]

As this passage vividly indicates, by the beginning of the 1970s, Song came under the strong influence of missiological thinking that had developed in the West since the 1950s. As critical of the Western missionary movement,

---

71. Ibid., 25.
72. Ibid., 27–29.
73. Song, "Confessing the Faith," 98.
74. Song, "Whither Protestantism?" 69.

he was naturally critical of the traditional understanding of Christian mission. Thus, the questions of Christian mission and its theological implication for the churches in Asia became his major preoccupation in the 1970s. These questions were dealt with extensively in his numerous articles published in this decade as well as in his first monograph entitled *Christian Mission in Reconstruction: An Asian Analysis* originally published in India in 1975.

A Search for a Missiological Alternative from an Asian Perspective

As mentioned earlier, Song moved to the West in the 1970s, first to New York and then to Geneva, and began his life as an overseas Taiwanese. Yet he did not cut himself off from the political development of Taiwan in the decade. To the contrary, he played a leading role in the political activity of the overseas Taiwanese Christian community, and this political involvement had a significant impact on his theological development. I will, however, deal with this point later. First, we need to survey Song's search for a missiological alternative from the Asian perspective because this search became the starting point for his theological construction.

A Critique of Christian Missions

As we have already seen, Song traced the cause for the inability of Asian churches to make a relevant theological response back to the nature of the Western foreign missions. As the ecumenical mission leaders recognized in the 1960s, the age of Western foreign missions had come to an end. He was, however, suspicious of the real impact of this recognition on the practice of contemporary missionary agents operating in Asia.[75] He thus launched into a sweeping attack on Western Christian missions.

To Song, the major problem of Western missions was the fact that their continuing presence in Asia had become a hindrance to the work of the Asian churches at a time when the latter were confronted with the task of looking into the meaning of God's salvation in their socio-political and cultural contexts.[76] This situation arose from the unique relationship between Christian missions and the Western way of life introduced by missionaries into the non-Western world. According to Song,

---

75. Song, *Christian Mission in Reconstruction*, 4.
76. Ibid., 2.

Western mission agencies have not been satisfied with the role of planting and giving water to Christian communities in the non-Western lands. They have shaped these Christian communities, moulded them and forced them to grow into 'White' churches in 'Black' Africa or 'Yellow' Asia. Thus, despite denominational differences and sectarian idiosyncrasies a great uniformity was achieved. It looked as if the non-Western world would soon be evangelized and Westernized. And in due course, many a devout Christian in the West even naively began to think that the Western Christendom came very close to being in possession of these non-Western lands.[77]

Song thought that this self-imposing expansion of the West by means of Christian missions was the product of the traditional view of mission as foreign missions.[78] In his mind, this view concealed behind itself an ethnocentric idea prevalent among Western Christians: "Our 'Western home' has totally come under the saving grace of God," and "it is those foreign lands in Asia and Africa inhabited by uncivilized peoples that need our mission." As a consequence of this "subtle identification" of the Gospel with the Western culture, Western Christians came to view the terms "uncivilized" and "unevangelized" as almost synonymous, and Western missionaries as bearers of the "civilized" way of life, thereby resulting in the "misconception and belittlement" of non-Western cultures. This observation prompted Song to conclude that the concept of Christian mission as foreign missions was "a misinterpretation of the missionary message of the Bible."[79]

To Song, the identification of the Gospel with the West was also the cause for the traditional missionary emphasis on the clean break of new converts from their "pagan" past. As he observed, this ethnocentrism

---

77. Ibid., 7.

78. Ibid., 2. According to Song, "for more than a century, Christian mission is known to the Christians in the West solely as foreign missions" (ibid.). In fact, the following passage from the founder of missiology Gustav Warneck provides us with a classical example for the understanding of mission as foreign missions aimed at the non-Christian world: ". . . Luther did not think of proper missions to the heathen, *i.e.* of a regular sending of messengers of the Gospel to non-Christian nations, with the view of Christianising them. For by 'missions' we understand, and we must not understand anything else than, this sending, continuing through every age of the church, which carries out the commandment, 'Go and make disciples of all nations,' *i.e.* of all nations which are still non-Christian" (*Outline of a History of Protestant Missions from the Reformation to the Present Time with an Appendix Concerning Roman Catholic Missions*, 3d English ed., ed. George Robson [New York: Fleming H. Revell Co., 1906.], 10).

79. Song, *Christian Mission in Reconstruction*, 2–3.

provided both Western missionaries and their native followers with the criteria of value judgement, making Western culture the norm for the attitude of converts towards their own culture.[80] A consequence was the self-complacent cultural, spiritual, and religious isolation of Asian Christians in their society, which Song considered as a cause for their inability to make a relevant theological response as we have already seen.

Seeing the churches in Asia deeply influenced by Western ethnocentrism, Song urged Asian Christians to have "the will and courage to break away from the bondage to the missionary ecclesiology developed in the West and transplanted to the East." Fortunately, the "sudden outburst of secularism" in the West had exposed "the 'secular nature of the 'Christian' West" and finally dissolved the "myth of Western Christendom." Song thus challenged Asian Christians to free themselves from "the myth of the Western man blessed with the long history of cultural and political influence of the West on the rest of the world"—the myth still prevailing in the "subconsciousness" of non-Western people.[81]

Song's criticism did not stop here. Having unmasked the ethnocentric identification of the Gospel with the Western culture lurking in foreign missions, Song further traced the roots of this identification back to the theological position that viewed the institutional Church as "the centre of God's redemptive activity," identifying God's salvation with the history of Israel and the Christian Church. As we will come back to this point later, it suffices here to say that Song also rejected this widely accepted Church-centric position. In his mind, such a view had already begun to collapse due to the rise of secular forces and revolutionary changes in the contemporary world. The Church, therefore, could no longer "claim to be the sole agent of God's saving grace" on behalf of the whole of humanity.[82] This way of thinking, inevitably, drove him to the effort to reformulate the entire concept of mission since the Church-centered view of salvation was an integral part of traditional missionary thinking in the West.[83]

---

80. Song, "Obedience of Theology," 11.

81. Song, *Christian Mission in Reconstruction*, 3, 5, 7.

82. Choan-Seng Song, "God's Mission with the Nations," in *A Vision for Man: Essays on Faith, Theology and Society in Honour of Joshua Russell Chandran*, ed. Samuel Amirtham (Madras: Christian Literature Society, 1978), 221–23, 227.

83. The missionary thought of the American Presbyterian Robert E. Speer serves as a good illustration for Song's observation regarding the traditional equation of salvation with the Christian church. This famous missionary statesman conceived Christian mission as foreign missions defined as "the effort of those who have heard of Christ to take what they have heard to the whole world in order that all men together may learn more of Him" (Robert E. Speer, *"Are Foreign Missions Done For?"* [N.p., 1928], 36–37). For Speer, Christ

Hoekendijk and Song

Song's critique of Western missions was essentially in the line of Hoekendijk's critique of the Church-centered mission in the 1950s. In his own criticism, Hoekendijk questioned the validity of the problematic identification of Christian mission with foreign missions, which had become an attempt to export the institutionalized Church from the West to the rest of the world. He also rejected the validity of the widely accepted division of the world into two distinct areas: "Christendom" dominated by the Church and viewed as the object of "home missions" or "evangelism," and the area outside of it that was the object of "foreign missions" or "missions."[84]

Hoekendijk, furthermore, felt that the call to evangelism had often degenerated into "a call to restore 'Christendom,' the *Corpus Christianum*,

---

was "the final and sufficient revelation of God" (ibid., 36) and "enough" and "adequate . . . to the full needs of each soul" since he was "the whole world's sufficient Saviour" (ibid., 45–46). All the truths of non-Christian religions were found in Christ. Foreign missions were the endeavor to make this Christ known to all humankind, "that all mankind together may live in Him" (ibid., 45). The fate of all other religions were ultimately the same as that of the old European religions that were almost totally replaced with Christianity (ibid., 38). This "triumphantalist" Christology of Speer's granted the Church a prominent status through the biblical concept of "the body of Christ," almost equating its salvific significance with Christ: "The Church is His [Christ's] body through which He does His work and in which as the Crucified and ever Living Lord, and in His spirit, He fulfills the work which in one sense He completed and in another sense began in His life and death on earth" (ibid., 37). This passage expresses Speer's highly Church-centric understanding of salvation that viewed the Church as the agent of God's redemptive activity in the world. According to him, furthermore, "Christ needs the whole of humanity for His full expression," and, therefore, "He needs a Church made up of every people and race and tongue" (ibid.). However, only when all humankind had received Christ would it become possible "to gather into the Holy City the perfected humanity, the wealth and honor of all the nations, the full glory of Christ" (ibid., 37–38). In Speer's view, the worldwide expansion of the Church was thus explained in terms of the universalizing nature of God's redemption in Christ. Foreign missions were seen as the agents of the expansion as Speer wrote: "Foreign Missions are indeed a great quest of the Church" (ibid., 37). Thus, one can clearly recognize in Speer's missionary thinking what Song considered the subtle identification of salvation, the church, and foreign missions.

84. Hoekendijk, "Church in Missionary Thinking," 333. Hoekendijk reworded the phrase "home and foreign missions" into "evangelism and missions" as follows: "What justification is there for the traditional policy of our churches in which this one apostolic task is carefully divided as the one (primary) task on this side of political/linguistic frontiers and the other task beyond these frontiers; how can we make a theologically relevant distinction between home and foreign missions (or evangelism and missions)?" (ibid.) This is another piece of evidence, thought indirect, that the term "mission" was traditionally used to designate only foreign missions.

as a solid, well-integrated cultural complex, directed and dominated by the church." Behind this call, he sensed an implicit identification of the Gospel, the Church, and "Christendom." Despite the fact that Christendom had already disintegrated, many Western Christians continued "as if they still live in Christendom." They were eager to regain the lost integration of this cultural and religious complex and the influence of the Church over against "the spirit of the age." This observation led Hoekendijk to say: "In fact, the word 'evangelize' often means a Biblical camouflage of what should rightly be called the reconquest of ecclesiastical influence."[85] Over against these problems of the traditional view of mission as foreign missions, Hoekendijk argued for the need to conceive the entire world "as a unity," as the scene of God's redemptive act directed towards the entire *oikumene* rather than towards a part of it.[86]

It is not difficult to recognize a resonance of Hoekendijk's thinking in Song's criticism of mission. A major difference between Song and Hoekendijk was that the former was far more articulate than the latter about the problem posed by the Westernness of foreign missions. Song criticized not just Christendom but *Western* Christendom and, therefore, the division of the world into the *Western* world and the *non-Western* world. He also criticized the identification of mission with *Western* foreign missions, and of the Gospel with the *Western* culture inherited from the *Western* churches. Though Song, like Hoekendijk, emphasized the wholeness of the world as the locus for God's redemptive act, such an emphasis was actually intended to legitimize his attempt to place the Asian world and, for that matter, the entire non-Western world in the direct relationship to the divine redemption. The emphasis on wholeness was, therefore, often overshadowed by the criticism of the West that remained more prominent in his thinking. Doubtlessly, this difference between Song and Hoekendijk was caused by their different origins.

Missio Dei: *God's Direct Act in World History*

As noted above, Song considered the concept of incarnation as central to the biblical message. To him, the incarnation meant God's self-identification with the world in the suffering and death of Jesus Christ by affirming the entire creation while negating its autonomy and self-righteousness and re-orienting humankind radically from self-centeredness towards

---

85. J. C. Hoekendijk, *The Church Inside Out*, ed. L. A. Hoedemaker and Pieter Tijmes, trans. Isaac C. Rottenberg (Philadelphia: Westminster Press, 1966), 15–16.

86. Hoekendijk, "Church in Missionary Thinking," 333.

God-centeredness. Because God was deeply engaged in the world in the incarnation, the God-centered life would inevitably lead to a "worldly occupied" life. Centering on the incarnation, therefore, required "the decentralising of the church as we experience her and of which we are members." The incarnation was a recognition: "The world, and not the church as such, is the arena of God's activity."[87] Accordingly, Song wrote:

> An ecumenical church therefore is the church which takes the world seriously. She is the church which realises that God is working in her through the world. An ecumenical church is thus a secularised church, namely, the church which truly and faithfully embodies in herself the incarnation of the Word.[88]

Thus, the concept of incarnation provided Song with the theological basis not only for his rejection of the centrality of the Church in salvation but also for his this-worldly holiness that recognized the priority of God's relationship with the world over that with the Church.

In his view of God's relationship to the world, Song was profoundly indebted to the missiological debate in the 1960s, particularly the world-centric concept of *missio Dei* as formulated by the study project "The Missionary Structure of the Congregation." In fact, Song began using the *missio Dei* concept in the early 1970s. In his 1972 article "Election for Mission," he argued that the essence of Christian mission was the mission of Christ who, chosen by God, emptied himself to become "the most willing servant of God's mission" of healing and hope,[89] and that the Church was likewise elected to be the source of healing and hope for the entire humanity in solidarity with rest of the world.

Song's understanding of Christian mission as *missio Dei* was well formulated in the following statement:

> Strictly speaking, the Church does not and should not have her own mission. The only mission there is the mission of God. The Church exists to serve God's mission. The task of Third World theology is to help the traditional churches enlarge their vision of God's mission.[90]

---

87. Song, "Whither Protestantism?" 72, 74–75.

88. Ibid., 72.

89. Choan-Seng Song, "Election for Mission," *South East Asia Journal of Theology* 13, no. 2 (1972): 41.

90. Song, "New Frontiers," 28. Also see Song, *Tell Us Our Names*, 12.

In other words, the subject of mission was none other than God, who initiated *missio Dei* in response to the cries for help coming from nations and peoples in the world.[91] The mission of the Church was determined by this *missio Dei* as Song wrote: "The mission of the Church must be derived from the mission of God within history with the nations and peoples. God's mission with the nations and peoples is the presupposition of the mission of the Church."[92] The God of *missio Dei* could not, however, be the God "ensconced in the Church hierarchically organized and doctrinally conditioned" because Song rejected the idea of the Church as the agent of God's salvation[93]; rather, he maintained that the mission of the Church obtained the meaning only insofar as the Church participated in the mission of the living God at work among nations and peoples.[94]

Song's concept of God's mission was characterized by an emphasis on the directness of God's relationship with the entire creation. In his 1974 article "New China and Salvation History: A Methodological Enquiry,"[95] Song tried to develop a framework for the theological interpretation of the history of non-Christian nations, in particular that of the Communist China. Criticizing Wolfhart Pannenberg's idea of universal history as revelation, Song argued that the theological meaning of world history had to be seen through "the direct relationship between God's acts and historical events."[96] By the "direct relationship," Song meant: "God acts in

91. Song, "New Frontiers," 28.

92. Song, "God's Mission with the Nations," 228–29.

93. Ibid., 228.

94. In Song, this way of thinking has remained unchanged. In one of his much later publications, he wrote: "Christian mission is 'Christian' insofar as it serves the mission of God to create a world in which Jesus would no longer be crucified and the power of the Spirit curtailed and suppressed." (Choan-Seng Song, "Christian Mission toward Abolition of the Cross," in *The Scandal of a Crucified World: Perspective on the Cross and Suffering*, ed. Yacob Tesfai [Maryknoll, N.Y.: Orbis, 1994], 148).

95. Choan-Seng Song, "New China and Salvation History: A Methodological Enquiry," *South East Asia Journal of Theology* 15, no. 2 (1974): 52–67.

96. Ibid., 58. Concerning Pannenberg's idea of universal history as revelation, Song admitted that this German theologian's approach freed "the biblical witness to God's love and salvation from the narrow confinement of the so-called *Heilsgeschichte* solely represented by ancient Israel and the Christian church" (ibid., 57). Song was, however, critical of Pannenberg's emphasis on the "indirect nature of revelation" (ibid., 58). Song also questioned the validity of the idea of universal history and asked whether the idea was not "a philosophical abstraction" that had "no immediate designation with respect to specific event, persons, or nations." Song went on to argue that the idea could be "dangerous" because this type of "universalistic language" could be "a projection of the West-centered Judeo-Christian understanding of history" (ibid.).

history universally in such a way that historical events in the extra-Jewish/ Christian traditions bear direct relationships with the historical events in the Bible."[97] In other words, the world had been "God's mission field" even before the Church was called to serve the mission, and it never "ceased to be God's mission field" after the Church came "to share that mission."[98]

Presenting the idea of God's direct act in the world, Song found support in the process theologian Schubert Ogden who presented an unconventional view of the relationship between God and the world in analogy to the relationship between the human brain and human body. Of God's action, Ogden wrote:

> The primary meaning of God's action is the act whereby, in each new present, he constitutes himself as God by participating fully and completely in the world of his creatures, thereby laying the ground for the next stage of the creative process. Because his love, unlike ours, is pure and unbounded, his relation to his creatures and theirs to him is direct and immediate.[99]

Song saw a breakthrough in this view and wrote:

> Here the narrow theological norms which Western theologians have imposed upon their systems are overcome. God relates himself directly to all creatures. The affirmation of such a direct relationship is very crucial because salvation history can no longer be regarded as an extension or an expansion of the *Heilsgeschichte* conceived in Western theological terms. Salvation history is present already in the histories of nations, . . . [100]

Song thus rejected the Neo-orthodox approach that regarded God's action merely as "supernatural intervention which bears only [a] tangential relation" with human history,[101] and joined Ogden in the affirmation: "Wherever or insofar as an event in history manifests God's characteristic action as Creator and Redeemer, it actually *is* his act in a sense in which

---

97. Ibid., 58.

98. Song, *Tell Us Our Name*, 13.

99. Schubert M. Ogden, *The Reality of God and Other Essays* (New York: Harper & Row, 1963; Dallas: Southern Methodist University Press, 1992), 177. This passage is from the chapter entitled "What Sense Does It Make to Say, 'God Acts in History'?" (ibid., 164–87). Published originally in 1963 as a journal article (ibid., xi), this chapter was Ogden's response to the conciliar debate concerning the emerging idea of God at work in secular history. As for the debate, see the discussion on Mexico City 1963 in pp. 45–46 above.

100. Song, "New China," 58.

101. Ibid., 59.

other historical events are not."[102] In other words, God's action was part of secular history and constituted its "texture"; world history contained "certain distinctively human words and deeds in which his characteristic action as Creator and Redeemer is appropriately re-presented or revealed."[103]

Supported by Ogden further, Song also argued that such revelatory words and deeds in history were not confined to ancient Israel and the early Church but could be present "anywhere and anytime."[104] Nor were these words and deeds hidden from human beings because, as Ogden insisted, human beings as "the creatures of meaning" possessed the "capacity to discern meaning and to give it symbolic expression"—the capacity that "lies behind the whole complex phenomenon of human culture."[105] Thus, Ogden's understanding of God's act in world history helped Song to break away from the ethnocentric identification of salvation, the Church, and the Western Christendom and embark on the search for a theology that would assume a positive approach to the cultures and history of Asian peoples. After the mid-1970s, the idea of God's direct relationship with the world remained one of the major components of Song's theology throughout the rest of his theological career.[106]

God's Mission of Incarnation as the Divine Response to Human Suffering

The rejection of the identification of salvation with Israel and the Church and the affirmation of God's direct relationship with the whole world

---

102. Ogden, *Reality of God*, 182. Song quoted this statement by Ogden, commenting that it was "an important theological criterion to deal with the relationship between God's acts and events in history" ("New China," 59).

103. Ibid., 59–60; Ogden, *Reality of God*, 184.

104. Song, "New China," 60.

105. Ogden, *Reality of God*, 181; Song, "New China," 60.

106. For instance, Song began his discussion of Christian mission in his *Christian Mission in Reconstruction* with a statement that expressed the idea of God's direct relationship with the world as follows: "From the beginning to end, one basic theme which runs through the Bible is the theme of God's personal dealings with man and the world *redemptively*. . . . He does not relate Himself to man and his world in a general sort of way. Whenever He acts, He acts personally, directly and concretely" (*Christian Mission in Reconstruction*, 19). The idea was also found in the second volume of Song's Christological trilogy published in the 1990s: "By saying that the reign of God is theirs, Jesus affirms the direct link between God's reign and people, particularly those men, women, and children, oppressed, exploited, downtrodden, marginalized, in body and in spirit, those human persons treated inhumanly, and to whom injustice is done" (C. S. Song, *Jesus and the Reign of God* [Minneapolis: Fortress, 1993], 21). These passages demonstrate that the idea remained basic to Song's thinking throughout his career.

meant seeing the entire creation as a unity under the sovereignty of one God. The world taken as a single entity was also the world with "the complexities reflected in diversity of race, history, culture, religion or geography"[107] The world that God directly deals with was, therefore, the world both in totality and diversity and not a certain part of the divided world, whether Western Christendom or the Christian Church.

Such an approach inevitably contradicted the traditional concept of election, and Song sought to reformulate it. According to him, the Bible indeed presented God as dealing with the world "through intense concentration" on Israel and the Christian Church.[108] This "concentration," however, did not mean that they were the sole object of the divine redemption; instead, it meant that God's saving love toward the world was manifested through the election of "one for many" culminating in the suffering and death of Jesus Christ.[109] As Christ was elected to be the source of healing and hope for entire humanity, Christian communities were also elected to follow Christ and become the being for humanity. Their task was to participate in human tragedies, as Jesus did, while acknowledging their own responsibility in face of destructive forces threatening human life.[110] As Song wrote, "Christian mission is the mission of suffering. . . . [T]he essence of Christian mission consists in the manifestation of healing through suffering. Through the suffering of few, the nations will be healed."[111] For him, this mode of Christian presence was what Bonhoeffer meant by "the church for others."[112]

107. Song, *Christian Mission in Reconstruction*, 10.

108. Ibid., 10.

109. Song, "Election for Mission," 43–44; idem, *Christian Mission in Reconstruction*, 9–16.

110. Song, "Election for Mission," 44.

111. Song, *Christian Mission in Reconstruction*, 13. Song wrote this passage in the first half of the 1970s. As we will see later, the PCT issued the "Public Statement on Our National Fate" in 1971 and became literally "the suffering few" for the sake of entire Taiwan. As Song was deeply involved in this political development, it is not difficult to hear in this quotation a voice of the Taiwanese Presbyterian who was theologically striving to make sense of this new situation.

112. Song quotes Bonhoeffer's words: "The church is her true self only when she exists for humanity. As a fresh start she should give away all her endowments to the poor and needy" (ibid., 16). In the German original, this passage reads as follows: "Die Kirche ist nur Kirche, wenn sie für andere da ist. Um einen Anfang zu machen, muß sie alles Eigentum den Notleidenden schenken" (Dietrich Bonhoeffer, *Widerstand und Ergebung: Briefe und Aufzeichnungen aus der Haft*, ed. Eberhard Bethge [Gütersloh, Germany: Gütersloher Verlagshaus Mohn, 1985], 193). See p. 47 above for the significance of this passage in the world-centric *missio Dei* concept developed in the WCC project "The Missionary Structure of the Congregation."

For Song, Christ was thus "decisive."[113] The meaning of God's redemption for creation was ultimately revealed in the life, death, and resurrection of Jesus Christ. According to him,

> The symbolic meaning of God taking human flesh is that God has always been with and in the world, that He has always been involved in history and that He has been the redemptive force which directs the course of the nations and peoples to His destination. The incarnation is therefore the Word of God, that is, His will, His purpose, His love, and His judgment, become flesh, become the inseparable part of human history.[114]

The meaning of Jesus Christ was thus "God's being with this world."[115] By becoming part of human history, God personally responded to the human cry for help out of their sufferings and pains. God's mission was "God's action in reply to the human need for help."[116] Song, therefore, called God's mission the "mission of incarnation" or "mission of enfleshment."[117]

---

113. In order to formulate a positive theological approach towards Asian cultures and non-Christian faiths, Song considered the concept of "absoluteness" as inadequate when applied to Jesus Christ because it does not express what the incarnation really meant, that is, "God relativizes himself in order that man may have access to him." Moreover, the claim of the absoluteness of Christ produced a negative attitude among Asian Christians towards their own cultures because the claim is "a typical product of Western theology" made "in utter disregard for culture and life outside the so-called Western Christendom." Song also rejects the concept of "uniqueness" as applied to Christ. In his mind "uniqueness" means "without comparison" or "without parallel," and it would be impossible for humans to know God's will if Christ is viewed as unique, that is, totally with no parallel with human beings. Finally, Song regards the concept of "finality" as inadequate too because to him the divine revelation in Jesus Christ continues "to unfold itself in history," despite the Christian belief in the fulfillment of God's revelation in Jesus Christ. Having rejected these concepts, Song came to adopt the word "decisive" in the sense that something decisive might "create a situation which will alter the course of events, change the tide of history, and give impact on the life and thought of mankind." To Song, the decisiveness of Christ for one's life or for a culture means: "The impacts of Jesus Christ brings out from man's life and his culture those qualities that are responsive to the love and justice. At the same time, the decisiveness of Christ puts under the judgment of God the distortions and corruptions of the gift of the divine creation and salvation by man and his culture." In other words, Song considered Christ as "decisive" because "his impacts on Asian cultures, and for that matter any culture, brings into light the dialectics of love and judgment at work in them." (Choan-Seng Song, "The Decisiveness of Christ," in *What Asian Christians Are Thinking: A Theological Source Book*, ed. Douglas J. Elwood [Quezon City: New Day Publishers, 1976], 242–47).

114. Song, "God's Mission with the Nations," 232.

115. Song, *Christian Mission in Reconstruction*, 53.

116. Song, *Tell Us Our Names*, 13.

117. Song, "God's Mission with the Nations," 232; idem, *Christian Mission in Reconstruction*, 51.

In Song's mind, God's mission of incarnation had two aspects: "the mission of the cross" and "the mission of the resurrection." The mission of the cross was the mission in which God's self-disclosure occurred, identifying God as God where God was crucified, over against a false God who was the cause for human suffering. God's mission of the cross, thus, revealed the true God as the God who was with the world in the midst of "the darkest abyss of human existence." God's mission of resurrection, in contrast, manifested the hope that stemmed from the fulfillment of the divine love here and now; it was "the mission of building a new life and planting a new hope and a new future." Through this mission, God brought about deliverance of people from social, economic, and political bondage and opened up "a new dimension of understanding the history of the nations and peoples."[118]

According to Song, the mission of the Church had to be a "reflection" of God's mission of incarnation; the Church was truly the Church insofar as it became mission, reflecting God's own mission in Christ in response to God's invitation. The Church was, thus, "an event rather than an organization, fellowship rather than church order."[119] Its mission had to be Christ-centered rather than Church-centered.

The mission of the Church, therefore, had also two aspects. Participating in God's mission of the cross, the Church had to discern and identify the true God wherever God was crucified, that is, in the midst of the pains, sufferings, and deaths. Song wrote:

> If God has chosen the cross where he is to be identified as God, where else can the mission of the Church point to God except the cross? Where acts of injustice and inhumanity are committed, God is there. When the crucifixion of the truth takes place, God is there. When people suffer at the hands of the economically and politically powerful, God is there. And when death occurs, God is there.[120]

This God who was with humankind in their predicaments was simultaneously the God who gave them new hope and life out of divine love. Thus, the task of the Church was also to become "a community of hope on behalf of the world" through participation in God's mission of resur-

---

118. Song, "God's Mission with the Nations," 232–34; idem, *Christian Mission in Reconstruction*, 120.

119. Song, "God's Mission with the Nations," 232; idem, *Christian Mission in Reconstruction*, 63.

120. Song, "God's Mission with the Nations," 234.

rection "to renew and recreate humanity in different religious, social and cultural contexts." The Christian presence in Asia was, thus, "the symbol of the incarnation" pointing to God's saving act for the sake of the entire humanity.[121]

The conception of Christian mission as God's mission in suffering humanity naturally brought Song to the question of discernment particularly in the history of Asian peoples. For Song, participation in God's mission in Asia presupposed the ability of the Church to learn the contents and forms of their mission from the nations and peoples in Asia who lived outside the direct influence of the Judeo-Christian traditions for centuries.[122] In other words, the Church had to be able "to discern how people in different cultural and historical situations can see and experience the hope of salvation in the sufferings which descend on them with cruel consistency." In Song's mind, such learning was possible because Asia was "a theatre of God's *direct* redemptive operation."[123] Thus, theological and missiological discernment became one of his major concerns.

A Search for a New Framework of Theology in Asia

As we have already seen, the historical tie between Christianity and Western civilization deeply disturbed Song. The problem created by the tie in the churches in Asia was a major factor that drove him into a critical theological reflection. This tie had a profound impact not only on Western missions but also Western theology.[124] In his *Third-Eye Theology* published

---

121. Song, *Christian Mission in Reconstruction*, 66; idem, "Election for Mission," 48; idem, "Whither Protestantism," 75.

122. Song, "God's Mission with the Nations," 230.

123. Choan-Seng Song, "From Israel to Asia: A Theological Leap," *Ecumenical Review* 28 (July 1976): 258.

124. In his works, Song tirelessly criticized "Western theology." He, however, seldom defined the term clearly. As a result, his arguments often give his reader an impression of ignoring the dynamic complexity and diversity of the West. The truth is that Song, like many other Asian Christian theologians, rather uncritically accepted the popular Asian perception that sees the West, namely, Europe and North America, as a single cultural and historical entity in opposition to the East or Asia. As for his critique of Western theology, it is rather obvious that the criticism was aimed at "Western theology" as a whole in the sense of the "theological framework" ("New China," 55) and formulations which had shaped in the experiences and thought forms of the European and later North American churches since the time of Constantine and had been transplanted into the rest of the world by Western missionaries. His questioning was even extended to "the validity and relevance of accepting the ethical, social, and cultural norms and ethos developed out of the experience of the church in the West" ("Decisiveness of Christ," 253). This fact does not negate another important fact that Song was under the heavy influence of Western

in 1979,[125] Song called the situation "the marriage between theology and Western norms of thought and life" and wrote that the marriage had become "the implicit assumption of doing theology in the West." The marriage was even reinforced in the churches outside the West, and the theological reflection of the Christian faith in Asia remained "mostly direct extensions of their Western traditions and practices." Thus, Confucius, for instance, had not become a part of theological thinking for the Chinese churches as Aristotle had become influential in Roman Catholic theology. Song felt that Christian theology built on such a marriage was doomed to be detrimental to the spiritual growth and development of the churches in Asia. To overcome this problem, one had "to reappraise critically the relationship between Christian faith and the cultural forms that shape the formulation of the faith."[126] This task became Song's main preoccupation in the 1980s.

The Problem of Salvation History

What Song saw at the core of the marriage between Western civilization and Christianity was the already mentioned theological position to identify salvation with the history of Israel and the Christian Church. To him, a classical example for this position was Cyprian's famous words, "Outside the Church there is no salvation."[127] In his *The Compassionate God* of 1982, Song called the position "centrism" and argued that traditional Western theology was too much accustomed to viewing human history with this bias of centrism.[128]

---

theology and often inspired by its representatives, such as Barth, Hoekendijk, Ogden, Bonhoeffer, Tillich, and others, in various manners.

125. Choan-Seng Song, *Third-Eye Theology: Theology in Formation in Asian Settings* (Maryknoll, N.Y.: Orbis, 1979). The references to this work in the subsequent footnotes are made to its revised edition published in 1991 (Choan-Seng Song, *Third-Eye Theology: Theology in Formation in Asian Settings*, rev. ed. [Maryknoll, N.Y.: Orbis, 1991]).

126. Ibid., 20–23.

127. Song, "From Israel to Asia," 255–56. The Second Helvetic Confession of 1566 explicitly makes reference to this phrase: "OUTSIDE THE CHURCH OF GOD THERE IS NO SALVATION. . . . so we believe that there is no certain salvation outside Christ, who offers himself to be enjoyed by the elect in the Church; and hence we teach that those who wish to live ought not to be separated from the true Church of Christ" (*The Constitution of the Presbyterian Church (U.S.A.)*, part 1, *Book of Confessions* [New York: Office of the General Assembly, 1983], 5.136).

128. C. S. Song, *The Compassionate God* (Maryknoll, NY: Orbis, 1982), 16.

Song regarded the concept of *Heilsgeschichte* or salvation history as the typical modern formulation of centrism.[129] In this concept, the meaning of world history was centered on the history of Israel and the Christian Church as the vessels of God's saving activity; the rest of the world was thought to have no direct link with salvation and to be brought into the sphere of salvation only when it was touched by Israel and the Church.[130] According to Song, the *Heilsgeschichte* concept was best articulated by Oscar Cullmann, who wrote in his *Christ and Time* as follows:

> The entire redemptive history unfolds in two movements: the one proceeds from the many to the One; this is the Old Covenant. The other proceeds from the One to the many; this is the New Covenant. At the very mid-point stands the expiatory deed of the death and resurrection of Christ. . . . Common to both movements is the fact that they are carried out according to the principle of election and representation. This principle then is decisive also for the present phrase of development, which proceeds from the mid-point. The Church on earth, in which the Body of Christ is represented, plays in the New Testament conception a central role for the redemption of all mankind and thereby for the entire creation.[131]

This passage summarizes Cullmann's idea of "presentation," that is, the "election of the minority for the redemption of the whole."[132] Reacting strongly against this Church-centric view of salvation, Song wrote:

> Election and representation of Israel and the church, and in Cullmann's view, especially the church, on behalf of all humankind! These two concepts have been the two solid pillars supporting the claim of Christianity to uniqueness among other faiths and religions. The main actors on the stage of redemptive history are Israel and the church.[133]

---

129. Song raised the question regarding the difficulty of the concept of salvation history in his 1974 article "New China and Salvation History." In this article, he tried to interpret the concept in a more universal and inclusive way. He, however, thoroughly criticized and rejected the concept later in his "From Israel to Asia" (1976) and *The Compassionate God* (1982).

130. Song, *Compassionate God*, 24.

131. Oscar Cullmann, *Christ and Time: The Primitive Christian Conception of Time and History*, rev. ed., trans. Floyd V. Filson (Philadelphia: Westminster Press, 1964), 117–18. This passage is quoted in Song, *Compassionate God*, 24–25.

132. Cullmann, *Christ and Time*, 115.

133. Song, *Compassionate God*, 25.

In other words, the concept of election was guilty of the centrist idea of salvation history. As we have seen above, Song earlier expressed the idea of election of the minority for the redemption of the whole or "one for many" in his criticism of Christian missions. Criticizing salvation history, he now distanced himself from this earlier position and made a distinction between "election as an experience of God's free grace" and election as a justification for centrism. The former was the expression of God's free grace experienced, for instance, by Israel in their covenant with God on Mount Sinai. The institutionalization of the biblical religion, however, distorted this original meaning, turning election into a claim for "monopoly right of salvation" and giving rise to the notion of salvation history. Song thus rejected both election and salvation history as the justification for the centrist claim by the institutionalized religion of the West.[134]

The Creation-Redemption Paradigm

The concept of salvation history, understandably, raises in the minds of many non-Western people, whether Christian or not, the question about the ultimate meaning of their own history and cultures left by the concept outside the scope of the Christian faith. The question Song asked in this regard was: "How do we as Christians view and interpret the cultural and historical activities and events of the nations and peoples not under the direct influence of the Judeo-Christian traditions?"[135]

As Preman Niles pointed out, Song's search in the 1970s led him to replace the connection traditionally advocated in Christian theology between election and redemption with the one between creation and redemption, thereby making creation "the point of entry into a new under-

---

134. Ibid., 32–33. The problem of the identification of salvation and Western culture was pointed out also by the conservative missiologist Harold Lindsell who maintained that one of the weaknesses of the church was its failure to distinguish between the Christian faith and western culture—"a product which has its roots in the Hebrew-Roman-Greek-Christian tradition," and that, due to this failure, "missionaries have somehow been left with the idea that western culture is an integral part of the gospel." According to him, "this error arose out of a false eschatology which posited the Christianization of the world and the advent of a golden age introduced by the permeation of the gospel as a leaven throughout the world." As for the Christianization of the world, Lindsell did not hold it was "the biblical goal," for "all men will not be saved" (*Missionary Principles and Practice* [Westwood, N.J.: Fleming H. Revell Co., n.d.], 22–23).

135. D. Preman Niles, Charles C. West, and Choan-Seng Song, "Reviewing and Responding to the Thought of Choan-Seng Song," *Occasional Bulletin of Missionary Research* 1 (July 1977): 14.

standing of cultures, religions, and histories" in theology.[136] Song's following statement well illuminates his new approach to theology:

> Creation in redemption and redemption in creation—these are the key concepts that enable me to see cultures and religions in a positive as well as negative light. At the same time, they put all cultures and religions, that is to say, all human activities, on an equal footing before God. On the basis of this, I have given up the concept of salvation history—the term often understood in a narrow sense of the history of Israel and of the Christian Church as alone representing God's redeeming values.[137]

Such an approach, naturally, required Song to reconceptualize the traditional doctrine of creation. The American Presbyterian theologian Charles Hodge (1792–1878), for instance, taught of creation that the universe "was not formed out of any preëxistence or substance; but was created *ex nihilo*." He also said: "Creation was not necessary. It was free to God to create or not to create, to create the universe as it is, or any other order and system of things according to the good pleasure of his will."[138] For Song, however, the doctrine of creation *ex nihilo* was not essential. Nor was creation "an act of God's free will"[139] that had nothing to do with human conditions. To him, the vital point in the biblical faith of creation was "the personal way in which God responds to the fear and predicament of a human community."[140] Regarding this point, Song wrote:

> God's dealing with man is radical in the sense that He goes to the root of man's need, namely, the need of being right with God and with his fellow creatures. Thus, God's timely act of redemption brings about new relationships in the ordering of the whole of creation. As a result, a new creation comes into being.[141]

Here, Song spoke of the new creation. Unlike Devanandan and Thomas, however, he did not conceive the new creation as something eschatological brought into history for the first time in Jesus Christ. To him, creation was by itself God's act of new creation. In fact, the story of creation in the first chapter of Genesis was not "the primeval history of the universe"; rather, it

---

136. Ibid., 10.
137. Ibid., 13.
138. Charles Hodge, *Systematic Theology*, vol. 1 (Reprint, Grand Rapids, Mich.: Eerdmans, 1989), 553.
139. Ibid., 555.
140. Song, *Third-Eye Theology*, 53.
141. Song, *Christian Mission in Reconstruction*, 20.

was a story composed by the Jewish people in exile to express their experience of God's saving acts and joy of liberation from the darkness of the present suffering and destruction.[142] Thus, "the experience of redemption is an experience ultimately related to the experience of creation."[143]

In this way, Song juxtaposed creation and redemption. For him, creation meant "God's redemptive response to the pain and suffering of this world."[144] Likewise, the creation story was the story of God's redemptive intervention in history that brought about a radically new reality in the midst of destructive power. Song, therefore, wrote:

> Creation and redemption are in reality two sides of the same coin. Where there is creation, there is redemption. Conversely, where there is redemption, there is creation. Or to put it another way, creation is God's redeeming act, while redemption is God's creating act.[145]

As we have already seen, Song maintained that God acts directly in the history of peoples and nations. By juxtaposing creation and redemption, Song articulated a theological foundation for this idea, placing the entire world under God's redemptive activity. God's direct relation could not be confined merely to the chosen people, whether Israel or the Christian Church. God was at work directly among all peoples and nations in the world; their history was, therefore, also to be seen as a history of the continual interaction between God and humankind, that is, as a

---

142. Ibid. This understanding of creation was not new to Song in the 1970s. In the mid-1960s, Song already expressed the basically same understanding as follows: "The creation story composed during the exilic period in a land far away from Jerusalem marks the final victory of Yahweh as the God of heaven and earth.... The creation story is a hymn of praise to the Maker of heaven and earth confessing that He is the only God. It is the affirmation of His lordship over the whole *seculum*" ("Confessing the Faith," 100–101).

143. Song, *Christian Mission in Reconstruction*, 20.

144. Song, *Third-Eye Theology*, 56.

145. Ibid. One may sense an echo of Schubert Odgen's language in Song's juxtaposition of creation and redemption. In his discussion of God's act in history, Ogden frequently designated God as "God as Creator and Redeemer" (*Reality of God*, 178–79, 181–87). It is likely that Song was influenced by Ogden when the former paid special attention to the relationship between creation and redemption and considered the twin notions "creation in redemption and redemption in creation" as "the key concepts" for his theological construction (Niles, West, and Song, "Reviewing and Responding," 13. See p. 171 above). Graham S. Ogden pointed out this connection between Schubert Ogden and Song as follows: "Both in his theology of history as well as in his selection of the Creation-Redemption model, we find Song in agreement with Schubert Ogden" ("The Old Testament in Asia: A Response to C. S. Song," *Taiwan Journal of Theology* 1 [March 1979]: 78–79).

history of the continual "acts of God in creation and redemption."[146] Song called this way of viewing God's activity in history "the creation-redemption paradigm." He maintained that such a paradigm would enable us "to gain the freedom to appreciate how God is at work in, say, China or India, both in judgment and redemption."[147]

Redemption as Interruption-Dispersion

In Song's creation-redemption paradigm, God's saving activity was seen as the continual work of creation and re-creation throughout history to rescue humankind from the dominion of the power of destruction. Redemption was, therefore, viewed as God's continuing engagement with world history, breaking down old orders and introducing new orders into human life, and God as the source of fundamental change and renewal in society.

This approach brought Song to the understanding of redemption as disruption-dispersion.[148] In this view, the meaning of history was considered to be revealed by the redemptive events that appeared to "disrupt" or "interrupt the normal course of life and history." These events would become "the bearers of meaning which brings something qualitatively new into the realm of history" and "takes us into the future and frees us from slavery to the sinful past and to absurd fate." In other words, Song regarded redemption as "God's revolution within his own creation" which would produce "radical interruptions and qualitative changes in the life and history of humankind."[149]

Song's primary scriptural basis for this understanding of redemption was the words uttered by God upon completion of the work of creation: "Be fruitful and multiply, and fill the earth and subdue it; and have dominion over the fish of the sea and over the birds of the air and over every living thing that moves upon the earth" (Gen. 1:28 NRSV). These words were God's command for humankind to multiply and disperse on the entire earth. To Song, the significance of this command was particularly evident in the story of the Tower of Babel built by humankind to resist God's command out of the fear of discontinuity. God, however, challenged this

---

146. Song, *Christian Mission in Reconstruction*, 35.

147. Niles, West, and Song, "Reviewing and Responding," 13.

148. Song developed this approach to redemption mainly in his article "From Israel and Asia" and *The Compassionate God*. See also Choan-Seng Song, "Theology of Transposition," *Northeast Asia Journal of Theology* 24–25 (March-September 1980): 6–28.

149. Song, "From Israel to Asia," 254.

resistance by disrupting the human effort and dispersed people into nations with diverse languages. Song, thus, regarded disruption and dispersion as crucial to the understanding of redemption.[150]

The prophetic tradition in the Old Testament was particularly important in this connection. According to Song, the people of Israel built a racially and religiously exclusive community in the name of the covenant on Mount Sinai, making election "their right over against other peoples." The prophetic tradition was essentially a rejection of such a Jewish centrism as well as the Jewish identity as God's only chosen people. The prophets were the people who tried to rescue Israel out of its centrism. They, indeed, admitted that God worked within the history of Israel; nonetheless, they urged the Israelites not to presume on God's saving love. Their refusal of the Jewish centrism meant the recognition that the whole world inhabited by nations was also within the scope of God's saving love. As Song wrote, the prophets thus "challenged . . . a narrow and exclusive theology of election and tried to help compatriots see how God was working in the wider arena of world history."[151]

Thus, Song found that the prophetic tradition paradoxically depicted God's redemptive acts within the Jewish history as radical interruptions of this very history. In this tradition, God's grace was seen as increasingly transcending the history of the elect through such interruptions and more fully embracing all nations in the world. Song found God's similar disruptive interventions in history in other biblical events, such as the call of Abraham, the Exodus, and the Babylonian exile of Israel.[152] These observations brought him to the idea that redemption as disruption and dispersion was the way God intermittently rebuffs the human effort to maintain identity and continuity through institutionalizing the experience of God's free grace into religious establishments.

According to Song, the most serious disruption in the history of Israel occurred in the death and resurrection of Jesus Christ. Seen from the perspective of redemption as disruption-dispersion, the cross of Jesus Christ was God's final rejection of the Jewish centrism. On the cross, God negated the Jewish expectation of a political messiah and affirmed Jesus as the suffering messiah whose significance was to go far beyond the borders of the Jewish community.[153] The cross was not simply God's judgment on

---

150. Song, *Compassionate God*, 22–23.
151. Ibid., 16, 32; idem, "From Israel to Asia," 257.
152. Song, *Compassionate God*, 28–38.
153. Ibid., 90–92.

the sins of the world; it was primarily God's judgment on the institutionalized elitist religion that concealed the true God—God of love who is always with the world—from people and misrepresented God to them by "erecting barriers between the saved and the unsaved, between the godly and the ungodly."[154] This disruption was not merely the negation of the Jewish messianism; completed by the resurrection of Jesus Christ, it decisively transferred God's redemptive presence from the Jewish religious establishment controlled by the religious elite to ordinary people, that is, to the suffering people in the whole world. Therefore, Song wrote:

> By becoming the suffering messiah, Jesus breaks with the elitist political culture that defends and serves the powerful ruling class and exploits the masses of powerless "plebeians." The transposition of Jesus from a political messiah to the suffering messiah is thus of decisive importance. Jesus as the suffering messiah becomes the prototype of "little suffering messiahs" throughout human history. He becomes embodied in the suffering messiahs of the suffering people of Israel, in Egypt, in France, in the United States, in China, in Brazil.[155]

Thus, though Jesus was born into Israel, he radically "interrupted the continuity of its life and history built on the dream of a national messiah." Jesus was "an interruption of a most fundamental kind" that occurred "in the life of people and in the history of the world."[156] He was, therefore, "the great disruption."[157] In other words, incarnation was the event in which God radically overcame God's own captivity to the centrism of Israel, and through which the meaning of redemption was forcefully revealed as God's solidarity with powerless suffering people in the whole world.

A Theological Leap

In Song's attempt to relate God's redemption to the history and cultures of Asian peoples, the view of incarnation as the great disruption of the history of Israel went together with another important idea, that is, the idea of "theological leap" or "transposition."

In his search for a better theological framework for interpreting human history, Song asked in the early 1970s whether one had to understand salvation history as the "absolute norm" as most Western theologians in-

---

154. Ibid., 95.
155. Ibid., 108.
156. Song, "From Israel to Asia," 255.
157. Song, *Compassionate God*, 17.

cluding Cullmann did, or as a "pattern" or a "type" for discernment.¹⁵⁸ His option was for the latter. In his mind, the limited experiences of Israel and the Christian Church could not be normative because God was freely at work among nations in the world. The significance of these experiences were rather interpretive and consisted in their function as the "proto-model of interpretation."¹⁵⁹ The concept of election would make sense insofar as the significance of Israel and the Christian Church was viewed as symbolic and not as the channel of God's salvation. According to Song,

> Israel is chosen not to present herself to the rest of the world as a nation through which God's redeeming love will be mediated, but to be a symbol, or an example, of how God is also at work among the nations in a redeeming way. In the light of the experiences unique to Israel, other nations should learn how their histories too are endowed with redemptive significance. The history of Israel experienced and interpreted redemptively provides a pattern of framework by which other nations may scrutinize their history for its redemptive quality and meaning. . . . A nation will thus find itself placed under the redemptive acts of God in the company of Israel and other nations. In this way, Israel is symbolically transported out of its original context to a foreign context. This is a theological leap which must be taken by Asian theologians. For them Asia is a theatre of God's *direct* redemptive operation.¹⁶⁰

Song thus argued that one could discern and identify the redemptive presence of God among all nations and peoples in the world in light of God's dealing with God's "chosen" people.

Obviously, the "theological leap" of which Song spoke in the above passage, or "transposition" as he called it in his *The Compassionate God*,¹⁶¹ was the theological method closely related to the concept of disruption.

---

158. In 1974, Song wrote as follows: "The crucial question is obviously this: Is the salvation history intensely exhibited or demonstrated in both the Old and the New Testament to be looked upon as the absolute norm by which events in secular world history get chosen arbitrarily to be incorporated into God's salvation in Christ, OR, is it to be regarded as a pattern or a type of God's salvation manifested in a massively concentrated way in ancient Israel and in the history of the church and therefore to be discovered in varied degrees of intensity and concentration in other nations and peoples also?" ("New China," 57). This passage is important because it reveals what kind of consideration regarding salvation history led Song to the methodological idea of "theological leap" or "transposition" which is being discussed here.

159. Song, "Decisiveness of Christ," 248.

160. Song, "From Israel to Asia," 258.

161. Song, *Compassionate God*, 1–17; idem, "Theology of Transposition," 10–21.

This leap was a "leap of faith" to follow God's great disruption of the history of Israel in Jesus Christ. The theological justification for transposition was, therefore, the incarnation, that is, "the Word become flesh."[162] The theological leap ultimately became possible and even imperative because, in Jesus' suffering and death, God took the initiative to break away from the centrism of the religion of Israel and manifest the universal nature of redemption as God's solidarity with suffering humanity. For Song as a Christian theologian, taking incarnation seriously did not simply mean rejecting Jewish centrism; it also meant rejecting the Christian claim of salvation monopolized by the Church and identified with its history as well as all other similar claims made by any religions in the world. Furthermore, taking the incarnation seriously meant engaging oneself in the task of elucidating the meaning of God's redemption in relation to the suffering men and women in the world, particularly in Asia.

In his *The Compassionate God*, Song applied the principle of transposition to Chinese history. Thereby, he attempted to give theological interpretations to ancient Confucianism, the arrival of Buddhism in China, the Taiping rebellion in the nineteenth century, and the pro-democracy movement in Communist China.[163]

The People-Centered Approach towards Christology

In Song's career, the decade that ended with the publications of *Third-Eye Theology* in 1979 and *The Compassionate God* in 1982 can be seen as the period of the search for a new approach to Christian mission and theology. Building on his rather methodological reflections in this period, Song attempted in the following decade to construct a people-centered Christian theology that took into account the cultures and history of Asian peoples.

The Movement for Taiwan's Self-Determination

The direction in which Song's theological construction developed was closely related with the historical experience of the people of Taiwan, in particular the Taiwanese Christians, from the early 1970s on.[164] This decade was a turbulent period in the history of Taiwan, marking the beginning of the dynamic political awakening and change of this island nation. The change was prompted by a series of political incidents surrounding Taiwan, begin-

---

162. Song, "From Israel to Asia," 261.
163. Song, *Compassionate God*, 145–241.
164. Kishimoto, postface to *Minwa no shingaku*, 205.

ning with the U.S. national security advisor Henry Kissinger's secret visit to China in July 1971. In October 1971, when the international community decided to give Beijing a seat in the United Nations, the Nationalist government in Taipei withdrew from it, claiming that Taipei was the only legitimate government representing the entire China. Taiwan was further shocked by the news of the U.S. president Richard Nixon's visit to China planned in the following year.[165]

Deeply troubled by the island's growing international isolation, the PCT broke out the political silence that the people of Taiwan had kept for twenty-five years under the Nationalist regime, and became the first under the regime to raise an open voice for Taiwan's democracy and self-determination.[166] Issuing the "Public Statement on Our National Fate" on December 30, 1971, the Executive Committee of the PCT declared:

> We oppose any powerful nation disregarding the rights and wishes of fifteen million people and making unilateral decisions to their own advantage, because God has ordained and the United Nations Charter has affirmed that every people has the right to determine its own destiny. . . . Therefore, we earnestly request that within the Taiwan area it hold elections of all representatives to the highest government bodies to succeed the present representatives who were elected 25 years ago on the mainland.[167]

This bold statement "brought down the wrath of the government on the Presbyterian Church."[168] The PCT was subsequently placed under the severe surveillance of the Nationalist authorities. Yet the Presbyterians refused to be silenced and issued a second statement entitled "Our Appeal" in 1975, following the government confiscation of the romanized Taiwanese Bible. Two years later, when the U.S. president Jimmy Carter's policy of normalizing the relations between Washington and Beijing became public, the PCT further challenged the Nationalist government, issuing the third statement entitled "A Declaration of Human Rights" in August 1977.[169]

---

165. O and Munakata, *Atarashii Taiwan*, 247–48; Cohen, *Taiwan at the Crossroads*, 251–53.

166. Choan-Seng Song, "Introduction: Building a Political Culture of Love," *in Testimonies of Faith: Letters and Poems from Prison in Taiwan*, selected, ed. and trans. with an introduction by Choan-Seng Song (N.p., [1984]), 17–19; O and Munakata, *Atarashii Taiwan*, 248; Cohen, *Taiwan at the Crossroads*, 192–93.

167. C. S. Song, ed., *Self-Determination: The Case for Taiwan* (Tainan, Taiwan: Taiwan Church Press, 1988), 6.

168. Song, "Building a Political Culture," 19.

169. Cohen, *Taiwan at the Crossroads*, 193–95; Song, "Building a Political Culture,"

In this declaration, the PCT explicitly referred to Taiwan's independence as the goal, thereby touching upon "the most sensitive political nerve of the ruling authorities" who had been denying independence to the island's residents under their "one China" policy.[170] This confrontation between the PCT and the Nationalist government eventually led to the imprisonment and trial of the PCT leadership, including the General Secretary C. M. Kao, after the Kaohsiung Incident in 1979.[171] Subsequently, many ministers and lay people were forced to leave Taiwan and live abroad until the late 1980s.[172] Song was one of those Taiwanese Christians who chose a life in exile escaping the repression of the Nationalist government.

While the PCT continued challenging the Nationalist regime courageously from within, its 1971 statement was "received with great excitement by the Taiwanese Christians in diaspora," whom Song himself had joined in 1970.[173] In response to the statement, Song, Shoki Coe, Tsung-yi Lin of Ann Arbor, Michigan, and Wu-tong Hwang of New York City formed a group called "Formosan (Taiwanese) Christians for Self-Determination" in Washington, D.C., in 1972, and initiated a movement for Taiwan's self-determination among the overseas Taiwanese communities in North America and Europe.[174] Song greatly contributed to the journal *Self-Determination* occasionally published by the group. In the editorial of its first issue, he wrote:

> We people of Taiwan, fifteen million of us, have an appeal to make. We have a cause to fight for. We have a claim to make. And we have a dream to dream. We appeal to the community of nations to respect our integrity and dignity as human beings. We claim that we People of Taiwan are entitled to determine for ourselves our own future and destiny just as any other group of people. We call upon all people of Taiwan to fight for this right of self-determination. And we dream of the day when Taiwan will play a responsible part as a nation-state in the world community of nations and peoples. . . . As Taiwanese Christians, we believe that the above claim is an inalienable part of our faith in God who

---

20–23; O and Munakata, *Atarashii Taiwan*, 251–52.

170. Song, "Building a Political Culture," 23.

171. Ibid., 25; O and Munakata, *Atarashii Taiwan*, 258–63; Cohen, *Taiwan at the Crossroads*, 196–97.

172. Nihon Kirisuto Kyodan Taiwan Kankei Iinkai, *Tomo ni nayami tomo ni yorokobu*, 199.

173. Song, "Building a Political Culture," 19.

174. Song, *Self-Determination*, vi–ix.

created human beings in God's image. Taiwanese, no less than men and women of other nationalities, are created by God for freedom, justice and equality.[175]

In his theological writing, Song has seldom touched upon the political issues of Taiwan. The political awakening of the people of Taiwan that began in the 1970s was, nonetheless, the historical background of his theological reflection with the emphasis on suffering and hope of people under the oppressive political regime. Song later wrote: "Political theology developed by some Christians of Taiwan has its roots in this historical situation. It is a theology born our of the history of the people of Taiwan."[176] Making this statement, he neither mentioned himself nor his own involvement in the movement. Yet this statement doubtlessly applies, above all, to Song's own theology because his theology has become the most prominent political Christian theology that has emerged out of the awakening of the people of Taiwan.

The Suffering People of Asia

As we have already seen, the incarnation meant to Song that the locus for God's redemptive work was transferred decisively to the suffering people in the world from the elitist religious establishment, whether Jewish or Christian, or for that matter, from any religious and political establishments. In the early 1970s, Song's understanding of Christian mission clearly reflected the situation confronting the PCT at the moment, and he considered the mission of the Church to serve as a chosen minority for the redemption of many. With the new method of transposition, however, he shifted the focus of his theology by the early 1980s from the Church onto the suffering people.[177] Song thought that people were also the key for understanding history, and wrote in a 1978 article: "The meaning of history comes from people—the people who . . . are created in the image of God and who struggle to retain the image of God in them."[178] To understand people in Asia and their history, he began to use folk stories in his reflec-

---

175. Ibid., 1.

176. C. S. Song, *Theology from the Womb of Asia* (Maryknoll, N.Y.: Orbis, 1986), 102.

177. This shift was expressed in his following words written in 1979: "The frontiers of our theology must move from the history of Israel and the history of Christianity in the West to the history in which we are involved in Asia" (Song, "New Frontiers," 17).

178. Choan-Seng Song, "Liberation of People in History," *South East Asia Journal of Theology* 19, no. 2 (1978): 16.

tion because he regarded them as sources of "popular history" that testified "the universal struggle of people to be human, free, and authentic."[179]

Song's emphasis on people can be traced back to the 1960s when his attempt to overcome Neo-orthodoxy drove him to an emphasis on humanity. In his 1965 article "The Possibility of Analogical Discourse of God," he suggested that both the knowledge of God and the analogical discourse of God were made possible by "the humanity of Jesus which we share in some basic form, namely, in the form of the *imago Dei* as God's gracious act of creation."[180] This idea of knowability of God through the humanity of Jesus Christ shared by other human beings turned to be one of Song's essential convictions affirmed by him on various occasions in various forms. The idea eventually brought him to declare: "Theology should not begin with the study of God. Rather it should start with the study of humanity, the study of people and the world, in short, the study of God's creation."[181]

Such a people-centered approach was reinforced by Song's suspicion of the religious and political establishment. As he wrote, "human perception of God is very much determined by social and cultural environments in which human beings live, and that perception in turn shapes their worldview and religious beliefs."[182] He, therefore, thought that theological tradition built up by the established churches in the West and endorsed by the institutionalized churches in Asia would not help to understand the meaning of Jesus Christ in relation to the suffering people in Asia. Thus, in his reflections that resulted in the publication of the Christological trilogy entitled *The Cross in the Lotus World* in the 1990s,[183] Song attempted to interpret Jesus Christ not through the eyes of the established theological tradition but through the eyes of people in Asia. In this work, he defined

---

179. Choan-Seng Song, "Asian Contribution to Ecumenical Theology," *Drew Gateway* 57 (Fall 1986): 26–27; idem, *Tears of Lady Meng*, 25. For Song's use of folk stories in theology, see his *Tears of Lady Meng* and *Tell Us Our Names*. See also pp. 80–82 above.

180. Choan-Seng Song, "The Possibility of Analogical Discourse of God," *South East Asia Journal of Theology* 7 (October 1965): 76.

181. Song, *Third-Eye Theology*, 112.

182. C. S. Song, *Jesus, the Crucified People*, vol. 1 of *The Cross in the Lotus World* (New York: Crossroad, 1990), 59.

183. Song's Christological trilogy *The Cross in the Lotus World* consists of *Jesus, the Crucified People* (1990); *Jesus and the Reign of God* (1993); and *Jesus in the Power of the Spirit* (Minneapolis: Fortress, 1994). Only the first volume carries the general title for the trilogy as part of the bibliographical information. Song, however, stated that these three books had been written as "a three-volume work under the general title *The Cross in the Lotus World*" (*Jesus, the Crucified People*, xi).

people as "human beings who are oppressed, exploited, disadvantaged, and marginalized, socially, politically, economically, culturally, and also religiously." In other words, people were those "with whom Jesus was associated during his ministry."[184] This definition of people clearly reveals the inspiration that Song received from *minjung* theology in Korea.[185]

This understanding of people also suggests the influence of liberation theology on Song. Such an influence, in fact, became evident in the mid-1970s while he was involved in the movement for Taiwan's self-determination. The 1974 open letter "Salvation Today for the People of Taiwan" signed by Coe, Song, and two other initiators of the movement explicitly mentioned Bangkok 1973, which placed the emphasis on liberation, and declared: "The issue of Liberation is an urgent one for the people of Taiwan at this critical period when its survival is at stake."[186] Salvation, of which Song used to speak rather abstractly in terms of "healing"[187] or "freedom to be human,"[188] also obtained a political implication in his thinking; by the second half of the 1970s, he came to describe salvation as the "liberation of people from history within history" or liberation of people from a tyrannical stage of history.[189] These tendencies were further accompanied by the shift in Song's attention from the problem of the West toward the social and political issues within Asia. Consequently, the problem of suffering of Asian people came to the fore. Song now perceived suffering as the chief characteristic of Asian history and wrote: "The history of Asian nations and peoples is the history of people's suffering and their experi-

---

184. Ibid., 210.

185. See p. 78 above. For Song's reference to *minjung* theology, see, for instance, Song, *Tears of Lady Meng*, 29–30; idem, *Theology from the Womb of Asia*, 70–71.

186. Song, *Self-Determination*, 33.

187. Song, "Election for Mission," 44. In this 1972 article, Song wrote: "What is of supreme importance is that the Christian community becomes the source of the healing of the world" (ibid.).

188. Song, "New China," 66–67. In this 1974 article in which Song attempted to interpret God's mission in the Communist China, he defined salvation as "the freedom to be human," saying: "The Incarnation is God's freedom to be human. In Jesus Christ God has shown what it means to be human. To be human, as Jesus demonstrated in life and in death, is to be open to God and to man. Openness is thus an essential nature of humanness" (ibid., 66). This definition of salvation reveals an echo of the view of salvation as defined by some ecumenical leaders of the older generation, including M. M. Thomas.

189. Song, "Liberation of People," 22. See also Song, *Christian Mission in Reconstruction*, x.

ence of deep bitterness of life."[190] Thus, the question of suffering became a major component of Song's theology.[191]

Jesus, the Crucified People

These new tendencies in Song's theology gradually evolved from the mid-1970s on and corresponded to the new theological and missiological emphases that formally emerged in the CCA at Singapore 1973.[192] In his people-centered Christology in *Jesus, the Crucified People* (1990), Song brought these new elements together to elucidate his central theological theme, namely, the incarnation.

As noted above, Song considered suffering as the chief reality characteristic of the history of Asian people. Suffering was a fruit of human sin, which he defined in terms of human destructiveness as follows:

> It is a demonic power hidden in the depths of human beings and lurking in the abyss of human community, biding its time to strike and to destroy. For its work of destruction it employs all means at its disposal—political, military, economic, ideological, even religious. Sin is human power turned demonic, inflicting pain, terror, and death on human persons and tearing apart human community.[193]

The power of sin was pervasive. No religion was exempted from it. While Song admitted that God was at work in any religions, he also insisted that the destructive power of sin was also at work among them.[194] All religions could and, in fact, had often become oppressive in the course of their history, perpetuating a no longer credible tradition, seeking to halt the effort

---

190. Song, *Theology from the Womb of Asia*, 74.

191. For his emphasis on suffering, Song was indebted to Bonhoeffer, Jürgen Moltmann, the Japanese theologian Kazo Kitamori, Buddhism, and the Chinese concept of *thun-ai* or "pain-love." (Choan-Seng Song, "Asia in Suffering and Hope," in *Asian Theological Reflections on Suffering and Hope*, ed. Yap Kim Hao [Singapore: Christian Conference of Asia, 1977], 51–52; idem, *Third-Eye Theology*, 75–79, 83–88, 119–41, 181–85; idem, *Compassionate God*, 9; idem, "Role of Christology," 29).

192. See pp. 75–77 above.

193. Song, *Jesus, the Crucified People*, 21.

194. Ibid., 24. As for God's presence in non-biblical religions, Song wrote that this question could be dealt with in terms of God's reign among them, and that "a theology of religions," therefore, had "to be a theology of God's reign." To him, the essence of God's reign was grace, and the manifestation of God's grace could be found in the figures, such as *Jizo Bosatsu* or the Buddhist guardian of children in Japanese Buddhism (Choan-Seng Song, "The Power of God's Grace in the World of Religions," *Ecumenical Review* 39 [January 1987]: 54–55).

to change, and demanding the submission to the God who was invoked to justify the status quo and human suffering. Therefore, Song wrote: "religion with its elaborate rituals, doctrinal systems, and hierarchical structures, can become a barrier that separates people from God."[195]

In his criticism of religion, Song particularly pointed out the problem of the idea that any misfortune was a result of God's punishment for human sin. To him, this idea, or the "doctrine of retribution" as he called it, was "deeply rooted in human religious consciousness" and could distort "the moral power at work in human community." The idea could also distort God, turning God "into a monster, an executioner, an avenger."[196] Song called this false God the "God of retribution" and distinguished it from the true God or "God in God's own self."[197] In his mind, the God of retribution was a God created by humans, in particular by the oppressive religious system that arose from the distorted moral power of human beings. The God in God's own self was, in contrast, the "Abba-God" of Jesus—the God of love who is with people, listening and responding to their cries and remembering their pains and sufferings. To Song, Jesus' earthly ministry was to carry out the mission of his Abba-God to unmask the cruelty and lie of the God of retribution in solidarity with the underprivileged people victimized in the name of this false God.[198]

Song's reflection on the Abba-God was based on his view of God's knowability through the humanity of Jesus shared by the rest of humankind and, therefore, focused on understanding Jesus as a human being. Because God became incarnate in Jesus of Nazareth, God was to be known through the life and work of Jesus who lived and ministered among the suffering people. To Song, however, the "gold-crowned Jesus" in the Korean Catholic poet Kim Chi Ha's play could not speak out without the search by "Leper" and "Beggar" for the real Jesus; similarly, the humanity of Jesus could not be understood apart from people's search for meaning amid their suffering because the thick garment of theological interpretations produced by the religious elite in the West had hidden the real Jesus deeply

---

195. Song, *Jesus and the Reign of God*, 22.

196. Song, *Jesus, the Crucified People*, 47–49.

197. Ibid., 59.

198. Ibid., 58–59, 71–73. The distinction of these two Gods arose from Song's basic view of religion. For him, the essential question regarding religion was. "Does it or does it not show to the world and to the people the true face of the God who forgives, comforts, and makes live, the face of God who is love, justice, and freedom?" (Song, *Jesus and the Reign of God*, 35). He applied this criterion not only to Christianity but also other Asian religions.

under itself for centuries.[199] Furthermore, since suffering was the essence of human existence, Jesus' humanity was fully revealed only in his extreme physical agony on the cross.[200] Jesus as a human being as well as the symbolic meaning of his cross could be, therefore, grasped only through relating them to the suffering people's lives and search for meaning in the midst of their agonies and struggle for freedom and dignity.[201]

Thus, Song declared: *"People are now clues to who the real Jesus is,"* and called such an approach to Christology "people hermeneutic."[202] As we have already seen, in *The Compassionate God*, Song had transposed God's redemptive presence from the Jewish religious establishment to the suffering people or "little suffering messiahs" in the world.[203] His attempt was now to understand Jesus from the perspective of these "little suffering messiahs" in Asia. From such a perspective, he interpreted the meaning of the cross as follows:

> The cross is the suffering of Jesus of Nazareth and it is the suffering of humanity. The cross means human beings rejecting human beings. It shows how human beings, in the grips of demonic powers, are inflicting injustice on each other, tearing each other apart, destroying each other. The cross is the plot of an organized religion blinded by its own power and orthodoxy and unable to tolerate those deeply and sincerely religious persons eager to restore faith in the God of love and mercy. And the cross discloses the complicity of sociopolitical powers ready to defend their self-interest at any cost, even at the expense of the law, even at the cost of the lives of those God-inspired persons faithful to the truth and devoted to love for others. . . . The cross, in short, is human violence and not divine violence.[204]

Song felt that the traditional "theological" interpretation of the cross was to play down the physical reality of the cross and the cruelty committed by humans in the name of the false God and merely beautify the cross, removing "the sting of pain and death" from it. He also felt that the traditional view ignored the Abba-God's incapability of demanding from humans the kind of physical agony Jesus experienced on the cross. Therefore, Song

---

199. C. S. Song, "Oh, Jesus, Here with Us!" *Ecumenical Review* 35 (1983): 59–74. This article was later revised and published as "Prologue" of his *Jesus, the Crucified People*, 1–14.

200. Song, *Jesus, the Crucified People*, 71.

201. Ibid., 61.

202. Ibid., 12.

203. Song, *Compassionate God*, 108. See p. 175 above.

204. Song, *Jesus, the Crucified People*, 99.

rejected the traditional explanation of the crucifixion as Jesus' voluntary act in obedience to God or as the Son being forsaken by the Father for the sins of the world.[205]

What then happened to the Abba-God when Jesus was crucified in the midst of the human rebellion in the name of the false God if this God of love was incapable of placing Jesus on the cross? According to Song, the Abba-God was stunned into silence by inhumanity inflicted on Jesus on the cross.[206] In a brief moment during this divine silence, Jesus suspected out of agony if his God might not actually be the God of retribution rather than the God of love, and cried: "My God, my God, why have you forsaken me?" (Mark 15:34 NRSV). In this experience of "abandonment by God in the depths of suffering," Jesus was "most fully human," sharing the experience of God's silence with numerous people in history.[207] This cry of Jesus' was, thus, people's cries coming from all parts of God's creation. Jesus' cry was joined and reinforced by all their cries.[208]

The silence of Jesus' God was, however, the silence out of *karuna* or compassion. Using the Buddhist imagery, Song compared it to the silence in a womb in which *karuna* struggled "to empower the embryo of life for the day of fulfillment."[209] In the silence, God's *karuna* was "empowering him [i.e., Jesus] during the last moments of his life and nourishing him for the resurrection of a new life from the tomb." Thus, in his last cry addressed to his Abba-God, "Father, into your hands I commend my spirit" (Luke 23:46 NRSV), Jesus again found himself intimately embraced by God's *karuna*, thereby overcoming the God of retribution ultimately. In this Jesus' last cry too, Song heard the cries of numerous suffering people, joining and reinforcing Jesus' cry. God's silence was broken not simply by Jesus' cry but by people's cries. Thus, Song wrote: "God's voice does not

---

205. Ibid., 59, 61.
206. Ibid., 111–16.
207. Ibid., 68–69, 71.
208. Ibid., 121.

209. *Karuna* is a Sanskrit word for compassion. Buddhism, particularly its Mahayana branch, considers compassion as one of the major virtues required from the *bodhisattvas*, that is, those who seek enlightenment (John Bowker, ed. *The Oxford Dictionary of World Religions*, [Oxford: Oxford University Press, 1997], s.v. "Karuṇā."). The "womb" or *garbha* in Sanskrit is a Mahayana symbol for the place in all living beings where the seed of the Buddhahood is believed to be conceived, nourished, and matured (Richard H. Robinson and Willard L. Johnson, *The Buddhist Religion: A Historical Introduction*, 4th ed., assisted by Sandra A. Wawrytko and Thanissaro Bhikkhu [Geoffrey DeGraff] [Belmont, Calif.: Wadsworth Publishing Company, 1997], 93–94).

come from heaven but from the earth. It is not communicated by angels in the sky but people in the streets and factories."[210]

Thus, in the crucified Jesus, Song saw people agonizing under the power of destruction, and in these people, he saw the crucified Jesus. Therefore, he said, Jesus was not the crucified God but "the crucified people."[211] Jesus was there wherever suffering people were throughout history. He was historical because people were historical. For Song, this Jesus who thus became incarnate among people was the Jesus who was "risen as the historical Christ."[212] This Jesus or "Jesus-Christ" did not need to be Jesus of Nazareth. He could be a man, a woman, a child, a Japanese, an Indian, a Chinese, and so forth. The suffering and death of such an individual Jesus-Christ or little suffering messiah had the redemptive power that could overcome the sin and empower human beings to live in the presence of suffering, pain, and death in anticipation of a full life in God.[213] Therefore, Song wrote:

> The reign of God, according to Jesus, is not an institution but people—people with dignity as human beings regardless of their backgrounds and entitled to freedom and justice, people affirming their full humanity and refusing to accept the conditions that belittle that humanity. The reign of God creates a new consciousness in them, emboldens them to claim to be full members of human community irrespective of their backgrounds and status, and enables them to experience God as a God who affirms them and shares their concerns and struggles.[214]

Thus, Song's reflection on God's direct presence in the world brought him to situate this presence among people. To him, God was there wherever and whenever people suffer and aspire for freedom, justice, and dignity. Their suffering and aspiration were as ancient and universal as people themselves were. Therefore, God's redemptive presence in the non-biblical world like Asia was also ancient and known by the existence of people's suffering and hope. In this way, Song provided Christians in Asia with a

---

210. Song, *Jesus, the Crucified People*, 119–22.
211. Ibid., 215.
212. Ibid., 215–17.
213. Ibid., 232. In his *The Tears of Lady Meng*, Song expressed this view as follows: "The critical point to remember is that powerlessness can transform into powerfulness through the power of tears, that is, the power of love and truth. And the reverse can also be true. Powerfulness, when confronted by the power of tears, that is, the power of love and truth, can turn into powerlessness" (*Tears of Lady Meng*, 59).
214. Song, *Jesus and the Reign of God*, 44.

new theological framework for the work of discernment of, and response to, God's mission at work in the history of the Asian world.

Conclusion

Song regarded his theology as a theology from an Asian perspective. His works, however, display a strong influence of the Western mode of thinking on him. As a result, he has sometimes been criticized for the "Westernness" of his "Asian" theology. Sheldon Sawatzky, for instance, wrote:

> Those who look to Song for an authentic, contextualized, Asian Christian theology will be disappointed. Song's thought largely reflects liberal theological trends of the West, and is steeped in Western categories. . . . [O]ne gets the impression that it has all been said before, only this time Western theology is reiterated by an Asian.[215]

As Moore rightly pointed out, this criticism is strong and would, if valid, "call into question the very identity of Song's theology."[216]

The influence of the West on Song was indeed inescapable and understandable, for he received theological education exclusively in the West and has spent most of his life in the West. As Moore suggested, however, one has to ask whether there exists pristine, purely Asian categories in today's multicultural and multilingual world.[217] In fact, the West has exercised a powerful influence on the intellectual and political life of Chinese society since the nineteenth century, and non-Christian intellectuals in postwar Taiwan, such as Hu Shih and Song's undergraduate mentor Thomé H. Fang, came under this influence in various degrees, no matter whether modernists or traditionalists.[218]

The Westernness of Song's thinking does not, therefore, disqualify him as an advocate of Asian theology. What is important is rather the fact that Song as an Asian theologian tirelessly strove to free himself from cap-

---

215. Sheldon Sawatzky, "Review and Critique of C. S. Song's Theology of Mission," *Taiwan Journal of Theology* 4 (March 1982): 245. See also G. R. Singh, Review of *Christian Mission in Reconstruction: An Asian Analysis*, by Choan-Seng Song, in *Religion and Society* 23 (June 1976): 117.

216. Moore, "Choan-Seng Song's Theology," 462.

217. Ibid., 463.

218. Fang wrote of himself: "I am a Confucian by family tradition; a Taoist by temperament; a Buddhist by religious inspiration; moreover I am a Westerner by training" (Thomé H. Fang, *Chinese Philosophy: Its Spirit and Its Development* [Taipei, Taiwan: Linking Publishing,1981], 525, quoted in Federschmidt, *Theologie*, 76).

tivity to Western theology and relate Christian theology to the history and cultures of peoples in Asia. This point is congruous with our observation made in the first chapter that contextual theology in Asia can be seen as an integrative discourse that tries to bridge and reconcile two conflicting legitimations, Asian and Christian. Song's theological construction provides us with an excellent example for such integrative discourse.

Furthermore, it is important to situate Song in the context of the overseas Taiwanese communities and their network. The Chinese emigration was already afoot in the ninth century during the T'ang dynasty, and overseas Chinese communities existed in various parts of Asia for centuries. In the nineteenth century, the number of Chinese emigrants increased dramatically, and their presence is today found in every corner of the world.[219] These emigrants are called *hua ch'iao* or overseas Chinese.[220] Their communities have played a crucial role in the history of modern China; particularly, they have often provided the politically-minded Chinese people with bases for their activities for revolution and democratization from the late-nineteenth century on.

Historically speaking, overseas Taiwanese communities should be understood against the background of this larger overseas Chinese presence. During the Japanese period, the majority of overseas Taiwanese lived in Japan, and Tokyo was the center of Taiwanese political activism. After the February 28 Incident, tens of thousands of people fled the island to escape the Nationalist "White Terror." Japan first provided them with a refuge and became the center of the Taiwanese movement for independence. In the 1950s, Taiwanese communities also grew in Europe and the Americas. As a result, the center of Taiwanese anti-Nationalist activism gradually moved from Japan to the United States, where the World United Formosans for Independence (WUFI) was organized in 1970.[221] Thus, as Mark J. Cohen

---

219. Chûkun Yû, *Kakyo* [Overseas Chinese] (Tokyo: Kodansha, Kodansha Gendai Shinsho, 1990), 30–38; J. Harry Haines, *Chinese of the Diaspora*, Research Pamphlets No. 14 (London: Edinburgh House Press for the World Council of Churches Commission on World Mission and Evangelism, 1965), 9–11.

220. Republic of China Government Information Office, "Foreign Relations," in *The Republic of China Yearbook 1998* [yearbook on-line], available from http://www.gio.gov.tw/info/yb97/html/ch9.htm, Internet, accessed 12 October 1998.

221. Cohen, *Taiwan at the Crossroads*, 279–306; O and Munakata, *Atarashii Taiwan*, 195–98; Ito, *Taiwan*, 160–62. In this junction, it is noteworthy that Song wrote in 1974: "The people of Taiwan in dispersion—this has been our lot for the past two decades" (Song, *Self-Determination*, 50). The word "dispersion" here suggests that Song's idea of redemption as disruption-dispersion somehow reflected the historical reality in which overseas Taiwanese communities existed.

wrote, "Taiwanese living outside the island have exerted an important influence on political life on Taiwan ever since" the Japanese period.[222]

Song's political commitment and theology must be seen in relation to this Taiwanese political activism abroad. Indeed, he did not attempt to build a "Taiwanese" contextual theology because his major theological interest was a reappraisal of the relationship between the Christian faith and Asian cultures as well as a construction of Christian theology based on this reappraisal. His approach to theology was, nevertheless, conditioned by the political awakening of the people of Taiwan, the impact of which was implicit and yet clearly discernible in Song's theological development from the 1970s on. In accordance with the political engagement of the PCT in the decade, Song initially understood Christian mission as the presence in society of the chosen minority who was to witness the ultimate reconciliation and hope in solidarity with the suffering of the rest of humanity. The emphasis on creation affirming the theological significance of people's cultures and history was to affirm the humanity and dignity of the people of Taiwan who had been deprived of their own culture and history by the Japanese and the Nationalist regimes. The tireless criticism of the religio-political power reflected his opposition against the Nationalist regime. Finally, his concentration on the suffering and hope of people oppressed and marginalized by the religio-political establishment was the expression of his solidarity with the people of Taiwan. These motifs doubtlessly expressed his personal cry, anger, and hope as a Taiwanese—the cry for freedom, justice, and equality; the anger towards the oppressive Nationalist regime and the world that continued ignoring the predicament surrounding his compatriots; and the hope for a free and independent Taiwan. Therefore, one has to conclude that Song's theology is truly Asian even though he has spent most of his life in the West.

This historical context of Song's theology made his this-worldly holiness radical. Indeed, he began his missiological reflection and the formulation of the idea of God's this-worldly presence under the influence of the world-centric *missio Dei* in the West; his writings do not contain much evidence that he was directly indebted to the preceding ecumenical discussions in Asia. Inspired by the world-centric *missio Dei*, however, he rejected the concept of salvation history and broke with the traditional identification of God's salvation with the Christian Church and Western civilization. This break also meant turning away from relating God's work in history with Westernization, modernization, and secularization. For Song, therefore, God's this-worldly presence was not confined merely

222. Cohen, *Taiwan at the Crossroads*, 279.

to the modernizing or modernized segment of traditional society, such as reform movements of traditional religions and secular political movements. Inspired by liberation theology and particularly *minjung* theology, he rather affirmed that God as the source of hope and awakening was directly present among those who suffered most as victims of history—even among those who had never been touched by these modern movements led by the awakened intellectuals. He even reversed the epistemological order and affirmed that the presence of the suffering and hoping people was the clue for recognizing God redemptively at work throughout human history.

This fact, however, did not mean a refusal of modernity. Song's strong concern for freedom, justice, and political change displays his fundamental preference for modernity. The spirit of modernity expressly manifested itself in his theological ideas, such as disruption, dispersion, and transposition. While maintaining this fundamental orientation, he, nonetheless, identified himself with the thus far submerged strata in the Asian world, recognizing the suffering and hope of people as the marks that would endow their lives with the true meaning and identity throughout history. Thus, the idea of God's this-worldly presence enabled Song to overcome the incapacity of traditional Christian theology for relating itself to Asia and develop a theology based on the primordial identification with "disfavored strata and groups" in Asian society.

CHAPTER 6

Conclusion

From our study on this-worldly holiness in the ecumenical movement in Asia with special concentration on Thomas and Song, we may conclude that ecumenism in Asia, institutionalized into the EACC/CCA, has always been characterized by a remarkable degree of this-worldly emphasis since the earliest period. At the core of such an emphasis, one can find the affirmation of God's this-worldly presence which views God's saving activity as operating on the history of Asian nations and peoples independently of Israel and the Christian Church. The *missio Dei* concept that has gained wide circulation among Asian Christians since the mid-1960s should primarily be seen as an expression of this emphasis peculiar to ecumenism in Asia. Our study also demonstrated that the affirmation of God's this-worldly presence was central both to Thomas and Song in their intellectual endeavors to articulate Christian theology relevant to the cultural, social, and political reality of the Asian world.

As early as 1949, the participants in the first Asian ecumenical meeting held in Bangkok conceived of God as the sovereign of all realms of life who was judgingly and redeemingly at work in the midst of the Asian revolution and made the idea of God's this-worldly presence the starting point for Christian mission in Asia. The subsequent meetings of the EACC/CCA repeatedly affirmed this idea and elaborated a Christian theology of social and political participation based on this understanding of the relationship between God and the world. The idea was thus both a product of, and the basis for, the tireless intellectual efforts by the Christian leaders in Asia to relate their religious belief and commitment inherited from the West to the reality and history of Asia. With the help of this idea, these leaders tried to make sense of the Christian faith and life in the world rooted in cultures and religions quite different from the Western ones. For the churches in Asia, the idea of God's this-worldly presence thus served as the cardinal symbolism in their efforts to reconcile and integrate the conflicting legitimations, Christian and Asian, in modernizing societies in Asia.

Initially, the Asian Christians sought to situate God's saving presence in the midst of the social revolution taking place in postwar Asia, that is, nation-building accompanied with rapid modernization projects. From the mid-1960s on, however, they gradually turned away from this position; the degeneration of nationalism and the increasing socio-political conflicts within the new nations drove them to rethink their ideological position and relocate the locus for God's presence into the struggle of the oppressed and poor people for freedom, justice, and dignity. In the 1970s, the liberation motif increasingly won popularity in the churches in Asia just as in other parts of the Third World. By the end of the 1980s, the ecumenical leaders in Asia developed an inclusive people-centered theology that affirmed that all the people of Asia were the people of God regardless of their religious affiliations.

Thomas's and Song's thinking can be compared, above all, against this development of the ecumenical movement in postwar Asia. Thomas primarily belonged to the first generation of the movement, though he also made a significant contribution to the shift in the mid-1960s. As early as the late 1930s, he expressed the idea of God's this-worldly presence during his commitment to the YCCA in Kerala. Though the idea was once suppressed under the influence of Neo-orthodoxy, it resurfaced after the shift in his ideological and theological position in 1948 and developed into the core of his thinking. Because of his deep involvement in the formation of the EACC and the formulation of its thinking, his intense intellectual struggle in search of an ideological and theological basis for the Christian participation in the Asian revolution had a direct and profound impact on Asian ecumenical thinking. The idea of God's this-worldly presence as formulated by him, subsequently, became the foundation of the approach of the EACC/CCA to mission and theology.

Song, in contrast, belonged to the younger generation of Christians who assumed the leadership of ecumenism in Asia in the 1970s. Many of these Christians were influenced by the new missiological trend that emerged in the WCC in the 1960s, that is, the world-centric theology of *missio Dei* to which this-worldly holiness in the EACC greatly contributed. These Christians widely accepted the expression "God's mission" and vigorously used this concept to widen the scope of God's redemption far beyond the walls of the Church and place the people of Asia in direct relationship with God's redemptive work. Song was one of the theologians who most tirelessly and constantly pursued theological engagement in this direction. Thus, the difference between Thomas and Song can be viewed as generational.

The difference between Thomas and Song is, however, more than generational. Their backgrounds also significantly differed from each other. Thomas was born and grew up in the princely state of Travancore, part of today's Kerala, in British India. Despite his lifelong commitment to the Mar Thoma Syrian Church and the worldwide ecumenical movement, Thomas was neither an ordained minister nor a professionally trained theologian. He majored in chemistry at college and never received a formal theological education except for the one-year study at Union Theological Seminary in New York in his late thirties. As a theologian, he was self-taught. Raised in the social evangelical piety of the Mar Thoma Church, he began his life as a Christian thinker with involvement in Christian political activism in Kerala prior to India's Independence. Kerala was ideologically dominated by Gandhism and Communism, and his dialogue with these ideologies drew him into the search for a political ideology adequate to the Christian participation in the revolutionary situation in modernizing India.

Theologically, Thomas came under the influence of Berdyaev and Western Neo-orthodox theologians in the 1940s through his personal readings. However, his concern for society and politics remained prominent and gave his theological reflections a highly anthropological inclination. Thus, whenever he addressed himself to a theological issue, he began his reflection not with the question of God but of humanity, more specifically with a sociological analysis of social, political, and cultural dimensions of human life.

After his ideological and theological shift in 1948, Thomas's anthropological tendency led him to go beyond Neo-orthodoxy in search of the theoretical basis for the Christian participation. Out of this search, he started formulating his "post-Barthian-Kraemerian" theology that emphasized the immanence symbolically expressed by the idea of God's this-worldly presence. Under the influence of Berdyaev's personalism, as well as Devanandan's idea of new creation, Thomas developed his emphasis on humanity into the theological concept of new humanity in Christ. He argued that the new humanity in Christ was at work within the social revolution, creating newness in a traditional society, and, therefore, served as the key to the discernment of God's presence in the contemporary world.

Song was born and raised in Taiwan under Japanese rule. In contrast to Thomas, he became a well trained professional theologian. Having studied Chinese philosophy at National Taiwan University, he went to the West and received theological education with special emphasis on the Old Testament and systematic theology at some of the best theological institutes in Europe and North America. Then, he was engaged in theological education, teaching and later serving as principal at a Presbyterian seminary in Taiwan.

Unlike Thomas, who kept his residence in Kerala despite his worldwide activities, Song soon left Taiwan again and has lived in the West, mostly in the United States, till now partly because the political development in Taiwan did not allow him to return home for many years. His move to the West, however, did not mean that he cut himself off from the Taiwanese society; to the contrary, he maintained a close relationship with the overseas Taiwanese communities and their network and played a leading role in the political activity of overseas Taiwanese Christians.

In this connection, his affiliation with the Presbyterian Church in Taiwan (PCT) was important. Founded prior to the Japanese period, the PCT historically maintained the Taiwanese identity and was critical of the Nationalist government relocated from the Chinese mainland after the Communist victory in the civil war. In the 1970s, the PCT led the political awakening of the Taiwanese people against the Nationalist regime. As a Presbyterian, Song also involved himself in the anti-Nationalist activity as a leader of the overseas Taiwanese Christian movement for Taiwan's self-determination.

As a systematic theologian, Song's chief concern was primarily "theological" in contrast to Thomas's anthropological one. Initially, he was heavily influenced by Neo-orthodoxy, particularly Barth and Tillich. He was, however, conscious of the distance between Western theology and the reality of Asia and became interested mainly in the construction of a theology capable of presenting the Gospel in relation to the cultures and history of the Asian world, interpreting the latter in light of God's redemption. Unlike Thomas's, Song's reflections did not usually go into the phenomenological analysis of social and cultural phenomena; the questions he raised and tried to answer regarding these phenomena were always related to their theological significance.

In his reflections, Song constantly went back to the Bible, particularly the Old Testament, and tried to ground his arguments on interpretations of the scriptural narratives. He was also inspired by many biblical and systematic theologians both in the West and Asia. Among others, the world-centric *missio Dei* concept developed in the West in the 1960s was important. Relating this concept to the incarnation, Song viewed the *missio Dei* as God's direct engagement with the world even outside the history of Israel and the Christian Church. Understood in this way, the *missio Dei* concept enabled him to link God's redemption directly to the history of Asia, particularly the history of the suffering people in Asia. Aided further by his interaction with the emerging contextual theologies in Asia, such as *minjung* theology, Song gradually developed a theology reconstructed from the perspective of the people of Asia rather than traditional Western theology.

The difference in Thomas's and Song's upbringings made their stances toward the West also different. Due to his deep immersion in Western theological tradition, Song's theological effort was motivated by his personal desire to free himself from the captivity to the West and bridge the intellectual chasm created by education between his theological mind and his own cultural heritage. As a result, Song was very critical of the West to the extent that the readers of his writings may even want to call into question the fairness of his verdicts on the problems the West allegedly created in the churches in Asia. Indeed, he did not reject Western theological tradition as a whole; he often looked for supports for his arguments in the works of Western theologians. The criticism of the West was, nonetheless, central to his thinking. As he continued his reflection, he narrowed the target of his criticism to the ethnocentric identification of salvation with the history of Israel and the Christian Church and came to consider the concept of salvation history as the modern expression of this identification. Thus, with the rejection of salvation history, he embarked on the reconstruction of theology based on the world-centric *missio Dei* that viewed the entire creation directly under God's saving activity.

Compared to Song's, Thomas's stance toward the West was more favorable and yet dialectical. While Taiwan was never ruled by the Western power except for the brief Dutch period in the seventeenth century, India came under the colonial rule of powerful Western nations for a sustained period. The people of India not only experienced the evils of Western colonialism but also became firsthand witnesses to the creative impact of the West that broke down the rigidity of traditional social systems and produced among people's minds the intense urge for a free, just, and humane society.

While critical of the evils of Western colonialism, as well as the missionary movement accompanied by it, Thomas was well aware of this creative aspect of the Western impact. In his youth, he was personally involved in the ideological fermentation of the Indian movement for independence and nation-building and gained profound intellectual inspiration from the movement. He was also well acquainted with the reform movements of traditional religions in India. These movements were deeply indebted to Western influence. Above all, his own Mar Thoma Church was a product of the Indian response to the Western ethos and worldview. His reflections constantly touched the question of newness the Western impact had produced in Asia. Thus, Thomas neither negated nor dismissed the West; rather, he critically built his thinking on the dialectical evaluation of the historical significance of the Western impact.

The difference between Thomas and Song in their attitudes toward the West resulted in their different approaches to God's this-worldly presence. The affirmation that God is at work in human history led both of them to a reappraisal of the doctrine of creation for the purpose of shedding a more favorable light on peoples and cultures in Asia than Western theologians did. Consequently, both Thomas and Song affirmed that God's redemptive activity extends to the entire creation, including the realms left outside the mediation of Israel and the Church. This affirmation was expressed by Thomas with the concept of cosmic redemption and by Song with his emphasis on the directness of God's relationship to the entire creation.

Once they affirmed the cosmic nature of God's redemption, they were confronted by the question of discernment of God's presence in the world. To respond to this question, Thomas proceeded with his emphasis on humanity. According to him, the essence of human personality was creative freedom in the communion with God and neighbors. Redemption was the new creation, that is, the ultimate restoration of humanity into human personality as created by God. In Jesus Christ, however, God offered to us this eschatological reality here and now. Jesus Christ was the New Humanity, and God in Christ was at work in today's world, unleashing human creativity and increasing human freedom and dignity. Thus, Thomas attributed a special theological significance to the newness emerging in Asia through the social revolution produced by the Western impact and viewed religious and secular movements for social renewal and humanization as the signs of God's redemptive presence in the world.

While Thomas considered redemption as the eschatological reality of new creation at work here and now in the creation, Song interpreted creation itself as redemption. For Song, creation was nothing but God's redemptive intervention in history that brought about a radically new reality to the world dominated by destructive powers. Creation was, therefore, nothing but God's new creation that disrupts the continuity of human history and changes its course. God's interventions in the history of Israel occurred as the repeated disruptions of Jewish ethnocentrism. The incarnation in Jesus Christ was God's final rejection of Jewish ethnocentrism. However, the incarnation was also the rejection of the monopoly claim of God and salvation by any established religions; it was, furthermore, a transposition of God's redemptive presence into the suffering people in the world. Thus, the incarnation revealed God as the God of love who is always with the downtrodden and disfavored, affirming their full humanity and creating among them the aspiration for freedom, justice, and dignity.

Such an approach of Song's to this-worldly holiness was related with his critical stance toward the established religious tradition in the West transplanted also to Asia by missionaries. While he was involved in the Taiwanese struggle against the Nationalist regime, this stance developed into criticism of the political and religious establishment in general. His solidarity with the silenced majority in Taiwan also changed into solidarity with the suffering people in the world, in particular in Asia. Song thus tried to relate God's presence to the suffering and aspiration of the oppressed majority throughout history rather than the newness emerging in a modernizing society.

Despite these various differences, Thomas and Song shared a common orientation toward modernity. In Thomas, this orientation is evident because he considered the newness emerging in society as crucial to the mission of the Church. Song, in contrast, considered the suffering people throughout history as the locus for God's presence. However, his view of redemption as God's radical interruption in history producing a qualitative change in human life definitely pointed to his preference for modernity. Both Thomas and Song constantly advocated the renewal of society, affirming and siding with the struggle for freedom and justice in Asian nations and peoples.

We can also compare our two theologians in relation to the modes of the Christian primordial identification with the attempts in society at large to respond to the modern dilemma caused by the conflict between identity and change. In the first chapter, I distinguished three types of identification: 1) the identification with the traditional identity of their society; 2) the identification with the modernization project; and 3) the identification with "disfavored strata and groups." Prior to India's Independence, Thomas was among those young Christians who, whether Gandhian or Marxist, identified themselves with the cause of the colonized, that is, the "disfavored strata and groups" in the land ruled by the Western colonial power. In the postwar period, he shifted his identification to support the modernization project of nation-building led by the nationalist elite in a new independent nation in Asia. When nationalism began to manifest signs of degeneration in the mid-1960s, he swiftly shifted his identification back to solidarity with the "disfavored strata and groups"—this time, however, with the poor and oppressed struggling for the structural transformation of society within a new nation as well as in international life.

In Song's case, his position also steadily moved from the beginning of the 1970s on toward the identification with "disfavored strata and groups" in the Asian world as he involved himself in the anti-Nationalist struggle of the people of Taiwan for freedom and justice.

All that was just said questions our previous observations regarding the concept of contextualization. In the first chapter, we followed the reasoning made by the TEF and Shoki Coe for their proposal to replace "indigenization" with "contextualization" and wrote that contextualization was, unlike indigenization, the idea that was primarily meant to designate the orientation toward modernity rather than tradition. After the survey on ecumenical thinking in Asia in the third chapter, we modified this view and concluded that the proposal of this concept was associated with the new orientation among Christians toward solidarity with the "disfavored strata and groups" in modern and modernizing society. The reason for the modification was the finding that the orientation toward modernity did exist among Asian Christians long before the term "contextualization" was proposed. This finding was further confirmed by our reflection on Thomas's thinking.

Our reflection on Thomas, however, has also made it clear that the Christian identification with "disfavored strata and groups" was not necessarily a new phenomenon that emerged in the 1970s; this type of identification did already exist among the Christians, including Thomas himself, who participated in the struggle of the colonized peoples against the colonial powers. The difference between the colonial and the post-colonial period may be found in the fact that the struggle of the disfavored people in a colonized society was directed against the foreign colonial powers, while their struggle in a new nation was directed against the ruling minority within the nation as well as the foreign neo-colonialist powers that gave backing to these national rulers.

We may, therefore, conclude that, when proposed in the early 1970s, the concept of contextualization indicated a new awareness among Christians of a need to identify themselves with "disfavored strata and groups" in a rather specific sense, that is, with the oppressed and poor within a society who suffered mostly from the growing internal conflicts the modernization process had created in many nations by the mid-1960s. Understood in this specific sense, the concept of contextualization obviously applies better to Song than to Thomas because Song's people-centered theology was shaped from the early 1970s onward out of his solidarity with those who suffer social discrimination and political oppression within their own society.

The comparison of Thomas and Song thus shows us that these two theologians significantly differ from one another in various aspects. They, nevertheless, shared commonly the basic belief that God is at work in the history of Asia with no mediation of the Church, and that the task of the Church is to discern this divine presence and respond faithfully to God's initiative to break down the rigidity and inhumanity of traditional society and bring about freedom, justice, hope, and reconciliation to the oppressed people in Asia. This fact points to the significance of the idea of God's this-worldly presence in the ecumenical movement in Asia. The idea has offered one common unifying vision to Asian Christians who have come from the region characterized by a tremendous cultural, ethnic, linguistic, social, and political diversity. The idea has helped them to see these diverse peoples and their lives under the sovereignty of one God who transcends their diversity and yet never dismisses it quickly. Thus, the idea has become so central to ecumenical thinking in Asia.

This conclusion, however, must be confirmed by further research that is beyond the scope of our study. Our scope has been confined to the period after the Second World War, particularly to the two figures who came from Kerala and Taiwan. We have touched the prewar period only insofar as it is related to their lives. Yet, as we have seen in the first chapter, Hans-Ruedi Weber pointed out that this-worldly holiness already existed among the early *samurai* converts of Japan and in the life of people like Cheng-ting Wang of China and K. T. Paul of India before the war. This observation raises a question that should be answered in a future study: In what way are these early Asian expressions of this-worldly holiness related to the development of the world-centric spirituality in postwar Asia?

Another question is, To what extent is this spirituality unique and indigenous to Asia? Where are its cultural roots? To answer this question, we probably need to look more closely into the interactions between Christianity and Asian cultures and religions. We also need to make a careful investigation into the interaction between social and mission thinking in the West prior to the emergence of the *missio Dei* thinking. In fact, Thomas's thinking displays certain affinities with the Social Gospel in North America and Christian Socialism in Europe. It may also be important to understand the role that the SCMs and the WSCF played in the dialogical interactions between Western and Asian Christians as well as between mission and social thinking. Certainly, one cannot easily dismiss the significance of the SCMs in the emergence of this-worldly holiness in Asia if one recalls that the YCCA of Kerala was formed at a SCM summer camp, and that Thomas first expressed the idea of God's this-worldly presence in his involvement in the YCCA.

Bibliography

Abbreviations Used in Bibliography

CCA   Christian Conference of Asia
CISRS Christian Institute for the Study of Religion and Society
CLS   Christian Literature Society
CTC   Commission on Theological Concerns
CWME   Commission on World Mission and Evangelism
DWME   Division of World Mission and Evangelism
EACC   East Asian Christian Conference
IMC   International Missionary Council
ISPCK Indian Society for Promoting Christian Knowledge
SPCK   Society for Promoting Christian Knkowledge
WCC   World Council of Churches

Aagaard, Johannes. "Some Main Trends in Modern Protestant Missiology." *Studia Theologica* 19 (1965) 238–59.

———. "Trends in Missiological Thinking during the Sixties." *International Review of Mission* 62 (1973) 8–25.

Abrecht, Paul. "The Development of Ecumenical Social Thought and Action." In *A History of the Ecumenical Movement.* 3rd ed. Vol. 2, *The Ecumenical Advance: 1948–1968,* edited by Harold E. Fey, 233–59. Geneva: WCC, 1993.

Ahn Byung Mu. "Jesus and the Minjung in the Gospel of Mark." In *Minjung Theology: People as the Subjects of History,* edited by Kim Yong Bock, 136–51. Singapore: CTC, CCA, 1981.

Allen, Roland. *The Spontaneous Expansion of the Church and the Causes Which Hinder It.* London: World Dominion, 1927.

Andersen, Wilhelm. *Towards a Theology of Mission: A Study of the Encounter between the Missionary Enterprise and the Church and its Theology.* IMC Research Pamphlet No. 2. London: SCM, 1955.

Anderson, Gerald A. "Introduction: The Theology of Mission among Protestants in the Twentieth Century." In *The Theology of the Christian Mission,* edited by Gerald A. Anderson, 3–16. New York: McGraw-Hill, 1961.

Ariarajah, S. Wesley. *Hindus and Christians: A Century of Protestant Ecumenical Thought.* Amsterdam: Editions Rodopi, 1991; Grand Rapids: Eerdmans, 1991.

"Asian Missions." In *The Christian Community within the Human Community: Containing Statements from the Bangkok Assembly of the EACC, Feb–March 1964,* Minutes, Part 2, 59–70. Bangalore: CLS, 1964.

Azariah, M. *Mission in Christ's Way in India Today.* Madras: CLS for the Church of South India, 1989.

Barrett, David B., ed. *World Christian Encyclopedia: A Comparative Study of Churches and Religions in the Modern World, AD 1900–2000*. Oxford: Oxford University Press, 1982.

Bassham, Rodger C. *Mission Theology: 1948–1975, Years of Worldwide Creative Tension Ecumenical, Evangelical, and Roman Catholic*. Pasadena, CA: William Carey Library, 1979.

———. "Seeking a Deeper Theological Basis for Mission." *International Review of Mission* 67 (1978) 329–37.

Bayly, Susan. *Saints, Goddesses and Kings: Muslims and Christians in South Indian Society 1700–1900*. Cambridge: Cambridge University Press, 1989.

Beaver, R. Pierce. "Rufus Anderson's Missionary Principles." In *Christusprediking: studiën op het terrien van de zendingswetenschap gewijd aan de nagedachtenis van Professor Dr. Johan Herman Bavinck*, 43–62. Kampen: Kok, 1965.

Bellah, Robert N. *Beyond Belief: Essays on Religion in a Post-Traditionalist World*. New York: Harper & Row, 1970; reprint, Berkeley and Los Angeles: University of California Press, 1991.

———. "Epilogue: Religion and Progress in Modern Asia." In *Religion and Progress in Modern Asia*, edited by Robert N. Bellah, 168–229. New York: Free, 1965; London: Collier-Macmillan, 1965.

———. "Ienaga Saburo and the Search for Meaning in Modern Japan." In *Changing Japanese Attitudes Toward Modernization*, edited by Marius B. Jansen, 369–423. Princeton, NJ: Princeton University Press, 1965.

Berdyaev, Nicolas. *The Beginning and the End*. London: Geoffrey Bles, 1953.

———. *The Destiny of Man*. Translated from the Russian by Natalie Duddington. London: Geoffrey Bles, 1937.

Berger, Peter L. *The Sacred Canopy: Elements of a Sociological Theory of Religion*. Garden City, NY: Doubleday, 1967; reprint, New York: Anchor, Doubleday, 1990.

Berger, Peter L., and Thomas Luckmann, *The Social Construction of Reality: A Treatise in the Sociology of Knowledge*. Garden City, NY: Doubleday, 1966; reprint, New York: Anchor, Doubleday, 1989.

Bevans, Stephen B. *Models of Contextual Theology*. Maryknoll, NY: Orbis, 1992.

Bonhoeffer, Dietrich. *Letters and Papers from Prison*. Edited by Eberhard Bethge. Enlarged edition. New York: Macmillan, 1972.

———. *Widerstand und Ergebung: Briefe und Aufzeichnungen aus der Haft*. Edited by Eberhard Bethge. Gütersloh, Germany: Gütersloher Verlagshaus Mohn, 1985.

Bosch, David J. *Transforming Mission: Paradigm Shifts in Theology of Mission*. Maryknoll, NY: Orbis, 1991.

Bottomore, Tom. *Élites and Society*. 2d ed. London: Routledge, 1993.

Bowker, John, ed. *The Oxford Dictionary of World Religions*. Oxford: Oxford University Press, 1997. s.v. "Karunā."

Boyd, Robin. *An Introduction to Indian Christian Theology*. Rev. ed. Delhi: ISPCK, 1989.

Bria, Ion. *The Sense of Ecumenical Tradition: The Ecumenical Witness and Vision of the Orthodox*. Geneva: WCC, 1991.

"The Calling of the Church to Mission and to Unity." *Ecumenical Review* 4 (October 1951) 66–71.

Carino, Feliciano V. "Partnership in Obedience." *International Review of Mission* 67 (July 1978) 316–28.

Castro, Emilio. "Bangkok, the New Opportunity." *International Review of Mission* 62 (April 1973) 136–43.

———. *Sent Free: Mission and Unity in the Perspective of the Kingdom*. Grand Rapids: Eerdmans, 1985.

Chander, N. Jose. "Political Culture." In *Dynamics of State Politics: Kerala*, edited by N. Jose Chander, 13–30. New Delhi: Sterling, 1986.

Chatterji, Saral K. "Introduction." In *The Asian Meaning of Modernization: East Asia Christian Conference Studies*, edited by Saral K. Chatterji, 1–18. Delhi: Indian Society for Promoting Christian Knowledge, CLS, and Lucknow Publishing House for the EACC, 1972.

Chi Myong-Kwan, "Theological Development in Korea." *International Review of Mission* 74 (1985) 73–79.

The Christian Community within the Human Community: Containing Statements from the Bangkok Assembly of the EACC, Feb–March 1964. Minutes. Part 2. Bangalore: CLS, 1964.

Christian Conference of Asia, Fifth Assembly, 6–12 June 1973, Singapore. Bangkok: CCA, 1973.

The Christian Prospect in Eastern Asia: Papers and Minutes of the Eastern Asia Christian Conference, Bangkok, December 3–11, 1949. New York: Friendship Press for the IMC and the WCC, 1950.

Chung, Archie Lee Chi. "Cross-Textual Hermeneutics in Asian Context." *PTCA Bulletin* 5, no. 1 (1992) 5. Quoted in R. S. Sugirtharajah, "Introduction," in *Frontiers in Asian Christian Theology: Emerging Trends*, edited by R. S. Sugirtharajah, 4. Maryknoll, NY: Orbis, 1994.

The Church for Others and the Church for the World: A Quest for Structures for Missionary Congregations, Final Report of the Western European Working Group and North American Working Group of the Department on Studies in Evangelism. Geneva: WCC, 1968.

"The Church in Social and Political Life." In *The Christian Prospect in Eastern Asia: Papers and Minutes of the Eastern Asia Christian Conference, Bangkok, December 3–11, 1949*, 114–17. New York: Friendship Press for the IMC and the WCC, 1950.

"Church Renewed in Mission: Report of Section III of the Bangkok Conference." *International Review of Mission* 62 (April 1973) 216–23.

Coe, Shoki. "Across the Frontiers: Text and Context of Mission." In *Christian Action in the Asian Struggle*, 70–80. Singapore: CCA, [1973?].

———. "In Search of Renewal in Theological Education." *Theological Education* 9 (Summer 1973) 233–43.

Cohen, Mark J. *Taiwan at the Crossroads: Human Rights, Political Development and Social Change on the Beautiful Island*. Washington, DC: Asia Resource Center, 1991.

Committee on Research in Foreign Missions, Division of Foreign Missions and the Central Department of Research and Survey, National Council of the Churches of Christ in the U.S.A. "The Missionary Obligation of the Church: Why Missions?" Report of Commission I on the Biblical and Theological Basis of Missions. 26 February 1952. Mimeographed.

The Common Evangelistic Task of the Churches in East Asia (Papers and Minutes of the East Asia Christian Conference) Prapat, Indonesia, March 17–26, 1957. n.p.: EACC, [1957?].

Cone, James H. *A Black Theology of Liberation*. C. Eric Lincoln Series in Black Religion. Philadelphia: Lippincott, [1970].

Confessing the Faith in Asia Today: Statement Issued by the Consultation Convened by the East Asia Christian Conference and Held in Hong Kong, October 26–November 3, 1966. Redfern, Australia: Epworth, 1967.

The Constitution of the Presbyterian Church (U.S.A.). Part 1, *Book of Confessions.* New York: Office of the General Assembly, 1983.

Copper, John F. *Taiwan: Nation-State or Province?* Boulder, CO: Westview, 1990.

Costa, Ruy O. "Introduction: Inculturation, Indigenization, and Contextualization." In *One Faith, Many Cultures: Inculturation, Indigenization, and Contextualization,* edited by Ruy O. Costa, ix–xvii. Maryknoll, NY: Orbis, 1988; Cambridge, MA: Boston Theological Institute, 1988.

Costas, Orlando E. *Christ Outside the Gate: Mission Beyond Christendom.* Maryknoll, NY: Orbis, 1982.

Cox, Harvey. *The Secular City: Secularization and Urbanization in Theological Perspective.* New York: Macmillan, 1965.

Crim, Keith, Roger A. Bullard, and Larry D. Shinn, eds. *The Perennial Dictionary of World Religions.* 1st Harper & Row paperback ed. Nashville, TN: Abingdon, 1981; reprint, San Francisco: HarperCollins, 1989. s.v. "Ahimsa," by G. R. Welbon.

Cullmann, Oscar. *Christ and Time: The Primitive Christian Conception of Time and History.* Rev. ed. Translated by Floyd V. Filson. Philadelphia: Westminster, 1964.

"Culture and Identity: Report of Section I of the Bangkok Conference." *International Review of Mission* 62 (April 1973) 185–97.

Dalton, Dennis. *Mahatma Gandhi: Nonviolent Power in Action.* New York: Columbia University Press, 1993.

Daly, Mary. *Beyond God the Father: Toward a Philosophy of Women's Liberation.* Boston: Beacon, 1973.

Davies, J. G. *Worship and Mission.* London: SCM, 1966.

"Death of Leading Asian Ecumenist at Age of 80." *ENI Bulletin* (13 December 1996) 15–16.

"Declaration of Korean Theologians, October 13, 1984 Seoul, Korea." *East Asia Journal of Theology* 3 (1985) 290–92.

Devanandan, P. D. "The Bangkok Conference of East Asia Leaders: An Impression." *International Review of Missions* 39 (1950) 146–52.

———. "Called to Witness." In *Preparation for Dialogue: A Collection of Essays on Hinduism and Christianity in New India,* edited by Nalini Devanandan and M. M. Thomas, 179–93. Devanandan Memorial Volume No. 2. Bangalore, India: CISRS, 1964.

———. *Christian Concern in Hinduism.* With a foreword by S. Radhakrishnan. Bangalore, India: CISRS, 1961.

———. *I Will Lift Up Mine Eyes unto the Hills: Sermons and Bible Studies.* Edited by S. J. Samartha and Nalini Devanandan. Bangalore, India: CISRS, 1963.

———. *Preparation for Dialogue: A Collection of Essays on Hinduism and Christianity in New India.* Edited by Nalini Devanandan and M. M. Thomas. Devanandan Memorial Volume No. 2. Bangalore, India: CISRS, 1964.

Dickinson, Richard D. N. *Poor, Yet Making Many Rich: The Poor as Agents of Creative Justice.* Geneva: WCC, Commission on the Churches' Participation in Development, 1983.

Douglas, J. D., ed. *Proclaim Christ Until He Comes: Calling the Whole Church to Take the Whole Gospel to the Whole World, Lausanne II in Manila, International Congress on World Evangelization, 1989.* Minneapolis: World Wide Publication, 1990.

Durkheim, Emile. *On Morality and Society.* Edited by Robert N. Bellah. Chicago: University of Chicago Press, 1973.

Eagleson, John, and Philip Sharper, eds. *Puebla and Beyond: Documentation and Commentary.* Translated by John Drury. Maryknoll, NY: Orbis, 1979.

East Asia Christian Conference, Fourth Assembly, 1968. *"In Christ All Things Hold Together": Statement and Findings from the Fourth Assembly of the East Asia Chritian [sic] Conference.* n.p.: [EACC?], [1968?].

East Asia Christian Conference. *Asian Conference on Church and Society, Seoul, Korea, October 10–16, 1967: Modernization of Asian Societies.* Seoul: EACC, 1967.

Eisenstadt, S. N. "Intellectuals and Tradition." *Daedalus* 101 (Spring 1992) 1–19.

Eliade, Mircea. *The Sacred and the Profane: The Nature of Religion.* Translated by Williard R. Trask. San Diego: A Harvest/HBJ Book, Harcourt Brace Jovanovich, 1987.

Elwood, Douglas J., ed. *Asian Christian Theology: Emerging Themes.* Philadelphia: Westminster, 1980.

Events and People. *Christian Century* 109 (11 March 1992) 272.

Fang, Thomé H. *Chinese Philosophy: Its Spirit and Its Development.* Taipei, Taiwan: Linking Publishing, 1981, 525. Quoted in Karl H. Federschmidt, *Theologie aus asiatischen Quellen: Der theologische Weg Choan-Seng Songs vor dem Hintergrund der asiatischen ökumenischen Diskussion*, with a foreword by Konrad Raiser, 76. Münster, Germany: Lit, 1994.

Federschmidt, Karl H. *Theologie aus asiatischen Quellen: Der theologische Weg Choan-Seng Songs vor dem Hintergrund der asiatischen ökumenischen Diskussion.* With a foreword by Konrad Raiser. Münster, Germany: Lit, 1994.

Firth, Cyril Bruce. *An Introduction to Indian Church History.* Rev. ed. The Christian Students' Library No. 23. Madras: CLS for the Senate of Serampore College, 1976.

"The Frankfurt Declaration." *Christianity Today*, 19 June 1970, 3–6.

Freytag, W[alter]. "Changes in the Patterns of Western Missions." In *The Ghana Assembly of the International Missionary Council, 28th December, 1957 to 8th January, 1958: Selected Papers, with an Essay on the Rôle of the I.M.C.*, edited by Ronald K. Orchard, 138–47. London: Edinburgh House Press for the IMC, 1958.

Fung Yu-lan. *A Short History of Chinese Philosophy.* Edited by Derk Bodde. New York: Free, 1948; Free Paperback, 1966.

Furuya, Yasuo, ed. and trans. *A History of Japanese Theology.* Grand Rapids: Eerdmans, 1997.

Geertz, Clifford. *The Interpretation of Cultures: Selected Essays.* New York: Basic, 1973.

Gerth, H. H., and C. Wright Mills, eds. and trans. *From Max Weber: Essays in Sociology.* New York: Oxford University Press, 1946.

Giddens, Anthony. *The Consequences of Modernity.* Stanford, CA: Stanford University Press, 1990.

Gill, David M. "The Secularization Debate Foreshadowed. Jerusalem 1928." *International Review of Missions* 57 (1968) 344–57.

Glasser, Arthur F., and Donald A. McGavran. *Contemporary Theologies of Mission.* Grand Rapids: Baker, 1983.

Goodall, Norman, ed. *Missions under the Cross: Addresses Delivered at the Enlarged Meeting of the Committee of the International Missionary Council at Willingen, in Germany, 1952; with Statements Issued by the Meeting.* London: Edinburgh House Press for the IMC, 1953.

———, ed. *The Uppsala Report 1968: Official Report of the Fourth Assembly of the WCC, Uppsala July 4–20, 1968.* Geneva: WCC, 1968.

Gutiérrez, Gustavo. *The Power of the Poor in History.* Translated by Robert R. Barr. Maryknoll, NY: Orbis, 1983.

———. *A Theology of Liberation: History, Politics, and Salvation.* Maryknoll, NY: Orbis, 1973.

———. *A Theology of Liberation: History, Politics, and Salvation.* Rev. ed. with a new introduction. Maryknoll, NY: Orbis, 1988.

Hadjor, Kofi Buenor. *Dictionary of Third World Terms.* London: Penguin Books, 1993. s.v. "Dependency Theory."

Haines, J. Harry. *Chinese of the Diaspora.* Research Pamphlets No. 14. London: Edinburgh House Press for the WCC CWME, 1965.

Haleblian, Krikor. "The Problem of Contextualization." *Missiology* 11 (January 1983) 95–111.

Hartenstein, Karl. *Die Mission als theologisches Problem: Beiträge zum grundsätzlichen Verständnis der Mission.* Berlin: Furche-Verlag, 1933.

———. "Theologische Besinnung." In *Mission zwischen Gestern und Morgen: Vom Gestaltwandel der Weltmission der Christenheit im Licht der Konferenz des Internationalen Missionsrats in Willingen,* edited by Walter Freytag, G. Brennecke, K. Hartenstein, C. Ihmels, A. Lehmann, and E. Verwiebe, 51–72. Stuttgart: Evang. Missionsverlag, 1952.

Hesselgrave, David J., and Edward Rommen. *Contextualization: Meanings, Methods, and Models.* Grand Rapids: Baker, 1989.

Hodge, Charles. *Systematic Theology.* Vol. 1. Reprint, Grand Rapids: Eerdmans, 1989.

Hodge, Robert, and Gunther Kress. *Language as Ideology.* 2d ed. London: Routledge, 1993.

Hoedemaker, Bert [Libertus A.]. "The Legacy of J. C. Hoekendijk." *International Bulletin of Missionary Research* 19 (October 1995) 166–70.

Hoedemaker, L[ibertus] A. "The People of God and the Ends of the Earth." In *Missiology: An Ecumenical Introduction: Texts and Contexts of Global Christianity,* edited by F. J. Verstraelen, A. Camps, L. A. Hoedemaker, and M. R. Spindler, 157–71. Grand Rapids: Eerdmans, 1995.

Hoekendijk, J. C. "The Call to Evangelism." *International Review of Missions* 39 (1950) 162–75.

———. "The Church in Missionary Thinking." *International Review of Missions* 41 (1952) 324–36.

———. *The Church Inside Out.* Edited by L. A. Hoedemaker and Pieter Tijmes. Translated by Isaac C. Rottenberg. Philadelphia: Westminster, 1966.

———. "Notes on the Meaning of Mission (-ary)." In *Planning for Mission: Working Papers on the New Quest for Missionary Communities,* edited by Thomas Wieser, 37–48. New York: U.S. Conference for the WCC, 1966.

Hollenweger, Walter J. "'Christus extra et intra muros ecclesiae.'" In *Planning for Mission: Working Papers on the New Quest for Missionary Communities,* edited by Thomas Wieser, 56–61. New York: U.S. Conference for the WCC, 1966.

The Humanum Studies 1969–1975: A Collection of Documents. Geneva: WCC, 1975.

Hwang, C. H. "God's People in Asia Today." *South East Asia Journal of Theology* 5 (October 1963) 5–17.

Hyun, Younghak. "Minjung Theology and the Religion of Han." *East Asia Journal of Theology* 3 (1985) 354–59.

India, Registrar General and Census Commissioner [M. Vijayanunni]. *Religion.* Census of India 1991. Series 1: India, Paper 1 of 1995. Delhi: Controller of Publications, 1995.

International Missionary Council. *"Madras Series": Presenting Papers Based upon the Meeting of the International Missionary Council, at Tambaram, Madras, India, December 12th to 29th, 1938.* vol. 1. *The Authority of the Faith.* New York: IMC, 1939.

———. "A New Study of the Missionary Obligation of the Church." TD [mimeographed]. n.d. The Missionary Obligation of the Church: (Papers and Reports). Speer Library, Princeton Theological Seminary, Princeton, NJ.

Ito, Kiyoshi. *Taiwan*. Tokyo: Chuokoron Sha, Chuko Shinsho, 1993.

John, George M. *Youth Christian Council of Action 1938–1954: The Story of a Dynamic Movement of Christian Youth*. CISRS Social Research Series No. 10. Madras: CLS for the CISRS, Bangalore, 1972.

John, Mathai. "The Reformation of Abraham Malpan: An Assessment." *Indian Church History Review* 24 (June 1990) 31–65.

Juergensmeyer, Mark. *The New Cold War?: Religious Nationalism Confronts the Secular State*. Berkeley and Los Angeles: University of California Press, 1993.

Kariyil, Antony. *Church and Society in Kerala: A Sociological Study*. New Delhi: International Publications, 1995.

Kim, Y. "Christian Koinonia in the Struggle and Aspirations of the People of Korea." In *Asian Theological Reflections on Suffering and Hope*, edited by Yap Kim Hao, 36–48. Singapore: CCA, 1977.

Kim Yong Bock. "Korean Christianity as a Messianic Movement of the People." In *Minjung Theology: People as the Subjects of History*, edited by Kim Yong Bock, 77–116. Singapore: CTC, CCA, 1981.

———. "Messiah and Minjung: Discerning Messianic Politics over against Political Messianism." In *Minjung Theology: People as the Subjects of History*, edited by Kim Yong Bock, 185–96. Singapore: CTC, CCA, 1981.

———, ed. *Minjung Theology: People as the Subject of History*. Singapore: CTC, CCA, 1981.

Kim Yong-Bock. "Keynote Address: The Mission of God in the Context of the Suffering and Struggling Peoples of Asia." In *Peoples of Asia, People of God: A Report of the Asia Mission Conference 1989*, 5–32. Osaka: CCA, 1990.

Kinnamon, Michael, ed. *Signs of the Spirit: Official Report, Seventh Assembly, Canberra, Australia, 7–20 February 1991*. Geneva: WCC, 1991; Grand Rapids: Eerdmans, 1991.

Kishimoto, Yoichi. Postface ("Kaisetsu—Atogaki ni kaete") to Choan-Seng Song, *Minwa no shingaku* [Theology of Folktale], translated by Yoichi Kishimoto and Keiichi Kaneko into Japanese. Tokyo: Shinkyo Shuppan Sha, 1984.

Koyama, Kosuke. *Mount Fuji and Mount Sinai: A Critique of Idols*. Maryknoll, NY: Orbis, 1985.

Kuepers, J. J. A. M. *The Dutch Reformed Church in Formosa 1627–1662: Mission in a Colonial Context*. Schriftenreihe der Neuen Zeitschrift für Missionswissenschaft. Immensee, Switzerland: Neue Zeitschrift für Missionswissenschaft, 1978.

Kumar, Suresh. *Political Evolution in Kerala: Travancore 1859–1938*. New Dehli: Phoenix, [1994?].

Kuribayashi, Teruo. "Recovering Jesus for Outcasts in Japan: From a Theology of the Crown of Thorns." *The Japanese Christian Review* 58 (1992) 19–32.

Kwok Pui-Lan. "Gospel and Culture." *Christianity and Crisis* 51 (15 July 1991) 223–24.

Lamley, Harry J. "The 1895 Taiwan Republic: A Significant Episode in Modern Chinese History." *Journal of Asian Studies* 27 (August 1968) 739–62.

———. "The 1895 Taiwan War of Resistance: Local Chinese Efforts against a Foreign Power." In *Taiwan: Studies in Chinese Local History*, edited by Leonard H. D. Gordon, 23–77. New York: Columbia University Press, 1970.

Latourette, Kenneth Scott. *A History of the Expansion of Christianity.* Vol. 3, *Three Centuries of Advance: A.D. 1500–A.D. 1800.* Grand Rapids: Zondervan, 1970.

Lee Jae-Won. "Spirit and Practice: A Radical Understanding." *Christianity and Crisis* 51 (15 July 1991) 226–27.

Lindsell, Harold. *Missionary Principles and Practice.* Westwood, NJ: Fleming H. Revell Co., n.d.

Lossky, Nicholas, José Míguez Bonino, John S. Pobee, Tom F. Stransky, Geoffrey Wainwright, and Pauline Webb. *Dictionary of the Ecumenical Movement.* Geneva: WCC, 1991; Grand Rapids: Eerdmans, 1991. s.v. "Christian Conference of Asia," by Tosh Arai and T. K. Thomas.

Mackie, Steven G. "God's People in Asia: A Key Concept in Asian Theology." *Scottish Journal of Theology* 42 (1989) 215–40.

Man's Disorder and God's Design. Vol. 1, *The Universal Church in God's Design: An Ecumenical Study Prepared Under the Auspices of the WCC.* London: SCM, 1948.

Mathew, C. P., and M. M. Thomas. *The Indian Churches of Saint Thomas.* Delhi: ISPCK, 1967.

McGavran, Donald A. "Salvation Today." In *The Evangelical Response to Bangkok*, edited by Ralph Winter, 27–32. South Pasadena, CA: William Carey Library, 1973.

"A Message from the First Assembly of the East Asia Christian Conference to Its Member Churches and Councils." In *"Witness Together": Being the Official Report of the Inaugural Assembly of the East Asia Christian Conference, Held at Kuala Lumpur, Malaya, May 14–24, 1959*, edited by U Kyaw Than, v–vi. Rangoon: EACC, [1959?].

Meyendorff, John. *Byzantine Theology: Historical Trends and Doctrinal Themes.* New York: Fordham University Press, 1979.

"Mission and Evangelism—An Ecumenical Affirmation." *International Review of Mission* 71 (October 1982) 427–51.

Moffett, Samuel Hugh. *A History of Christianity in Asia.* Vol. 1, *Beginnings to 1500.* San Francisco: HarperCollins, 1992.

Moon, Chris Hee-Suk. "Culture in the Bible and the Culture of the Minjung." *Ecumenical Review* 39 (1985) 180–86.

Moore, Michael S. "A Critical Profile of Choan-Seng Song's Theology." *Missiology* 10 (October 1982) 461–70.

Murthy, K. G. Krishna, and G. Lakshmana Rao. *Political Preferences in Kerala.* New Delhi: Radha Krishna, 1968, 17. Quoted in V. A. Pankratova, *Khristiane Keraly: rol' v sotsial'no-politicheskoy zhizni shtata* [Christians of Kerala: Role in Socio-Political Life of the State], 63. Moscow: Izdatel'stvo Nauka, 1982.

Nacpil, Emerito. "Mission and Modernization." In *What Asian Christians Are Thinking: A Theological Source Book*, edited by Douglas J. Elwood, 277–88. Quezon City, Phillipines: New Day, 1976.

———. "Renewing the Church for Christian Action." In *Christian Action in the Asian Struggle*, 31–37. Singapore: CCA, [1973?].

Neely, Alan. *Christian Mission: A Case Study Approach.* American Society of Missiology Series, No. 21. Maryknoll, NY: Orbis, 1995.

Neill, Stephen. *A History of Christian Missions.* 2d ed. Revised by Owen Chadwick. London: Penguin, 1986.

The New Delhi Report: The Third Assembly of the WCC, 1961. New York: Association Press, 1962.

New Encyclopaedia Britannica. 15th ed. s.v. "Kerala," by V. R. Pillai.

Newbigin, J. E. Lesslie. "The Work of the Holy Spirit in the Life of the Asian Churches." In *A Decisive Hour for the Christian Mission: The East Asia Christian Conference 1959 and the John R. Mott Memorial Lectures,* by Norman Goodall, J. E. Lesslie Newbigin, W. A. Visser't Hooft, and D. T. Niles, 18–33. London: SCM, 1960.

Newbigin, Lesslie. "The Call to Mission—A Call to Unity?" In *The Church Crossing Frontiers: Essays on the Nature of Mission in Honour of Bengt Sundkler,* edited by Peter Beyerhaus and Carl F. Hallencreutz, 254–65. Studia Missionalia Upsaliensia 11. Uppsala [Lund?]: Gleerup, 1969.

———. *One Body, One Gospel, One World: The Christian Mission Today.* London: IMC, 1958.

———. *The Relevance of Trinitarian Doctrine for Today's Mission.* CWME Study Pamphlets No. 2. London: Edinburgh House Press for the WCC, CWME, 1963.

———. *Unfinished Agenda: An Autobiography.* Grand Rapids: Eerdmans, 1985.

Nida, Eugene A. *Message and Mission: The Communication of the Christian Faith.* New York: Harper & Row, 1960.

Nihon Kirisuto Kyodan Taiwan Kankei Iinkai, ed. *Tomo ni nayami tomo ni yorokobu: Nihon Kirisuto Kyodan to Taiwan Choro Kyokai no kyoyaku teiketsu no tame ni* [Suffering Together, Rejoicing Together: Towards the Agreement between the United Church of Christ in Japan and the Presbyterian Church in Taiwan]. Tokyo: Nihon Kirisuto Kyodan, 1984.

Niles, D. Preman. "Christian Mission and the People of Asia." *Missiology* 10 (July 1982) 279–300.

Niles, D. Preman, Charles C. West, and Choan-Seng Song. "Reviewing and Responding to the Thought of Choan-Seng Song." *Occasional Bulletin of Missionary Research* 1 (July 1977) 9–15.

Niles, D. T. "A Church and Its 'Selfhood.'" In *A Decisive Hour for the Christian Mission: The East Asia Christian Conference 1959 and the John R. Mott Memorial Lectures,* by Norman Goodall, J. E. Lesslie Newbigin, W. A. Visser't Hooft, and D. T. Niles, 72–96. London: SCM, 1960.

———. *Upon the Earth: The Mission of God and the Missionary Enterprise of the Churches.* New York: McGraw-Hill, 1962.

Niles, Preman. "Towards a Framework of Doing Theology in Asia." In *Asian Theological Reflections on Suffering and Hope,* edited by Yap Kim Hao, 16–28. Singapore: CCA, 1977.

———, ed. "Report: The Consultation of Theologians, Hong Kong, October 10–15, 1976." In *Asian Theological Reflections on Suffering and Hope,* edited by Yap Kim Hao, 7–14. Singapore: CCA, 1977.

Nissen, Karsten. Review of *Missio Dei,* by H. H. Rosin. In *International Review of Mission* 62 (1973) 495–97.

Nossiter, T. J. *Communism in Kerala: A Study in Political Adaptation.* London: Hurst for the Royal Institute of International Affairs, London, 1982.

O Ikutoku [Wang Yü-te] and Takayuki Munakata. *Atarashii Taiwan: Dokuritsu e no rekishi to mirai-zu* [The New Taiwan: A History towards Independence and Its Future]. Tokyo: Kobundo, 1990.

O'Dea, Thomas F., and Janet O'Dea Aviad. *The Sociology of Religion.* 2d ed. Englewood Cliffs, NJ: Prentice-Hall, 1983.

Ogden, Graham S. "The Old Testament in Asia: A Response to C. S. Song." *Taiwan Journal of Theology* 1 (March 1979) 77–87.

Ogden, Schubert M. *The Reality of God and Other Essays*. New York: Harper & Row, 1963; Dallas: Southern Methodist University Press, 1992.

Orchard, Ronald K., ed. *The Ghana Assembly of the International Missionary Council, 28th December, 1957 to 8th January, 1958: Selected Papers, with an Essay on the Rôle of the I.M.C.* London: Edinburgh House Press for the IMC, 1958.

———, ed. *Witness in Six Continents: Records of the Meeting of the Commission on World Mission and Evangelism of the WCC Held in Mexico City, December 8th to 19th, 1963.* London: Edinburgh Press for DWME of the WCC, 1964.

Park Sang Jung. "An Ecumenical Understanding of the Mission of the Church in Asia." In *Outcry!: Report of the North-East Asia Church Leaders' Meeting, October 12–16, 1987*, 1–13. Hong Kong: CCA, 1988.

Parratt, John. "Recent Writing on Dalit Theology: A Bibliographical Essay." *International Review of Mission* 83 (April 1994) 329–38.

Paton, David M., ed. *Breaking Barriers, Nairobi 1975: The Official Report of the Fifth Assembly of the WCC, Nairobi, 23 November–10 December, 1975.* London: SPCK, 1976; Grand Rapids: Eerdmans, 1976.

Pauck, Wilhelm. "Theology in the Life of Contemporary American Protestantism." In *Religion and Culture: Essays in Honor of Paul Tillich*, edited by Walter Leibrecht, 278. New York: Harper, 1959. Quoted in Gerald H. Anderson, ed. *The Theology of the Christian Mission*, 3–4. New York: McGraw-Hill, 1961.

Peoples of Asia, People of God: A Report of the Asia Mission Conference 1989. Osaka: CCA, 1990.

Philip, T. M. *The Encounter between Theology and Ideology: An Exploration into the Communicative Theology of M. M. Thomas.* Madras: CLS for the Newday Publication of India, 1986.

Philip, T. V. "Christian Conference of Asia: A Historical Overview." *Asia Journal of Theology* 9 (April 1995) 2–29.

Pieris, Aloysius. *An Asian Theology of Liberation*. Maryknoll, NY: Orbis, 1988.

Potter, Philip. "Christ's Mission and Ours in Today's World: Director's Report." *International Review of Mission* 62 (April 1973) 144–57.

Rayan, Samuel. "Reconceiving Theology in the Asian Context." In *Doing Theology in a Divided World: Papers from the Sixth International Conference of the Ecumenical Association of Third World Theologians, January 5–13, 1983, Geneva, Switzerland*, ed. Virginia Fabella and Sergio Torres, 124–42. Maryknoll, NY: Orbis, 1985.

Republic of China Government Information Office. "Foreign Relations." In *The Republic of China Yearbook 1998* [yearbook on-line]. Available from http://www.gio.gov.tw/nfo/yb97/html/ ch9.htm, Internet, accessed 12 October 1998.

———. "Geography." In *The Republic of China Yearbook 1998* [yearbook on-line]. Available from http://www.gio.gov.tw/info/ yb97/html/ch1.htm, Internet, accessed 16 October 1998.

———. "History." In *The Republic of China Yearbook 1998* [yearbook on-line]. Available from http://www.gio.gov.tw/info/ yb97/html/ch4.htm, Internet, accessed 12 October 1998.

———. "People." In *The Republic of China Yearbook 1998* [yearbook on-line]. Available from http://www.gio.gov.tw/info/ yb97/html/ch2.htm, Internet, accessed 19 October 1998.

———. "Religion." In *The Republic of China Yearbook 1998* [yearbook on-line]. Available from http://www.gio.gov.tw/info/ yb97/html/ch25.htm, Internet, accessed 12 October 1998.

Robinson, Richard H., and Willard L. Johnson. *The Buddhist Religion: A Historical Introduction*. 4th ed. Assisted by Sandra A. Wawrytko and Thanissaro Bhikkhu (Geoffrey DeGraff). Belmont, CA: Wadsworth, 1997.

Rosales, Gaudencio B., and C. G. Arévalo, eds. *For All the Peoples of Asia: Federation of Asian Bishops' Conferences, Documents from 1970 to 1991*. Maryknoll, NY: Orbis, 1992; Quezon City, Philippines: Claretian, 1992.

Rosin, H. H. *'Missio Dei': An Examination of Origin, Contents and Function of the Term in Protestant Missiological Discussion*. Leiden: Interuniversity Institute for Missiological and Ecumenical Research, Department of Missiology, [Foreword 1972].

Rouse, Ruth, and Stephen Charles Neill, eds. *A History of the Ecumenical Movement 1517–1948*. 4th ed. Geneva: WCC, 1993.

Rubinstein, Murray A. *The Protestant Community on Modern Taiwan: Mission, Seminary, and Church. Taiwan in the Modern World*. Armonk, NY: M.E. Sharpe, 1991.

Ruether, Rosemary Radford, ed. *Religion and Sexism: Images of Women in Jewish and Christian Tradition*. New York: Simon and Schuster, 1974.

Russell, Letty M. *Human Liberation in a Feminist Perspective—A Theology*. Philadelphia: Westminster, 1974.

Ryerson, Charles. *Regionalism and Religion: The Tamil Renaissance and Popular Hinduism*. Madras: CLS for the CISRS, Bangalore, 1988.

Samartha, S. J. "Paul David Devanandan (1901–1962): A Biographical Introduction." In P. D. Devanandan, *I Will Lift Up Mine Eyes unto the Hills: Sermons and Bible Studies*, edited by S. J. Samartha and Nalini Devanandan, 1–11. Bangalore, India: CISRS, 1963.

Saniel, Josefa M. "The Mobilization of Traditional Values in the Modernization of Japan." In *Religion and Progress in Modern Asia*, ed. Robert N. Bellah, 124–49. New York: Free, 1965; London: Collier-Macmillan, 1965.

"Salvation and Social Justice: Report of Section II of the Bangkok Conference." *International Review of Mission* 62 (April 1973) 198–201.

Sano, Roy. "'Holy Moments' at Canberra." *Christianity and Crisis* 51 (15 July 1991) 227–28.

Sawatzky, Sheldon. "Review and Critique of C. S. Song's Theology of Mission." *Taiwan Journal of Theology* 4 (March 1982) 229–48.

Scherer, James A. "Church, Kingdom, and *Missio Dei*: Lutheran and Orthodox Correctives to Recent Ecumenical Mission Theology." In *The Good News of the Kingdom: Mission Theology for the Third Millennium*, edited by Charles Van Engen, Dean S. Gilliland, and Paul Pierson, 82–88. Maryknoll, NY: Orbis, 1993.

———. *Gospel, Church, and Kingdom: Comparative Studies in World Mission Theology*. Minneapolis: Augsburg, 1987.

Schmemann, Alexander. "The Problem of the Church's Presence in the World in Orthodox Consciousness." *St. Vladimir's Theological Quarterly* 21 (1977) 3–17.

Schoonhoven, Evert Jansen. "Tambaram 1938." *International Review of Mission* 67 (July 1978) 299–315.

Sharpe, Eric J. "New Directions in the Theology of Mission." *Evangelical Quarterly* 46 (January–March 1974) 8–24.

Shi Mei [Shih Ming]. *Taiwan wa Chugoku no ichibu ni arazu: Taiwan shakai hatten 400 nen shi* [Taiwan is not part of China: The 400 Year History of Taiwan's Social Development]. Translated by Masaru Shiga into Japanese. Tokyo: Gendaikikakushitsu, 1991.

Singh, G. R. Review of *Christian Mission in Reconstruction: An Asian Analysis*, by Choan-Seng Song. In *Religion and Society* 23 (June 1976) 114–17.

Soedjatmoko. "Memorandum on Scope and Purpose of Seminar." Quoted in Robert N. Bellah. "Introduction." In *Religion and Progress in Modern Asia*, edited by Robert N. Bellah, x–xiv. New York: Free, 1965; London: Collier-Macmillan, 1965.

Song, C. S. *The Compassionate God*. Maryknoll, NY: Orbis, 1982.

———. *Jesus and the Reign of God*. Minneapolis: Fortress, 1993.

———. *Jesus in the Power of the Spirit*. Minneapolis: Fortress, 1994.

———. *Jesus, the Crucified People*. Vol. 1 of *The Cross in the Lotus World*. New York: Crossroad, 1990.

———. "Oh, Jesus, Here with Us!" *Ecumenical Review* 35 (1983) 59–74.

———. "Political Theology of Living in Christ with People." In *A Call to Vulnerable Discipleship: Living in Christ with People*, by CCA Seventh Assembly, 1981, 5–24. Singapore: CCA, 1982.

———. *The Tears of Lady Meng: A Parable of People's Political Theology*. Geneva: WCC, 1981.

———. *Theology from the Womb of Asia*. Maryknoll, NY: Orbis, 1986.

———, ed. *Self-Determination: The Case for Taiwan*. Tainan, Taiwan: Taiwan Church Press, 1988.

Song, Choan-Seng. "An Analysis of Contemporary Chinese Culture and Its Implication for the Task of Theology." *South East Asia Journal of Theology* 4 (April 1963) 9–25.

———. "Asia in Suffering and Hope." In *Asian Theological Reflections on Suffering and Hope*, edited by Yap Kim Hao, 50–59. Singapore: CCA, 1977.

———. "Asian Contribution to Ecumenical Theology. " *Drew Gateway* 57 (Fall 1986) 1–39.

———. *Christian Mission in Reconstruction: An Asian Analysis*. Madras: CLS, 1975; reprint, Maryknoll, NY: Orbis, 1977.

———. "Christian Mission toward Abolition of the Cross." In *The Scandal of the Crucified World: Perspectives on the Cross and Suffering*, edited by Yacob Tesfai, 130–48. Maryknoll, NY: Orbis, 1995.

———. "Confessing the Faith in Today's World," *South East Asia Journal of Theology* 8 (July–October 1966) 95–107.

———. "Curriculum Vitae." In "The Relation of Divine Revelation and Man's Religion in the Theologies of Karl Barth and Paul Tillich." ThD diss., Union Theological Seminary, New York, 1965.

———. "The Decisiveness of Christ." In *What Asian Christians Are Thinking: A Theological Source Book*, edited by Douglas J. Elwood, 240–64. Quezon City, Phillipines: New Day Publishers, 1976.

———. "Election for Mission." *South East Asia Journal of Theology* 13, no. 2 (1972) 40–48.

———. "From Israel to Asia: A Theological Leap." *Ecumenical Review* 28 (July 1976) 252–65.

———. "God's Mission with the Nations." In *A Vision for Man: Essays on Faith, Theology and Society in Honour of Joshua Russell Chandran*, edited by Samuel Amirtham, 221–37. Madras: CLS, 1978.

———. "Introduction: Building a Political Culture of Love." In *Testimonies of Faith: Letters and Poems from Prison in Taiwan*, selected, edited, and translated with an introduction by Choan-Seng Song, 10–30. n.p., [1984].

———. "Liberation of People in History." *South East Asia Journal of Theology* 19, no. 2 (1978) 14–25.

———. "New China and Salvation History: A Methodological Enquiry." *South East Asia Journal of Theology* 15, no. 2 (1974) 52–67.

———. "New Frontiers of Theology in Asia: Ten Theological Theses." *South East Asia Journal of Theology* 20, no. 1 (1979) 13–33.

———. "The Obedience of Theology in Asia." *South East Asia Journal of Theology* 2 (October 1960) 7–15.

———. "The Possibility of Analogical Discourse of God." *South East Asia Journal of Theology* 7 (October 1965) 55–76.

———. "The Power of God's Grace in the World of Religions." *Ecumenical Review* 39 (January 1987) 44–62.

———. "The Relation of Divine Revelation and Man's Religion in the Theologies of Karl Barth and Paul Tillich." ThD diss., Union Theological Seminary, New York, 1965.

———. "The Role of Christology in the Christian Encounter with Eastern Religions." *South East Asia Journal of Theology* 5 (January 1964) 13–31.

———. "Taiwan: Theology of the Incarnation." In *Asian Voices in Christian Theology*, edited by Gerald H. Anderson, 147–60. Maryknoll, NY: Orbis, 1976.

———. *Tell Us Our Names: Story Theology from an Asian Perspective*. Maryknoll, NY: Orbis, 1984.

———. "Theology of Transposition." *Northeast Asia Journal of Theology* 24–25 (March-September 1980) 6–28.

———. *Third-Eye Theology: Theology in Formation in Asian Settings*. Maryknoll, NY: Orbis, 1979.

———. *Third-Eye Theology: Theology in Formation in Asian Settings*. Rev. ed. Maryknoll, NY: Orbis, 1991.

———. "Whither Protestantism in Asia Today?" *South East Asia Journal of Theology* 11 (Spring 1970) 66–76.

Speer, Robert E. *"Are Foreign Missions Done For?"* n.p., 1928.

Stackhouse, Max L. "Contextualization, Contextuality, and Contextualism." In *One Faith, Many Cultures: Inculturation, Indigenization, and Contextualization*, edited by Ruy O. Costa, 3–13. Maryknoll, NY: Orbis, 1988; Cambridge, MA: Boston Theological Institute, 1988.

Stroope, Michael W. "Eschatological Mission: Its Reality and Possibility in the Theology of Karl Barth and Its Influence on Modern Mission Theology." PhD diss., Southwestern Baptist Theological Seminary, 1985.

Sugirtharajah, R. S. "Introduction." In *Frontiers in Asian Christian Theology: Emerging Trends*, edited by R. S. Sugirtharajah, 1–8. Maryknoll, NY: Orbis, 1994.

Suh Nam Dong. "Historical References for a Theology of Minjung." In *Minjung Theology: People as the Subjects of History*, edited by Kim Yong Bock, 155–84. Singapore: CTC, CCA, 1981.

———. "Hutatsu no monogatari no goryu" [The Confluence of Two Stories]. In *Minjun no shingaku* [Minjung Theology], edited by I In-ha and Kida Ken'ichi, 261–320. Tokyo: Kyo-Bun-Kwan, 1984.

Suh, David Kwang-sun. "Minjung and Theology in Korea: A Biographical Sketch of an Asian Theological Consultation." In *Minjung Theology: People as the Subjects of History*, edited by Kim Yong Bock, 17–40. Singapore: CTC, CCA, 1981.

Suresh, C. P. "Electoral Politics." In *Dynamics of State Politics: Kerala*, edited by N. Jose Chander, 152–203. New Delhi: Sterling, 1986.

Tai Kuo Fei [Tai Kuo-hui]. *Taiwan*. Tokyo: Iwanami Shoten, Iwanami Shinsho, 1988.

Tai, Michael Cheng-tek. *In Search of Justice: The Development of the Social Teachings in Asian Churches*. Chilliwack, B.C., Canada: Julia Griffith Insticol of Language Arts, 1985.

Takenaka, Masao. "Christ's Ministry and Ours." *South East Asia Journal of Theology* 3 (January 1962) 10–39.

———. "A New Understanding of the World and the Need of Theological Renewal." In *"Witness Together": Being the Official Report of the Inaugural Assembly of the East Asia Christian Conference, Held at Kuala Lumpur, Malaya, May 14–24, 1959*, edited by U Kyaw Than, 33–42. Rangoon: EACC, [1959?].

Theological Education Fund. *Ministry in Context: The Third Mandate Programme of the Theological Education Fund (1970–77)*. Bromley, England: Theological Education Fund, 1972.

Thomas, M. M. *The Acknowledged Christ of the Indian Renaissance*. London: SCM, 1969.

———. "A Christ-Centered Humanist Approach to Other Religions in the Indian Pluralistic Context." In *Christian Uniqueness Reconsidered: the Myth of a Pluralistic Theology of Religions*, edited by Gavin D'Costa, 49–62. Maryknoll, NY: Orbis, 1990.

———. "Christ-Centred Syncretism." *Religion and Society* 26 (March 1979) 26–35.

———. "Christ's Promise within the Revolution: The Meaning of Evangelism and Service in the Post-War World." *Religion and Society* 8 (April 1961) 15–25.

———. "Christian Action in the Asian Struggle." In *Christian Action in the Asian Struggle*, 1–10. Singapore: CCA, [1973?].

———. *The Christian Response to the Asian Revolution*. London: SCM, 1966.

———. "Christianity and the Indian Situation: Nicolas Berdyaev and Gandhism." TMs [photocopy]. 1941–42. United Theological College Archives, Bangalore, India.

———. "The Church: What I Owe to It; and My Complaint against It." TMs [photocopy]. December 1939. United Theological College Archives, Bangalore, India.

———. "The Churches in the Political Struggles of Our Day." *Ecumenical Review* 3 (January 1951) 121–26.

———. "Faith Seeking Understanding and Responsibility." Unpublished manuscript. 1971. United Theological College Library, Bangalore, India, 1. Quoted in T. M. Philip, *The Encounter between Theology and Ideology: An Exploration into the Communicative Theology of M. M. Thomas*, 2. Madras: CLS for the Newday Publication of India, 1986.

———. *Ideological Quest within Christian Commitment 1939–1954*. Indian Christian Thought Series No. 16. Madras: CLS for the CISRS, Bangalore, 1983.

———. "Indian Nationalism: A Christian Interpretation." *Religion and Society* 6 (June 1959) 4–26.

———. *Man and the Universe of Faiths*. Inter-religious Dialogue Series No. 7. Madras: CLS for the CISRS, 1975.

———. "The Meaning of Salvation Today—A Personal Statement." *International Review of Mission* 62 (April 1973) 158–69.

———. *My Ecumenical Journey 1947–1975*. Trivandrum, India: Ecumenical Publishing Centre, 1990.

———. "My Pilgrimage in Mission." *International Bulletin of Missionary Research* 13 (January 1989) 28–31.

———. *New Creation in Christ: Twelve Selected Sermons Given on Various Occasions*. With a foreword by S. J. Sadiq. Delhi: ISPCK, 1976.

———. "Persons and Social Institutions: A Biblical Approach." In *Human Person, Society and State*, edited by P. D. Devanandan and M. M. Thomas, 130–40. Bangalore, India: Committee for Literature on Social Concerns, 1957.

———. *The Realization of the Cross (Fifty Thoughts and Prayers Centred on the Cross)*. Madras: CLS, 1972.

———. *Recalling Ecumenical Beginnings*. Delhi: ISPCK., 1987.

———. "A Rewarding Correspondence with the Late Dr. Hendrik Kraemer." *Religion and Society* 13 (June 1966) 5–14.

———. *Risking Christ for Christ's Sake: Towards an Ecumenical Theology of Pluralism*. Geneva: WCC, 1987.

———. *Salvation and Humanisation: Some Crucial Issues of the Theology of Mission in Contemporary India*. Madras: CLS for the CISRS, 1971.

———. "The Significance of the Thought of Paul D. Devanandan for a Theology of Dialogue." In *Inter-religious Dialogue*, edited by Herbert Jai Singh, Devanandan Memorial Volume No. 3, 1–37. Bangalore, India: CISRS, 1967.

———. "The Situation in Asia—II." In *Man's Disorder and God's Design: The Amsterdam Assembly Series*, vol. 3, *The Church and the Disorder of Society: An Ecumenical Study Prepared under the Auspices of the WCC*, 71–79. New York: Harper & Row, 1948.

———. "Some Notes on a Christian Interpretation of Nationalism in Asia." *South East Asia Journal of Theology* 2 (October 1960) 16–26.

———. *Some Theological Dialogues*. Madras: CLS for the CISRS, Bangalore, 1977.

———. "Some Trends in Contemporary Indian Christian Theology." *Religion and Society* 24, no. 4 (1977) 4–18.

———. "Spiritual Penetration: Revolts of the Poor and the Oppressed." *Religion and Society* 27 (March 1980) 10–20.

———. "Theological Aspects of the Relationships Between Social Action Groups and Churches." *Religion and Society* 31 (June 1984) 17–23.

———. "Toward an Indigenous Christian Theology." In *Asian Voices in Christian Theology*, edited by Gerald H. Anderson, 11–35. Maryknoll, NY: Orbis, 1976.

———. *Towards a Theology of Contemporary Ecumenism: A Collection of Addresses to Ecumenical Gatherings (1947–1975)*. Madras: CLS, 1978.

———. "Towards an Adequate Doctrine of Creation." *Religion and Society* 5, no. 1 (1958) 37–50.

———. *Towards an Evangelical Social Gospel: A New Look at the Reformation of Abraham Malpan*. Madras: CLS, 1977.

———. "Two Kinds of Messianism: Report of the Chairman of the Executive Committee." *Ecumenical Review* 26 (October 1974) 546–62.

———. "The World in Which We Preach Christ." In *Witness in Six Continents: Records on World Mission and Evangelism of the WCC Held in Mexico City, December 8th to 19th, 1963*, edited by Ronald K. Orchard, 11–19. Edinburgh: Edinburgh House Press for the DWME of the WCC, 1964.

Thomas, M. M., and J. D. McCaughey. *The Christian in the World Struggle: A Grey Book of the World's Student Christian Federation*. Geneva: World's Student Christian Federation, [1951?].

Thomas, M. M., and Lesslie Newbigin. "Salvation and Humanization: A Discussion." In *Mission Trends No. 1: Crucial Issues in Mission Today*, edited by Gerald Anderson and Thomas F. Stransky, 217–29. New York: Paulist, 1974; Grand Rapids: Eerdmans, 1974.

Thomas, M. M., and Paul E. Converse. *Revolution and Redemption.* New York: Friendship, 1955.
Thomas, T. Jacob. *Ethics of a World Community: Contributions of Dr. M. M. Thomas Based on Indian Reality.* Calcutta: Punthi Pustak, 1993.
Tong, Hollington K. *Christianity in Taiwan: A History.* Taipei: China Post, 1961.
Tovey, Philip. "Abraham Malpan and the Amended Syrian Liturgy of CMS." *Indian Church History Review* 29 (June 1995) 38–55.
Tsurumi, E. Patricia. "Colonial Education in Korea and Taiwan." In *The Japanese Colonial Empire, 1895–1945*, edited by Ramon H. Myers and Mark R. Peattie, 275–311. Princeton, NJ: Princeton University Press, 1984.
U Kyaw Than, ed. *"Witness Together": Being the Official Report of the Inaugural Assembly of the East Asia Christian Conference, Held at Kuala Lumpur, Malaya, May 14–24, 1959.* Rangoon: EACC, [1959?].
Van Leeuwen, Arend Th. *Christianity in World History: The Meeting of the Faiths of East and West.* Translated by H. H. Hoskins. London: Edinburgh House, 1964.
Verkuyl, Johannes. *Contemporary Missiology: An Introduction.* Translated and edited by Dale Cooper. Grand Rapids: Eerdmans, 1978.
Vicedom, Georg F. *Missio Dei: Einführung in eine Theologie der Mission.* Munich: Chr. Kaiser Verlag, 1958.
———. *The Mission of God: An Introduction to a Theology of Mission.* Translated by Gilbert A. Thiele and Dennis Hilgendorf. St. Louis: Concordia, 1965.
Visser't Hooft, W. A. "Asian Churches." *Ecumenical Review* 2 (Spring 1950) 229–40.
———. "The Asian Churches in the Ecumenical Movement." In *A Decisive Hour for the Christian Mission: The East Asia Christian Conference 1959 and the John R. Mott Memorial Lectures*, by Norman Goodall, J. E. Lesslie Newbigin, W. A. Visser't Hooft, and D. T. Niles, 46–58. London: SCM, 1960.
———. *Memoirs.* Geneva: WCC, 1973.
Wachman, Alan M. *Taiwan: National Identity and Democratization.* Taiwan in the Modern World. Armonk, NY: Sharpe, 1994.
Warneck, Gustav. *Outline of a History of Protestant Missions from the Reformation to the Present Time with an Appendix Concerning Roman Catholic Missions.* 3d English ed. Edited by George Robson. New York: Revell, 1906.
Weber, Hans-Ruedi. *Asia and the Ecumenical Movement 1895–1961.* London: SCM, 1966.
———. "Out of All Continents and Nations: A Review of Regional Developments in the Ecumenical Movement." In *The Ecumenical Advance: A History of the Ecumenical Movement, Volume 2, 1948–1968*, edited by Harold E. Fey, 63–92. 3d ed. Geneva: WCC, 1993.
Weber, Max. *The Protestant Ethic and the Spirit of Capitalism.* Translated by Talcott Parsons. With an Introduction by Anthony Giddens. New York: Scribner, 1976.
Werner, Dietrich. "Missionary Structure of the Congregation." In *Dictionary of the Ecumenical Movement*, edited by Nicholas Lossky, José Míguez Bonino, John S. Pobee, Tom F. Stransky, Geoffrey Wainwright, and Pauline Webb. Geneva: WCC, 1991; Grand Rapids: Eerdmans, 1991.
West, Charles C. "Culture, Power and Ideology in Third World Theologies." *Missiology* 12 (October 1984) 405–20.
Western European Working Group. "Mission in God's Mission." In *Planning for Mission: Working Papers on the New Quest for Missionary Communities*, edited by Thomas Wieser, 48–53. New York: U.S. Conference for the WCC, 1966.

Wickremesinghe, Lakshman. "Living in Christ with People." In *A Call to Vulnerable Discipleship: Living in Christ with People,* by CCA Seventh Assembly, 1981, 25–49. Singapore: CCA, 1982.
Wieser, Thomas. "Report on the Salvation Study." *International Review of Mission* 62 (April 1973) 170–79.
Wilson, Frederick R. ed. *The San Antonio Report: Your Will Be Done, Mission in Christ's Way.* Geneva: WCC, 1990.
"The Witness of the Churches amidst Social Change (An EACC Study Document)." *Religion and Society* 6 (June 1959) 27–50.
Witvliet, Theo. *A Place in the Sun: An Introduction to Liberation Theology in the Third World.* Maryknoll, NY: Orbis, 1985.
Wolf, Eric R. *Europe and the People without History.* Berkeley and Los Angeles: University of California Press, 1982.
Wolpert, Stanley. *A New History of India.* 3d ed. New York: Oxford University Press, 1989.
Wolters, Hielke T. *Theology of Prophetic Participation: M. M. Thomas' Concept of Salvation and the Collective Struggle for Fuller Humanity in India.* With a foreword by K. C. Abraham. Delhi: ISPCK/UTC, 1996.
World Conference on Church and Society, Geneva 1966. *Christians in the Technical and Social Revolutions of Our Time: World Conference on Church and Society, Geneva, July 12–26, 1966: The Official Report.* With a description of the conference by M. M. Thomas and Paul Abrecht. Geneva: WCC, 1967.
Worsley, Peter. *The Three Worlds: Culture and World Development.* Chicago: University of Chicago Press, 1984.
Wuthnow, Robert. *Meaning and Moral Order: Explorations in Cultural Analysis.* Berkeley and Los Angeles: University of California Press, 1987.
———. *Rediscovering the Sacred: Perspectives on Religion in Contemporary Society.* Grand Rapids: Eerdmans, 1992.
Yamamoto, Tatsuro, ed. *Indo shi* [A History of India]. Sekai kakkoku shi 10. Tokyo: Yamakawa Shuppan Sha, 1960.
Yates, Timothy. *Christian Mission in the Twentieth Century.* Cambridge: Cambridge University Press, 1994.
Your Kingdom Come: Mission Perspectives, Report on the World Conference on Mission and Evangelism, Melbourne, Australia, 12–25 May 1980. Geneva: CWME, 1980.
Yû, Chûkun. *Kakyo* [Overseas Chinese]. Tokyo: Kodansha, Kodansha Gendai Shinsho, 1990.

Index

Aagaard, Johannes, 36–37n20
Acknowledged Christ of the Indian Renaissance, The (Thomas), 121
adaptation, 14
ahisma, 101–2, 103
Allen, Roland, 14, 41n45
Andersen, Wilhelm, encouraging search for mission's theological base, 35–36
Anderson, Rufus, 14, 35
Andrews, Charles F., 125, 128
apostolate, as basic function of the Church, 40
Asia
    Christian presence in, as symbol of the incarnation, 167
    God's redemptive act in, 77
    growing power of elite in, 76
    post–World War II conditions in, 64–65
    suffering people of, 180–88
    theological framework for social witness in, 65
Asia Mission Conference, Cipanas 1989, 82
Asian Christian churches
    need of, to recover foreignness and strangeness of kerygma, 152
    problem of theology in, 146–49
    world-centric orientation of, 24
Asian Christians
    change- and modernity-oriented, 86
    living with distinct identity problems, 23
    search for identity and meaning, relating to society at large, 22
    self-complacent isolation of, 157
    sense among, of double belonging, 18–19
    social isolation of, 147–49

Asian Christians (*continued*)
    tendency of, to ignore the Old Testament, 151
Asian ecumenical movement, shift to people-centered paradigm, 83
Asian mission thinking, focus on, on social concerns, 43
Asian revolution. *See also* revolution
    leading to increase in good-evil conflict, 124–25
    missiological significance of, 123–25
    preparing Asia for the gospel, 126
    situating God's saving presence in, 194
    theological implications of, 123–27
Asian theologies
    distinct among contemporary Third World theologies, 15, 17
    dual emphasis on religio-cultural and socio-political issues, 17
authority, new attitude toward, 5

Barr, James, 145
Barth, Karl, 36, 42, 145
Bassham, Rodger C., 45–46, 69–70
Bayly, Susan, 92
Bellah, Robert N., 4–5, 10, 11–12, 22
Berdyaev, Nicolas, influence of, on Thomas, 101–2, 114, 126, 133
Berger, Peter, 7–8
Beyerhaus, Peter, 128n183
Black theology, 53
Black Theology of Liberation, A (Cone), 52
Bonhoeffer, Dietrich, 164
Bosch, David J., 25
Bottomore, Tom, on intellectuals, 10–11
Buber, Martin, 18
Byerhaus, Peter, 55

Index

Candidus, Georgius, 139
Carter, Jimmy, 178
Castro, Emilio, 55
CCA (Christian Conference of Asia), 15–16, 63
   Penang 1977, 76–77
   Urban-Industrial Mission (UIM) Committee, 65
   Urban-Rural Mission (URM) Committee, 65
centrism
   bias of, in viewing human history, 168–69
   prophetic tradition as rejection of, 174
Chandran, Russell, 38
change
   identity and, 10, 20
   modern conception of, integrating with conception of identity, 10
   openness toward, 5, 9
   viewed negatively, 9
Chatterji, Saral K., 74–75
Chenchiah, Pandippedi, 128
Cheng Ch'eng-kung, 139
Cheng-ting Wang, 28, 201
Chiang Kai-shek, 142–43
Chi Myong-Kwan, 79
Chinese Christians, narrow treatment of the Bible, 151
Chinese history, applying principle of transposition to, 177
Ch'ing dynasty, 139–41
Christ. *See also* Jesus, Jesus Christ
   concept of absoluteness applied to, negative results of, 165n113
Christavasram, 96
Christendom
   decline of, 36
   Hoekendijk critical of, 158–59
   Song critical of, 159
Christian communities, emergence of, in Asia, 2
Christian Conference of Asia. *See* CCA
Christian faith, related to traditional Asian legitimations, 22
Christian Institute for the Study of Religion and Society (CISRS), 112
Christianity, introduced to Taiwan, 139–40, 141

Christian Mission in Reconstruction: An Asian Analysis (Song), 77, 155
Christian missions
   merging concepts of *missio Dei* and new creation, 127–28
   mission of Christ as essence of, 160
   as mission of suffering, 164–67
   mistakenly viewed as foreign mission, 156–59
   search for theological foundation of, 34–42
Christians
   increasing irrelevance of, in Asia, 13
   Newbigin urging to unity, 41
Christian social action, 33–34
Christian symbols, giving new meaning to, 20
Christian theology
   in Asia, taking shape in midst of intersecting identities, 23
   built on ties to West, 167–68
   in modernizing Asia, 12–23
   rift of, with missionary enterprise, 34
Christian in the World Struggle, The (the Grey Book) (Thomas and McCaughey), 107–11
Christology
   centrality of, for Song, 153–54
   people-centered approach to, 177–88
Christ and Time (Cullman), 169
Christus extra muros ecclesiae, 47
Chung, Archie Lee Chi, 20n69
Chung Hyun Kyung, 19–20n67, 60–61
Church, as bearer of the apostolate, 40
Church-centric approach to mission, 58–59
church planting, 34–35
Coe, Shoki, 20–22, 76, 145, 179
Cohen, Mark J., 189–90
Commission of World Mission and Evangelism. *See* CWME
Compassionate God, The (Song), 168, 176–77, 185
Cone, James H., 52
confessing, total act of, 72
confessing theology, 72–73
confluence, of Christian and Korean *minjung* traditions, 81–82
Congress on World Evangelism, 55

contextuality, Asian Christians' search for, 76
contextualization, 13–14, 15
  chief agents of, from disfavored elements of society, 87
  Coe's introduction of, to replace indigenization, 21–22
contextual theology, 13–14, 15, 26, 53
  Asian, 63–64, 73
  as integrative discourse, 189
  missio Dei concept contributing to, 85
  recognized need for, 76
Converse, Paul E., 110
conversion, 55–56
Cox, Harvey, 47
creation
  as ongoing process, 117
  as starting point for doing theology in Asia, 77
creation-redemption paradigm, 170–73
creative co-operation, 102n68
Cross in the Lotus World, The (Song), 181–82
Cullman, Oscar, 169
cultural adaptation, to local conditions, 17
cultural ethos, new, quest for, 120–22
culture
  defined, 7n17
  as factor for Christian mission, 53
  Western, 1–2, 126
CWME (Commission of World Mission and Evangelism), 41–42
  Bangkok 1973, 52–56
  Bucharest 1974, 56
  first meeting of (Mexico City 1963), 43, 45–46
  Nairobi 1975, 56–57
  San Antonio 1989, 59–60

Davies, J. G., criticizing disunity of worship and mission, 57n119
Declaration of Korean Theologians (1984), 79
de Nobili, Robert, 17
dependency theory, 1n1
Devanandan, Paul D., 43, 65n3
  affirming God's active presence in Asia, 84

Devanandan, Paul D. (*continued*)
  centrality of new creation to thought of, 117
  collaboration with Thomas, 112–13
  developing emphasis on humanity, 128
  question of, regarding resurgence of traditional religions and secular ideologies, 123
  three basic affirmations of, 112n122
  use of term "God's mission," 129
discernment, 58
  hesitation to address, 56
  as a major concern in Asian ecumenical thinking, 85
  questions of, after Bangkok 1949, 66
  of the signs of God in Christ at work in history, 112–32
  Song's approach to, 167
  theology urged in engagement of, 50
disruption, 176–77
divine presence, search for signs of, as a central issue among Asian Christian leaders, 66
doctrine of retribution, 184
double belonging (dual identity), 18–20
Duff, Alexander, 125
Durkheim, Emile, 3

East Asian Christian Conference (EACC), 15–16, 63
  Asian Conference on Church and Society (Seoul 1967), 72
  Bangkok 1964, 70–71
  Bangkok 1968, 72
  Consultation on Faith and Order (Hong Kong 1966), 72
  formative period of, coinciding with upheaval in postwar Asia, 64
  Kuala Lumpur 1959, 67–70, 111
  origins of, 63
  shift in, in late 1960s, 74–75
  Singapore 1973, 75–77
  this-worldly orientation of, 64
Eastern Asia Christian Conference, 63
  Bangkok 1949, 64–66, 84
Eastern Orthodox Churches, growing influence of, on mission thinking, 56

223

Index

ecumenical movement
  Asian, 28, 32–34, 69, 193
  distinct branches of, 34
  domination of, by Western languages, 32n2
  linking mission and unity, 33
  reasserting Church-mission relationship, 41–42
  this-worldly spirituality of, 31
  Western domination of, coming to an end, 55
ecumenical thinking
  Asian, distinct from Western, 63–64
  contribution to world-centric missionary approach, 46
  Western approach to, 46n68
Eisenstadt, S. N., 3n3
election, concept of, guilty of centrist idea of salvation history, 170
Eliade, Mircea, 7
ethno-religious conflict, growth of, 3
ethos, shift from sacred to secular, 121
evangelical leaders
  criticizing Uppsala 1968's report on mission, 55
  reaffirming place of Church in mission, 56
evangelism, concern about, in postwar Asia, 64–65

faith
  as basis for political participation, 110
  significance of, in discerning God's activity in history, 110
"Faithful Lady Meng, The," 80
Fang, Thomé H. (Fang Tung-mei), 145, 188
February 28 Incident, 143
Federschmidt, Karl, 153
feminist theology, 52
freedom
  Berdyaev's distinctions between types of, 114
  Thomas's understanding of, 114–15, 118
Fung Yu-lan, 150

Gandhi, Mahatma, 96–97n37, 99, 101–2, 153

Gandhism, Thomas's involvement with, 99–103, 106
Geertz, Clifford, 6–7, 10, 23
General Conference of Latin American Bishops (Puebla 1979), 57
Giddens, Anthony, 2
globalization, 1
God
  directly at work among all nations and peoples, 172–73
  presence of, in contemporary historical process, 109
Gospel, mistakenly identified with Western culture, 159
Graham, Billy, 55
Gutiérrez, Gustavo, 52

han, 78
Hartenstein, Karl, 36–38
Heilsgeschichte, Song's impressions of, 169–70
history
  emphasis on, 47, 48
  as process toward greater differentiation, 3
Hodge, Charles, 171
Hodge, Robert, 32n2
Hoedemaker, L. A., 36
Hoekendijk, J. C.
  advocating attention to history, 47
  call for *missio Dei*'s "full identification with man in the modern world," 42
  critical of Christendom, 158–59
  ex-centeredness of Church, 49
  influence of, 50
  radical view of mission, 37–38, 39
  similarities with of Song's approach, 158–59
holiness, this-worldly and other-worldly, 27–28
holistic meaning, 12, 20
holy living, 70–71
hua ch'iao, 189
humanization, 48–49
  as central concept of approach to Christian mission (Uppsala 1968), 50–51
  related to salvation, 129–32

Index

humankind
  centrality of, 113–16
  final destiny of, 130
  re-orienting from self-centeredness to God-centeredness, 159–60
human nature, renewal of, 118
human rights, quest for, implying discovery of individual personality, 120
Hu Shih, 148, 153, 188
Hwang, C. H. *See* Coe, Shoki

identity
  Asian Christians' search for, 86
  change and, 10, 20
  Christian search for, 20–21
  related to double focus on God and the Asian world, 85
  traditional vs. primordial, 23
Ideological Quest (Thomas), 99n
Ienaga, Saburo, 12
IMC (International Missionary Council), 14, 34
  integrating with WCC, 41–43
  Tambaram 1938, 35, 63
  Willingen 1952, 37–39
incarnation
  central to biblical message, 159–60
  as divine response to human suffering, 163–67
  as model for discerning God, 81
  replacing indigenization, 152
incorporation, of Asian and Judeo-Christian people's stories, 81
India, independence of, from British rule, 96–97n37
"Indian Nationalism: A Christian Interpretation" (Thomas), 111–12
indigenization, 13–15
  concept of, replaced with contextualization, 21
  Song's suspicion of, 151–52
indigenous churches
  embodying search for new cultural ethos, 122
  planting of, 35
industrialization, as progressive fulfillment of God's command, 72
Innere Mission, 33–34

integrative discourse, 23
integrative revolution, 23
intellectuals
  converting to Christianity as response to pressures of modernity, 12
  peculiar relationship of, with culture, 10–11
  responding to identity-change dilemma, 10–11
International Missionary Council. *See* IMC
Inter-religious Student Fellowship, 95
Israel, status of, linked to conditions in Asia, 77

Jacobite Church, 93, 94
Jesus, understanding humanity of, 184–85
Jesus, the Crucified People (Song), 183–88
Jesus Christ. *See also* Christ
  death and resurrection of, as God's final rejection of Jewish centrism, 174–75
  as New Humanity, 117–18
Juergensmeyer, Mark, 6

Kao, C. M., 179
karuna, 186
Kerala (South India), 90–91, 133
  Marxist influence in, 97–98n41
Kim Yong-Bock, 82–83
Kingdom of God, understood in terms of Jesus' earthly ministry, 57
Kissinger, Henry, 178
koinonia, 129–32
Koyama, Kosuke, 18–20
Kress, Gunther, 32n2

laity, as bearers of Christian mission, 70
language, linked to ideology, 32n2
Lausanne Movement, 55
Lee Jae-Won, 60–61
legitimations, 7–9
Lehmann, Paul, 38
liberation
  deepening of concept, for mission, 37
  focus shifting toward, 75
  popularity of motif, 194

Index

liberation theology, 17, 52
   influence of, on Song, 182, 191
Life and Work movement, 34, 43
Lindsell, Harold, 170n134
Lin Yu-tang, 153
logical analysis, as West's permanent contribution to Chinese philosophy, 150n58
Luckmann, Thomas, 7–8

Mackay, George L., 141
Mackie, Steven G., 15–16
Malpan, Abraham, 93–94, 122
Mar Thoma Church, 122, 133
   rejecting Thomas for ordination, 104n77
   Thomas's loyalty towards, 94n21
Mar Thomas Students' Conference, 98
Marxism
   utopian tendency in, 104
   Thomas's preference for, 106
   victory of, 36
Mathai, K. I., 96
Mathew, K. A., 95
Maxwell, James L., 141
McCaughey, Davis, 107, 108–11
McGavran, Donald A., 55
meaning
   holistic, 12
   problems of, 11–12
mediatory mission, 56–57, 59
Message and Mission (Nida), 14–15
messianism, types of, inherent in messianic faiths, 127
Miller, William, 125
Ministry in Context (Theological Education Fund of the WCC), 13
minjung, shift from *minjok*, 78–79n59
minjung theology, 77–83
   influence of, on Song, 182, 191
Minjung Theology: People as the Subject of History, 78
missio Dei
   acceptance of, among missionary circles, 43
   in Asia, preexisting introduction of concept from the West, 83–84

missio Dei (continued)
   continuing tensions between church-centric and world-centric view, 51–61
   emergence of, 25, 36–37
   first official appearance of concept in EACC Assembly, 71
   as God's direct act in world history, 159–63
   key to reorienting theology and missiology of ecumenical movement in Asia, 83
   placing notion of people within theology of, 81–82
   popularity of concept, among Third World theologians, 26
   releasing churches from preoccupation with the Church, 83
   shift from Church-centrism to theocentrism, 39–40
   Song's view of, 196
   theocentric conception of, 129
   this-worldly connotation of, 71
   world-centric view of, 26–28, 42–51, 85, 98
Missio Dei (Vicedom), 40
missiological alternative, search for, from Asian perspective, 155–67
mission
   Church-centric approach to, 40, 41–42
   continuing Christ's work through, 40
   defined as participation in Christ's mission, 111
   dialectical approach to, 104
   given new definition for Asia, 69–70
   grounded in creation and covenant, 44
   indissolubly related to Church, 35
   mistakenly identified with Western missions, 159
   pneumatological approach to, 41
   theological basis for, of little concern to Asia's Christian leaders, 84
   Thomas's narrow definition of, 129
   Trinitarian foundation for, 38–39
missionaries, emphasis of, on individualistic piety, 148–49
missionary movement, little early interest of, in theology, 34

missionary obligation, source of, for the Church, 39
"Missionary Structure of the Congregation," 46–47
mission of the cross, 166
mission of the resurrection, 166
modernity
  confidence in, weakening of, 3
  confronting rest of the world, 6
  defining, 3–4, 5
  impact of, 5–7, 18
  pressures of, conversion to Christianity as response to, 12
  significance of, 2–3
  Song's preference for, 191
  Song's and Thomas's common orientation toward, 199
  spiritual orientation of, 5
  undermining function of religion, 9
modernization
  conflicts resulting from, recognition of, 74–75
  defining, 3–5
  effects of, 1, 3
  growing ambivalence toward, 74
  increasing disillusionment with, 85–86
  in newly independent Asian nations, 4
  optimistic attitude toward, 72–74
  relationship of, with traditional values, 4–5
  in Taiwan, 140
modernization theory, 1n1
Moody, Dwight L., 33
Moore, Michael S., 146, 188
Mount Fuji and Mount Sinai (Koyama), 18–20

Nacpil, Emerito, 75
National Christian Youth Council, 97, 99
National Council of Churches in Korea, Seoul 1979, 77–78
nationalism, 2
  in Asia, result of Western impact, 126
  betraying the Asian revolution, 132
  defined, 6n14
  resulting in alienation of Christian coverts, 13
  rise of, in Third World, 36

new creation, 113, 116–19
  cosmic character of, 118–19
  idea of, traced back, 127–28
  resurfacing in Thomas's thinking, 116, 134
  Song's approach to, 171–72
new humanity, 113, 134
  idea of, traced back, 127–28
Newbigin, Lesslie, 38, 40–41, 42, 50
Nida, Eugene A., 14–15
Niebuhr, Reinhold, 103
Niles, D. T., 42, 72–73n33
Niles, Preman, 77, 85, 170–71
Nixon, Richard, 178
Nossiter, T. J., 90–91

ochlos, relation of, to *minjung* theology, 79
Ogden, Schubert, 162–63, 172n145
One Body, One Gospel, One World (Newbigin), 40
Orthodox Syrian Church, 93
other-worldly view of salvation, 33

Palakunnathu, Abraham (Abraham Malpan), 93–94
Pannenberg, Wolfhart, Song's criticism of, 161
Parthenios, 60
participation
  Eastern Orthodox concept of, 102n68
  in Thomas's thinking, 108
Pauck, Wilhelm, 34
Paul, K. T., 28, 125, 201
PCT. *See* Presbyterian Church in Taiwan
people of God, in Asia, 77
people-oriented theology, 25, 194
personality
  discovery of, leading to quest for human rights, 120
  as likeness and image of God, 114
personal salvation, 33
Philip, T. M., 97
Pieris, Aloysius, 17
plantatio ecclesiae, 34–35, 59
political action, Christian quest for, 104
political systems, call for mass actions to address changes of, 74, 75

Index

poor
  increased focus on, 57–58
  liberation of, 76
Potter, Philip, 52
preferential option for the poor, 57
preparatio evangelica, for Asia, 125
Presbyterian Church in Taiwan (PCT), 141, 143–44, 146
  advocating democracy and self-determination for Taiwan, 178–80
  as suffering few for Taiwan's sake, 164n111
presentation, concept of, in salvation history, 169
primordial attachments, 6–7, 23
primordial identification (identity), 20–22, 23
primordial sentiments, 19
progress, liberal belief in, 102–3
Puritanism, 5, 31
purna swaraj, 97n

Radhakrishnan, 153
Realization of the Cross, The (Thomas), 95–96, 113
redemption
  cosmic and social, biblical basis for, 109, 110–11
  embracing the entire cosmos, 109
  as interruption-dispersion, 173–75
  restoring humans' creative freedom, 115, 118
religion
  importance of, as legitimation, 8–9
  as mechanism for producing identity, 7
  as primordial attachment, 7
  rationalization of, intellectuals' role in, 11
religious nationalism, 2
religious reform movements, emerging as responses to Western values, 2
responsible society, 110n111
revolution. *See also* Asian revolution
  language of, emerging within ecumenical movement, 46
  as *preparatio evangelica* for Asia, 125
  as theological concept, 108–9

Revolution and Redemption (Thomas), 110–11
Ricci, Matteo, 17
Romo-Syrian Church, 93
Ryerson, Charles, 3–4

sacred-secular dichotomy, rejected, 44
salvation
  four sociopolitical dimensions of, 54
  holistic nature of, 53–54
  mission of, seeking the Christ-centered *koinonia*, 129–32
  other-worldly view of, 33
  related to humanization, 129–32
  as source of *koinonia* in India's religious community, 131
  this-worldly orientation of, 54
salvation history, problem of, 168–70
Salvation and Humanisation (Thomas), 128–32
Samartha, Stanley J., 52, 112
Saniel, Josefa M., 4
Sano, Roy, 19n67
Sawatsky, Sheldon, 188
Scherer, James A., 26–27, 28, 52–53, 59
Schiff, Leonard, 100, 101n60
science and technology, role of, in social revolution, 119–20
second liberation, 75
secularism, 121
secularization
  positive attitude toward, 44
  process of, as fundamental feature of contemporary world history, 47
secular nationalism, 6
secular world, service to God in, 67
Sen, Keshub Chunder, 128, 153
sending and receiving churches, role reversal of, 36
shalom, as goal of mission, 49
sin, destructive power of, 183–84
Singh, Surjit, 128
social concerns, related to mission thinking, 43
social *diakonia*, 67
social history, fallenness of, 103
social justice, focus shifting toward, 75
"Social Manifesto for the Church, A" (Thomas), 98

social revolution
   meaning of, for Asian nations, 119–22
   significance of, for missiology, 120
social thinking, integration of, with mission thinking, 51
social witness, grounded in God's sovereignty over the whole world, 65–66
society, traditional and modern, 3
socio-political engagement, emphasis on, for salvation, 53–54
solidarity, 86
Song, C. S. (Choan-Seng), 2, 24
   acceptance of distinction between Jesus Christ and Christianity as a religion, 153
   advocating democracy and self-determination for Taiwan, 179–80
   affirming God's direct relationship with world, 25
   affirming mission as key to reformation of Protestant churches in Asia, 154–55
   arguing for radical re-formation in life of Asian churches, 149
   attempting to interpret God's mission in Communist China, 182n188
   building on Ogden's approach to God's actions in history, 162–63
   centrality of incarnation in understanding of God's this-worldly presence, 153n70
   on Christian mission as mission of suffering, 164–67
   Christology's centrality for, 153–54
   compared to Thomas, 195–201
   concept of theological leap (transposition), 175–77
   considering concept of absoluteness as inadequate when applied to Jesus Christ, 165n113
   constructing people-centered approach to Christology, 177–88
   on creation-redemption paradigm, 170–73
   critical of Christendom, 159
   critical of Western missionary movement, 154–57

Song, C. S. (*continued*)
   critical of Western theology, 167–68n124
   criticized for Westernness of his Asian theology, 188
   differentiating between "Taiwanese" and "Chinese," 148n51
   discernment in thought of, 167
   distinguishing between confessing the faith and a confession of the faith, 150
   on doctrine of retribution, 184
   disturbed by historical tie between Christianity and Western civilization, 167–68
   early life and theological formation of, 137–38, 144–46
   emphasis on people, 180–83
   emphasizing directness of God's relation with entire creation, 161
   envisaging Christological transformation of Asian societies and religions, 154
   focused on understanding of Jesus as human being, 184
   folk stories used in theological reflections, 180–81
   on God's mission of incarnation as response to human suffering, 163–67
   on God's presence in non-biblical religions, 183n194
   heavily influenced by Barth and Tillich, 196
   historical context of his theology, 190–91
   on importance of the Bible, especially the Old Testament, 151
   on importance of methodology, 150–51
   incarnation as central to biblical message, 152, 159–60
   on incarnation and suffering people in the world, 180, 181–83
   on individual Jesus-Christs, 187
   influence of, on Taiwanese political Christian theology, 180
   influences on, for emphasis on suffering, 183n191

Index

Song, C. S. (*continued*)
  inspired by world-centric *missio Dei*, 190–91
  on Jesus' earthly mission, 184
  on knowability of God, 181, 184
  liberation theology's influence on, 182, 191
  living in exile to escape repression of Nationalist government in Taiwan, 179
  minjung theology's influence on, 182, 191
  on mission of the Church, 180
  on Old Testament prophetic tradition, 174
  opposed to separation of person and work of Jesus Christ, 153–54
  on Pannenberg's idea of universal history as revelation, 161n96
  part of younger generation of ecumenical movement, 194
  people-centered Christology of, 183–88
  playing leading role in Taiwan's political development in 1970s, 155
  preference of, for modernity, 191
  primordial identification of, with disfavored in Asian society, 191
  on problem of salvation history, 168–70
  proposal of, to replace indigenization with incarnation, 152
  proposing creation as starting point for doing theology in Asia, 77
  reacting against Church-centric view of salvation, 169–70
  reconceptualizing traditional doctrine of creation, 171
  reflection on Abba-God and treatment of Jesus, 184–87
  rejecting Church-centric position, 157
  searching for new framework for theology in Asia, 167–77
  searching for true theological response in Asia, 150–55
  shifting attention from the West to Asian issues, 182–83
  similarities with Hoekendijk, 158–59

Song, C. S. (*continued*)
  situating, in Taiwanese history, 189–90
  suspicious of Asian theology and theologians, 146–48
  suspicious of indigenization concept, 151–52
  suspicious of religious and political establishment, 181
  suspicious of theology inspired by nationalism, 147n47
  theological basis for this-worldly holiness, 160
  theological basis for understanding of redemption, 173–74
  theological concerns, personal nature of, 146
  on theological meaning of world history, 161–62
  on traditional theological interpretation of the cross, 185–86
  understanding of Christian mission as *missio Dei*, 160–63
  understanding redemption as interruption-dispersion, 173–75
  using people's stories as source for theological reflections, 80–81
  viewing Church as event, rather than organization, 166
  viewing Jesus Christ's death and resurrection as God's final rejection of Jewish centrism, 174–75
  viewing salvation history as a "type" for discernment, 175–76
  Western influence on, 188–89
  Western theological training, effects of, 146
Speer, Robert E., missionary thought of, 157–58n83
spirituality, types of, among Asian Christians, 27
Stott, John R. W., 55
St. Thomas Christians (Syrian Christians), 91–94
Student Christian Movement (SCM), 95, 96
suffering, as chief reality in Asian people's history, 183
Suh Nam Dong, 81–82

symbolic universes, 8
symbolism, role of, in Asian Christians' search for identity, 23–24
syncretism, fear of, among Christians, 131–32

Taiwan
  history of, 138–44
  movement for self-determination, 177–80
  overseas communities of, 189
  persecutions of Christians in, 141–42
  Roman Catholicism in, 141n18
Taiwanese popular religion, 138
Takenaka, Masao, 67–68, 84, 28n96, 43
Tears of Lady Meng, The (Song), 187n213
theological leap, in Song's approach to incarnation, 175–77
Theology of Liberation, A (Gutiérrez), 52
Third World
  emergence of voices from, at Bangkok 1973, 52–53
  opposing motives of, 10
Third-Eye Theology (Song), 167–68
this-worldly holiness
  defined, 31
  development of, 28–29
  in ecumenical thinking, 31–32
  evident at CWME Mexico City 1963 meeting, 45–46
  in mission thinking, motivation for, 33
  Song's theological basis for, 160
this-worldly presence of God
  advocacy of concept, 24
  central theological motif in Asian ecumenical thinking, 84
  concept of, embraced by conciliar mission thinkers, 25
Thomas, M. A., 95
Thomas, M. M. (Madathiparampil Mammen), 2, 24, 28, 46, 54, 65
  accepting Marx's historical materialism, 100–101, 103–4
  acknowledging significance of discernment task, 68
  addressing theology of mission, 128–32

Thomas, M. M. (*continued*)
  affinity with Social Gospel and Christian Socialism, 201
  affirming God's active presence in Asia, 84
  asserting social justice as primary ecclesiological concern, 99
  belonging to first generation of ecumenical movement, 194
  Berdyaev's influence on, 114, 126, 133
  birth of, 89–90
  collaboration with Devanandan, 112–13
  compared to Song, 195–201
  conception of personality, transcendental nature of, 116n141
  consultant to WCC study project on Rapid Social Change, 112
  criticizing evolutionary view of progress, 103
  defining mission narrowly, 129
  early life of, 94–96
  elected moderator of WCC Central Committee, 50
  emphasis on humanity, 113–16, 134
  formulating basis for Christian participation in Asian revolution, 24
  Gandhism, involvement with, 99–103, 106
  growing conviction of God's this-worldly presence, 116
  holistic vision of ecumenical movement, 32–33
  identification of, with disfavored groups, 133
  ideological and theological shift (1948), 104–7
  ideology of, roots for, 133
  inability to accept inherent goodness of human nature, 102
  increasing awareness of ambiguity of the Church and the world, 115–16
  initial focus on similarities of Jesus' and Gandhi's ethics, 99
  interpretations of Indian social and political reality, 107
  introducing revolution as theological concept, 108–9

Index

Thomas, M. M. (*continued*)
  keynote address at Singapore 1973, 75
  motif of God's this-worldly presence, in thinking of, 104–12
  moving toward liberation movement, 132–33
  on nationalism betraying the Asian revolution, 132
  new creation concept resurfacing in thinking of, 116–17, 134
  organizer of National Christian Youth Council, 97, 99
  overview of theology and thinking, 132–35
  principal interest of, searching for adequate Christian response to Asian revolution, 128
  proponent of social democracy, 105–7
  proposing redemption as new theological emphasis, 106–7
  on quest for new cultural ethos, 120–22
  on redemption restoring human beings to their original personality, 115
  rejected for ordination in Mar Thoma Church, 104n77
  on restoration of divine-human community, 117–18
  rethinking pro-Communist stance, 105–6
  secretary of Youth Christian Council of Action, 97
  significance of modern quest for a fuller human life, 130
  on the spirit of modernity and the messianic faiths, 126–27
  suggesting Christ-centered fellowship outside the Church, 131
  suspicious of Devanandan's emphasis on religion, 113n123
  suspicious of utopianism, 103
  syncretism viewed negatively, 131–32n203
  tempered optimism of, regarding the revolution, 124–25
  theological and ideological search, early stage of, 96–104

Thomas, M. M. (*continued*)
  on theological implications of Asian revolution, 123–27
  on the true end of human beings, 115
  two main theological emphases, 107
  on types of messianism inherent in messianic faiths, 127
  understanding of freedom, 114–15, 118
  view of God at work in history, criticized, 123–24n165
  viewing revolution as *preparatio evangelica* for Asia, 125
  view of social revolution and its meaning for Asian nations, 119–22
  warning of danger in this-worldly emphasis, 104
  wary of utopianism, 103, 109
  working for WSCF, 104–5
  youth secretary of Mar Thoma Church, 97
Thomas, T. Jacob, 95
three-self movement, 14
Torrance, Thomas F., 145
tradition, sociological conception of, 3n3
traditional identity, 23
traditional religions, resurgence and renaissance of, 121–22
traditional societies
  confrontation with modernity, 5–7
  coping with change, 10
  missionary critique of, 13
tragic destiny, 101, 103, 104, 134
transnational organizations, 15
transposition, in Song's approach to incarnation, 175–77
trinitarianism, effect of, on mission, 38–39
Trinitarian language, missing from *missio Dei* concept, 43–44
True Jesus Church (Taiwan), 144n31
Tsung-yi Lin, 179

Uniate Church, 93
United Church of Christ in Japan, 141–42

van Leeuwen, Arend Th., 47
Venn, Henry, 14, 35

Vicedom, Georg F., 40, 50, 55
Visser't Hooft, W. A., 42, 65n3

Warneck, Gustav, 156n78
WCC (World Council of Churches)
    Canberra 1991, 60
    endorsing secular approach to mission, 50
    formation of, 35
    integrating with IMC, 41–43
    "Missionary Structure of the Congregation," 25
    New Delhi 1961, beginning of new climate in ecumenical mission thinking, 42–43
    Prapat 1957, 66
    Theological Education Fund (TEF), 13
    Uppsala 1968, 50, 127
Weber, Hans-Ruedi, 27–28, 201
Weber, Max, 3, 10, 11, 31
Wei, Francis, 153
Werner, Dietrich, 26, 28
West
    differences in Song's and Thomas's approach to, 197–98
    Gospel identified with, 156–57
Western Christian missions, embodying search for new cultural ethos, 122
Western colonial rule
    collapse of colonialism, 36
    political complications resulting from, 6
Western culture
    producing new ideas in Asian revolution, 126
    spread of, 1–2
Whorf, Benjamin L., 32n2
Wickremesinghe, Lakshman, 80
Wieser, Thomas, 53
Williams, Daniel T., 145
witness, concern for, tied to social changes, 67
"Witness of the Churches amidst Social Change, The" (Kuala Lumpur 1959), 111
Wolf, H. H., 123–24n165
world, as locus for God's redeeming act, 47–48. *See also* this-worldly *entries*

World Conference on Church and Society (Geneva 1966), 46
World Conference on Mission and Evangelism (Melbourne 1980), 57–59
World Student Christian Federation
    Strasbourg conference (1960), shift to mission's focus on the world, 42
    Thomas working for, 104–5
World United Formosans for Independence (WUFI), 189
Wu-tong Hwang, 179

Youth Christian Council of Action (YCCA), 96–99

Zacharias, H. C., 125

www.ingramcontent.com/pod-product-compliance
Lightning Source LLC
Chambersburg PA
CBHW051638230426
43669CB00013B/2352